Guatemala

Richard Arghiris & Claire Boobbyer

Credits

Footprint credits
Editor: Felicity Laughton
Production and layout: Emma Bryers
Maps: Kevin Feeney

Managing Director: Andy Riddle
Commercial Director: Patrick Dawson
Publisher: Alan Murphy
Publishing Managers: Felicity Laughton, Nicola Gibbs
Digital Editors: Jo Williams, Tom Mellors
Marketing and PR: Liz Harper
Sales: Diane McEntee
Advertising: Renu Sibal
Finance and Administration: Elizabeth Taylor

Photography credits
Front cover: Ralf Broskvar / Shutterstock
Back cover: Burnhills / Shutterstock

Printed in Great Britain by CPI Antony Rowe, Chippenham, Wiltshire

Publishing information
Footprint *Focus Guatemala*
1st edition
© Footprint Handbooks Ltd
September 2011

ISBN: 978 1 908206 23 7
CIP DATA: A catalogue record for this book is available from the British Library

® Footprint Handbooks and the Footprint mark are a registered trademark of Footprint Handbooks Ltd

Published by Footprint
6 Riverside Court
Lower Bristol Road
Bath BA2 3DZ, UK
T +44 (0)1225 469141
F +44 (0)1225 469461
footprinttravelguides.com

Distributed in the USA by Globe Pequot Press Guilford, Connecticut

The content of Footprint *Focus Guatemala* has been taken directly from Footprint's *Central America Handbook* which was researched and written by Richard Arghiris and Peter Hutchison.

Contents

Guatemala has a monopoly on colour – from the red lava tongues of the volcanoes in the western highlands to the creamy shades of the caves in the southern Petén, and from the white sand of the Caribbean coast near Lívingston to the black sand and fabulous orange sunsets over the Pacific. And that's just nature's palette. Completing this work of art are traditional Maya fiestas, arcane religious rituals where idol worship and Roman Catholicism merge, and jungle temples where ancient ruins tell of long-lost civilizations. Deep in Guatemala's northern jungle, the majestic cities of the Maya are buried. Temples, stelae and plazas have been discovered here, along with evidence of human sacrifice and astronomical genius, to reveal their dynastic history and traditions.

Antigua is the colonial centre of the New World. Gracefully ruined after an 18th-century earthquake, its cobbled streets are lined with columned courtyards, toppled church arches, preserved pastel-coloured houses, flowers and fountains galore.

Formed by an explosion that blew the lid off the top of a volcanic mountain, Lake Atitlán and its three volcanoes are truly breathtaking. Further west, the bustling city of Quetzaltenango makes an excellent base from which to explore the volcanoes, markets and villages of the western highlands, such as the mountain community of Todos Santos, where the colourful clothes of the Maya and the All Saints' Day horse race are major attractions. In the Verapaces, rivers run through caves stuffed with stalagmites and stalactites. On the humid lower slopes of the Pacific, Olmec-influenced ruins are buried among coffee bushes and turtles nest on the shore, while on the Caribbean coast, the Garífuna rock to the sound of the punta and dolphins frolic in the sea.

Planning your trip

Where to go

Guatemala City is a modern, polluted capital. It is the main entry point for travellers by air and long-distance bus. While there are some sites of interest, a couple of excellent museums in the city centre and some great nightlife, few stay long, preferring to head west to the clean air and relaxed atmosphere of **Antigua**. Once the capital, Antigua was built by the Spanish conquistadors. Later destroyed by several huge earthquakes, the grand ruins of colonial architecture remain, the dramatic location at the foot of three volcanoes and its prominence as a centre for Spanish studies, make Antigua a justifiably popular destination.

Heading northeast from Guatemala City, lie the highlands of the Verapaz region. **Cobán** is the main focus, with access to nearby traditional villages, the caves at Lanquín, the natural bridge of Semuc Champey and, at Purulhá, the Mario Dary Rivera Reserve which protects the habitat of the quetzal, Guatemala's national bird. Skirting the northern shores of Lago de Izabal is the Bocas del Polochic Wildlife Reserve, which is full of monkeys, avifauna and other wildlife.

South of the lake, the highway runs close to **Quiriguá**, which once competed with Tikal and nearby Copán, in Honduras, for dominance of the Maya heartlands. On Guatemala's short Caribbean shore is **Lívingston**, popular with young travellers and, near **El Golfete Biotopo Chocón–Machacas**, a manatee and wildlife reserve and the fabulous Río Dulce gorge. From Lívingston boats go inland to Río Dulce, north to Punta Gorda in Belize, or head for Puerto Barrios for Placencia in Belize, or south overland to Honduras.

The forested northern lowlands of **El Petén** hide most of Guatemala's archaeological sites. The majestic **Tikal** is the most developed for tourism, but many others can be reached including Uaxactún, Yaxhá and El Ceibal. **Flores**, sitting on an island in Lago Petén Itzá, is the centre for exploring El Petén with routes from here to Belize and Mexico.

West of Guatemala City, beyond La Antigua, the mountainous highlands overflow with Maya communities. Market days filled with colour, fiestas crammed with celebrations, and each community characterized by unique clothes and crafts. Several villages are dotted around the shores of **Lago de Atitlán**, a spectacular and sacred lake protected on all sides by silent volcanic peaks. From **Panajachel**, ferries and trails link the small communities. **San Pedro La Laguna** is the chief chill-out and hang-loose spot on the lake's shores, with **San Marcos** the favourite for true relaxation; but there are other less touristy and more interesting options to explore.

An hour north of Lake Atitlán is the famous market of **Chichicastenango**, a town where Maya and visitors converge in a twice-weekly frenzy of buying general goods and produce, alongside textiles and tapestry. The market is alive with colour and is a must for any visitor.

Towards the Mexican border, the towns of **Quetzaltenango**, **Retalhuleu** and **Huehuetenango** provide good opportunities for discovering the charms of western Guatemala, including volcanoes and Maya towns. To the north, in the heart of the Cuchumatanes mountains, **Todos Santos Cuchumatán** stands firm as a town that has restricted Western influences and is increasingly popular as a place to learn about the

Don't miss ...

Numbers relate to map on page 4.

Mam way of life, including language and weaving classes. Along the Pacific coastline, the turtle-nesting sites of **Monterrico** are attracting visitors to this little-explored district of Guatemala.

Suggested itinerary

The most natural trip in Guatemala, if you're travelling through the region, is to enter the country from the north from Mexico or Belize, visit Tikal and then head south. After some time in La Antigua and around Lake Atitlán, explore the towns of the Guatemalan highlands. Continuing south, there are many options for crossing the border. Head for El Florido, for best access to Copán, or out to the Caribbean and the crossing at Entre Ríos–Corinto near Puerto Barrios for the Bay Islands. Three to four weeks is a good stay in Guatemala; any less and you'll have to rush around.

When to go

Climate is dependent upon altitude and varies greatly. Most of the population lives at between 900 m and 2500 m, where the climate is healthy – with warm days and cool nights, so you'll need warm clothes at night. The majority of visitors spend most of their time in the highlands, where the dry season lasts from November to April. The central region around Cobán has an occasional drizzle-like rain called *chipi chipi* in February and March. Some places enjoy a respite from the rains (the *canícula*) in July and August. On the Pacific and Caribbean coasts you can expect rain all year round, heaviest on the Pacific in June and September with a dry spell in between, but with no dry season on the Caribbean. In the lowlands of El Petén, the wet season is roughly May to October, when the mosquitoes are most active. December to February are cooler months, while March and April are hot and dry. All of this is increasingly settled, according to Guatemalans, who say that the clear divisions of the seasons are blurring. In terms of festivals, the key events are **Semana Santa** at Easter in Antigua, see page 39, and **All Saints' Day** in Todos Santos, see page 89.

What to do

Archaeology

Archaeology is the big attraction. Consequently there are numerous organizations offering tours. Some companies operate out of Flores and Santa Elena in the Petén using local villagers to help with expeditions.

Explorations, in the USA, T1-239-992-9660, www.explorationsinc.com, has tours led by archaeologist and Maya specialist Travis Doering.

Maya Expeditions, 15 Calle "A", 14-07, Zona 10, Guatemala City, T2363-4955, www.mayaexpeditions.com, offers trips to **Piedras Negras** (with archaeologists who worked on the 1990s excavation of the site), **Río Azul**, the Petexbatún area, **El Mirador**, led by Dr Richard Hansen (the chief archaeologist of the site) and a trip to the more recently discovered **Cancuén** site, led by its chief archaeologist, Dr Arthur Demarest.

Mountain biking

Mountain biking is an increasingly popular activity in Guatemala. There are numerous tracks and paths that weave their way across the country, passing hamlets as you go.

Old Town Outfitters, 5 Av Sur 12 "C", Antigua, T7832-4171, www.adventure guatemala.com, is a recommended operator, offering mountain bike tours starting at US$25 for a half day. They also deals in the gear.

Mountain and volcano climbing

Guatemala represents a wealth of opportunity for climbers, with more than 30 volcanoes on offer. There are also the heights of the Cuchumatanes Mountains in the highlands, which claims the highest non-volcanic peak in the country at 3837 m, and those of the relatively unexplored Sierra de Las Minas in eastern Guatemala close to the Río Motagua Valley.

Fundación Defensores de la Naturaleza, 2a Av 14-08, Zona 14, Guatemala City, T2310-2929, are the people to contact for a *permiso* to climb in the Sierra de las Minas Biosphere Reserve.

Turismo Ek Chuah, 3 Calle 6-24, Zona 2, www.ekchuah.com, offer volcano-specific tours, see page 30. For other operators offering volcano climbing around Guatemala City and Antigua, see page 48.

Nature tourism

The majority of tour operators listed in this guide will offer nature-oriented tours. There are several national parks, *biotopos* and protected areas in Guatemala, each with their highlights. **CECON** (Centro de Estudios Conservacionistas) and **INGUAT** have set up conservation areas for the protection of Guatemalan wildlife (the quetzal, manatee, jaguar, etc) and their habitats. Several other national parks (some including Maya archaeological sites) and forest reserves have been set up or are planned.

CONAP (Consejo Nacional de Areas Protegidas) Av, 6-06, Zona 1, Guatemala City, T2238-0000, http://conap.online.fr, is the national parks and protected areas authority.

Proyecto Ecológico Quetzal, 2 Calle, 14-36, Zona 1, Cobán, T7952-1047, www.eco quetzal.org, a non-profit-making project, is another useful organization.

Spiritual interest

There is a spiritual centre on the shores of Lake Atitlán that offers courses in accordance with the cycle of the moon: **Las Pirámides del Ka**, in San Marcos La Laguna, offers yoga and meditation as well as spiritual instruction year round (see also page 72). At the **Takilibén Maya Misión** in Momostenango, day keeper Rigoberto Itzep (leave a message for him on T7736-5537), 3 Av "A", 6-85, Zona 3, offers courses in Maya culture.

Textiles and weaving

It is possible to get weaving lessons in many places across the highlands. Weaving lessons can also be organized through Spanish schools.

Watersports
Diving

La Iguana Perdida, Santa Cruz La Laguna, T5706-4117, www.laiguanaperdida.com, for diving in Lake Atitlán with **ATI Divers**.

Kayaking

Old Town Outfitters, Antigua, www.adventureguatemala.com, run kayaking tours.

Waterskiing

La Iguana Perdida, Santa Cruz La Laguna, see above for contact info, also organize waterskiing.

Whitewater rafting

Rafting is possible on a number of rivers in Guatemala across a range of grades. However, none of the trips are turn-up-and-go – they have to be arranged in advance. In general, the larger the group, the cheaper the cost.

Maya Expeditions, see address under Archaeology, above, is the country's best outfitter. It rafts the **Río Cahabón** in Alta Verapaz (Grade III-V), the **Río Naranjo** close to Coatepeque (Grade III), the **Río Motagua** close to Guatemala City (Grade III-IV), the **Río Esclavos**, near Barbarena (Grade III-IV), the **Río Coyolate** close to Santa Lucía Cotzumalguapa (Grade II-III) and the **Río Chiquibul** in the Petén (Grade II-III). It also runs a rafting and caving tour in the Petén and a combined archaeology and rafting tour where you would raft through a canyon on the **Río Usumacinta** (Grade II). For a little extra excitement, Maya Expeditions also arrange bungee jumping in Guatemala City.

Getting there

Air

From the USA American (Atlanta; Chicago; Dallas Fort Worth; Miami), **Continental** (Houston), **Delta** (Atlanta), **United** (Los Angeles), **Grupo Taca** (Miami).

From Canada Connections are made through San Salvador, Los Angeles or Miami.

From Europe Iberia flies directly from Madrid and via Miami, with connecting flights from other European cities. Long-haul operators from Europe will share between airlines, taking passengers across the Atlantic normally to Miami, and using **Taca**, for example, to link to Guatemala City.

From Central America Connections available throughout Central America, in most cases travelling through the capital city. There are exceptions with connections to Belize from Flores. **Taca** from the Caribbean and **Cubana** from Havana.

From South America Lacsa from Bogotá via San José, **Copa** via Panama.

Road

There are good road crossings with all of Guatemala's neighbouring countries. There are several crossing points to southern **Mexico** from western Guatemala with additional routes through the jungle from Palenque. From **Belize** it is possible to cross from Benque Viejo del Carmen. Links with **Honduras** are possible on the Caribbean near Corinto, and for the ruins at Copán the best crossing is El Florido. There are four road routes into El Salvador.

An unofficial tourist tax (10-30 quetzales) is sometimes charged on leaving or entering overland at some borders (borders may not be open 24 hours). Bribery is now less common at border crossings. Ask for a receipt and, if you have time and the language ability, do not give in to corrupt officials. Report any problems to INGUAT.

Sea

Connections by sea with daily boats between **Punta Gorda** in Guatemala and **Lívingston**.

Getting around

Air

Grupo Taca, www.taca.com, links Guatemala City with Flores/Santa Elena. TAG, www.tag.com.gt, also flies this route daily, US$135 one way. See page 147 for (overland) services to Tikal. Private charters are on the increase.

Road

Bus There is an extensive network of bus routes throughout the country. The chicken buses (former US school buses) are mostly in a poor state of repair and overloaded. Faster and more reliable Pullman services operate on some routes. Correct fares should be posted. We receive regular complaints that bus drivers charge tourists more than locals, a practice that is becoming more widespread. One way to avoid being overcharged is to watch for what the locals pay or ask a local, then tender the exact fare on the bus. Many long-distance buses leave very early in the morning. Make sure you can get out of your hotel/*pensión*. For international bus journeys make sure you have small denomination local currency or US dollar bills for border taxes. At Easter there are few buses on Good Friday or the Saturday and buses are packed with long queues for tickets for the few days before Good Friday. Many names on bus destination boards are abbreviated: (Guate – Guatemala City; Chichi – Chichicastenango; Xela/Xelajú – Quetzaltenango, and so on). On many tourist routes there are **minibus shuttles**; quick, comfortable, and convenient, they charge a little more than the regular buses, but can be useful. They can be booked through hotels and travel agencies and will pick you up from your hotel.

Car and motorcycle Think carefully before driving a vehicle in Guatemala as it can be hazardous. Of the 14,000 km of roads, the 30% that are paved have improved greatly in recent years and are now of a high standard, making road travel faster and safer. Even cycle tracks (*ciclovías*) are beginning to appear on new roads. However, a new driving hazard in the highlands is the deep gully (for rainwater or falling stones) alongside the road. High clearance is essential on many roads in remoter areas and a 4WD vehicle is useful.

Bringing a vehicle into Guatemala requires the following procedure: presentation of a valid International Driving Licence; a check by **Cuarantena Agropecuaria** (Ministry of Agriculture quarantine) to check you are not importing fruit or veg; at **Aduana** (Customs) you must pay US$4.50 for all forms and a tourist vehicle permit for your vehicle. A motorcycle entry permit costs the same as one for a car. The description of your vehicle on the registration document must match your vehicle's appearance exactly. You must own the car/motorcycle and your name must be on the title papers. When entering the country, ask the officials to add any important accessories you have to the paper. Car insurance can be bought at the borders.

On leaving the country by car or motorcycle, two stamps on a strip of paper are required: surrender of the vehicle permit at customs and the **Cuarantena Agropecuaria** (quarantine) inspection, which is not always carried out. It is better not to import and sell foreign cars in Guatemala, as import taxes are very high.

Gasoline 'Normal' costs US$3.80, 'premium' US$3.90, and diesel is US$3.50 for the US gallon, though prices are rising constantly (prices correct as of January 2011). Unleaded (*sin plomo*) is available in major cities, at Melchor de Mencos and along the Pan-American Highway, but not in the countryside, although it is gradually being introduced across the country.

Security Spare no ingenuity in making your car or motorbike secure. Try never to leave the car unattended except in a locked garage or guarded parking space. Lock the clutch or accelerator to the steering wheel with a heavy, obvious chain or lock. Street children will generally protect your car fiercely in exchange for a tip. Don't wash your car: smart cars attract thieves. Be sure to note down key numbers and carry spares of the most important ones. Try not to leave your fully laden motorbike on its own. An Abus D or chain will keep a bike secure. A cheap alarm gives you peace of mind if you leave the bike outside a hotel at night. Most hotels will allow you to bring the bike inside. Look for hotels that have a courtyard or more secure parking and never leave luggage on the bike overnight or whilst unattended. Also take a cover for the bike. Just about all parts and accessories are available at decent prices in Guatemala City at FPK, 5 Calle 6-75, Zona 9.

Border crossings From Mexico to Western Guatemala: **Ciudad Tecún Umán/Ciudad Hidalgo** is the main truckers' crossing. It is very busy and should be avoided at all costs by car. **Talismán**, the next border crossing north, is more geared to private cars. **La Mesilla** is the simplest for private cars and you can do your own paperwork with ease. All necessary documents can be obtained here.

Car hire Average rates are US$35-100 per day. Credit cards or cash are accepted for rental. Local cars are usually cheaper than those at international companies; if you book ahead from abroad with the latter, take care that they do not offer you a different vehicle claiming your original request is not available. Cars may not always be taken into neighbouring countries (none are allowed into Mexico or Belize); rental companies that do allow their vehicles to cross borders charge for permits and paperwork. If you wish to drive to Copán, you must check this is permissible and you need a letter authorizing you to take the vehicle in to Honduras. **Tabarini** and **Hertz** allow their cars to cross the border.

Cycling The scenery is gorgeous, the people friendly and colourful, but the hills are steep and sometimes long. The Pan-American Highway is OK from Guatemala City west; it has a shoulder and traffic is not very heavy. Buses are frequent and it is easy to load a bicycle on the roof; many buses do so, charging about two-thirds of the passenger fare. On the road, buses are a hazard for cyclists; Guatemala City is particularly dangerous. Look out for the cycle tracks (*ciclovías*) on a few main roads.

Hitchhiking Hitching is comparatively easy, but risky, especially for single women. Also beware of theft of luggage, especially in trucks. The best place to try for a lift is at a bridge or on a road out of town; be there no later than 0600, but 0500 is better as that is when truck drivers start their journey. Trucks usually charge US$1-1.50 upwards for a lift/day. Travellers have suggested it can be cheaper by bus. In remote areas, lifts in the back of a pickup are usually available; very crowded, but convenient when bus services are few and far between, or stop early in the day.

Sea

You can get around Lake Atitlán and from Puerto Barrios to Lívingston by public boat services. Private boat services are possible from Puerto Barrios to Belize and Honduras and around El Estor and Río Dulce and around Lake Petén Itzá.

Sleeping

The tourist institute INGUAT publishes a list of maximum prices for single, double and triple occupancy of hundreds of hotels throughout the country in all price ranges, though the list is thin at the budget end. They will deal with complaints about overcharging if you can produce bills or other proof. Room rates should be posted in all registered hotels. Ask if taxes (*impuestos*) are included when you are given the room rate. INGUAT tax is 10% and service charge is usually an additional 12%. Busiest seasons are Easter, December and July to August. Most budget hotels do not supply toilet paper, soap or towels. There are no official campsites in Guatemala.

Eating and drinking

Traditional Central American/Mexican food such as tortillas, tamales, tostadas, etc, are found everywhere. Tacos are less spicy than in Mexico. *Chiles rellenos* (chillies stuffed with meat and vegetables) are a speciality in Guatemala and may be *picante* (spicy) or *no picante*. *Churrasco*, charcoal-grilled steak, is often accompanied by *chirmol*, a sauce of tomato, onion and mint. Guacamole is also excellent. Local dishes include *pepián* (thick meat stew with vegetables) in Antigua, *patín* (small fish from Lake Atitlán wrapped in leaves and served in a tomato-based sauce) from Lake Atitlán, *cecina* (beef marinated in lemon and bitter orange) from the same region. *Fiambre* is widely prepared for families and friends who gather on All Souls' Day (1 November). It consists of all kinds of meat, fish, chicken, vegetables, eggs or cheese served as a salad with rice, beans and other side dishes. Desserts include *mole* (plantain and chocolate), *torrejas* (sweet bread soaked in egg and *panela* or honey) and *buñuelos* (similar to profiteroles) served with hot cinnamon syrup. For breakfast try *mosh* (oats cooked with milk and cinnamon), fried plantain with

Sleeping and eating price codes

Sleeping

$$$$ over US$150   **$$$**   US$66-150

$$ US$30-65   **$**   under US$30

Price codes refer to a standard double/twin room in high season.

Eating

$$$ over US$15   **$$**   US$8-15   **$**   under US$8

Price codes refer to the cost of a two-course meal, not including drinks.

cream, black beans in various forms. *Pan dulce* (sweet bread), in fact bread in general, and local cheese are recommended. Try *borracho* (cake soaked in rum).

Drink

Local beers are good (Monte Carlo, Cabra, Gallo and Moza, a dark beer); bottled, carbonated soft drinks (*gaseosas*) are safest. Milk should be pasteurized. Freshly made *refrescos* and ice creams are delicious made of many varieties of local fruits; *licuados* are fruit juices with milk or water, but hygiene varies, so take care. Water should be filtered or bottled. By law alcohol cannot be consumed after 2000 on Sundays.

Festivals and events

Although specific dates are given for fiestas, there's often a week of jollification beforehand.

1 Jan New Year.

Mar/Apr Holy Week (4 days). Easter celebrations are exceptional in Antigua and Santiago Atitlán. Bus fares may be doubled.

1 May Labour Day.

15 Aug Public holiday Guatemala City only.

15 Sep Independence Day.

12 Oct Discovery of America. Not a business holiday.

20 Oct Revolution Day.

1 Nov All Souls' Day. Celebrated with abandonment and drunkeness in Todos Santos. In Santiago Sacatepéquez, the *Día de los Muertos* is characterized by colourful kite-flying (*barriletes*).

24 Dec Christmas Eve. From noon, although not a business holiday.

25 Dec Christmas Day.

31 Dec Public holiday from noon.

Shopping

Visiting a market in Guatemala can be one of the most enjoyable and memorable experiences of any trip. Bartering in the markets is the norm and is almost expected and unbelievable discounts can be obtained. You won't do better anywhere else in Central America, but getting the discount is less important than paying a fair price. Woven goods are normally cheapest bought in the town of origin. Try to avoid middlemen and buy direct from the weaver. Guatemalan coffee is highly recommended, although the best is exported; coffee sold locally is not vacuum-packed.

Essentials A-Z

Customs and duty free

You are allowed to take in, free of duty, personal effects and articles for your own use, 2 bottles of spirits and 80 cigarettes or 100 g of tobacco. Temporary visitors can take in any amount in quetzales or foreign currencies. The local equivalent of US$100 per person may be reconverted into US dollars on departure at the airport, provided a ticket for immediate departure is shown.

Drugs

If caught with drugs you'll wind up in prison where the minimum penalty is 5 years. A number of police have been installed in the traditional laid-back travellers' drug haven of San Pedro on Lake Atitlán.

Electricity

Generally 110 volts AC, 60 cycles, US-style plug. Electricity is usually reliable in the towns but can be a problem in more remote areas like Petén.

Embassies and consulates

Belgium, Av Winston Churchill 185, 1180, Brussels, T(+322) 345-9058 (also covers Luxembourg).
Belize, 8 A St, Belize City, T223-3150.
Canada, 130 Albert St, Suite 1010, Ottawa, Ontario, K1P 5G4, T613 233-7188.
Costa Rica, del Gimnasio Fitsimons 100 m sur, 50 m oeste Sabana Sur, San José, T2291-6208.
El Salvador, 15 Av Norte No 135, between C Arce and 1 C Pte, San Salvador, T2271-2225.
France, 66 Rue Grignan, 13001, Marseille, T8866-3012 (also covers Portugal and Switzerland).
Germany, Joachim-Karnatz-Allee 45-47 D-10557, Berlin, T30 206-4363.
Honduras, C Arturo López Rodezno No 2421, Col Las Minitas, Tegucigalpa, T2232-1580.

Israel, Medinat Hayeydim 103, Ackerstein building, entry B, floor 2, Herzliya Pituah, T957-7335.
Italy, Vía dei Colli della Farnesina 128, 1-00194, Rome, T3638-1143.
Japan, 38 Kowa Bldg, 9th floor, room 905, Nishi-Azabu, Tokyo 106-0031, T3 3400-1830.
Mexico, Av Explanada No 1025, Col Lomas de Chapultepec, 11000 México DF, T5540-7520.
Nicaragua, Km 11.5 on road to Masaya, Managua, T2799-609.
Panama, Edif Altamira, 9th floor, office 925, Vía Argentina, El Cangrejo, Corregimiento de Bella Vista, Panama City, T2369-3475.
Spain, C Rafael Salgado No 3, 10a derecha, 28036, Madrid, T1-344-1417 (also covers Morocco).
UK, 13 Fawcett St, London, SW10 9HN, T020-7351-3042, embaguategtm@btconnect.com.
USA, 2220 R St NW, Washington DC, 20008, T202 745-4952, www.guatemala-embassy.org.

Health

Guatemala is healthy enough if precautions are taken about drinking water, milk, uncooked vegetables and peeled fruits; carelessness on this point is likely to lead to amoebic dysentery, which is endemic. In Guatemala City 2 good hospitals are **Bella Aurora**, 10 C, 2-31, Zona 14, T2368-1951 and **Herrera Llerandi**, 6 Av, 8-71, Zona 10, T2334-5959, but you must have full medical insurance or sufficient funds to pay for treatment. English and other languages are spoken. Most small towns have clinics. At the public hospitals, which are seriously underfunded and where care for major problems is not good, you may have an examination for a nominal fee, but drugs are expensive.

Internet
Internet cafés are found in all tourist destinations, ask around in the cities for the best rates. Rates are US$0.50-1.50 per hr.

Language
The official language is Spanish and Guatemala is one of the biggest centres for learning Spanish in Latin America. Outside the main tourist spots few people speak English. There are over 20 Mayan languages.

Regarding pronunciation in Guatemala, 'X' is pronounced 'sh', as in Xela (shay-la).

Media
The main newspaper is *Prensa Libre* (www.prensalibre.com). The *Guatemala Post*, www.guatemalapost.com, is published in English online. *Siglo Veintiuno*, www.sigloxxi. com, is a good newspaper. Mega popular is *Nuestro Diario*, a tabloid with more gory pics than copy. The *Revue*, www.revuemag.com, produced monthly in Antigua, carries articles, maps, advertisements, lodgings, tours and excursions, covering Antigua, Panajachel, Quetzaltenango, Río Dulce, Monterrico, Cobán, Flores and Guatemala City.

Money → *US$1=7.80 quetzales (Aug 2011)*
The unit is the quetzal, divided into 100 centavos. There are coins of 1 quetzal, 50 centavos, 25 centavos, 10 centavos, 5 centavos and 1 centavo. Paper currency is in denominations of 5, 10, 20, 50, 100 and 200 quetzales.

There is often a shortage of small change; ask for small notes when you first change money to pay hotel bills, transport, etc.

ATMs and exchange
There are numerous banks in Guatemala and in cities and towns most have ATMs (*cajeros automáticos*). All will change US dollars cash into quetzales, the majority will accept Visa and MasterCard to obtain cash, and some will change TCs, up to US$5000, although they are becoming less commonly accepted. **Banco Industrial** in Guatemala City and at the international airport will change sterling, Canadian dollars and yen. **Banco Uno** will change euros and Mexican pesos.

Banks usually charge up to 2% per transaction to advance quetzales on a credit card. Citicorp and Visa TCs are easier to change outside the main cities than Amex. Your passport is required and in some cases the purchase receipt as well, especially in the capital.

Credit cards
Visa and MasterCard are the most widely recognized and accepted bank cards. Some establishments may make a charge for use of credit cards – usually about US$3. Check before you sign. In the main it is only higher-class hotels and restaurants that accept cards. **Visa assistance**, T1-800-999-0115/T2331-8720; **MasterCard**, T1-800-999-1480/T2334-0578. **American Express**, T1-800-999-0245/T2470-4848. Amex cards are not very widely accepted.

Cost of living and travelling
Guatemala is one of the cheapest Central America countries, and those travelling on a tight budget should be able to get by on US$25 a day or less. With shorter distances, especially compared with Mexico to the north, travel becomes much less of a demand on your budget with the exception of the trip north to Tikal.

Opening hours
Banks Mon-Fri 0900-1500, Sat 0900-1300. Some city banks are introducing later hours, up to 2000; in the main tourist towns and shopping malls, some banks are open 7 days a week. **Shops** 0900-1300 and 1500-1900, often mornings only on Sat.

Post

Airmail to **Europe** takes 10-14 days. Letters cost US$1.10 for the first 20 g, US$3.40 for up to 100 g and US$37 for up to 2 kg. Airmail letters to the **US and Canada** cost US$0.1.10 for the first 20 g. Airmail parcel service to US is reliable (4 to 14 days) and costs US$2.70 for up 100 g and US$30 for up to 2 kg. Parcels over 2 kg can be sent from Guatemala City, Correos y Telégrafos, 7 Av y 12 C, Zona 1, and Antigua US$55 for up to 4.5 kg. See under Panajachel and Chichicastenango (pages 82 and 83) for alternative services.

Prohibition

Take care with gambling in public places and do not take photos of military installations. See also Drugs, page 14.

Safety

In some parts of the country you may be subject to military or police checks. Local people can be reluctant to discuss politics with strangers. Do not necessarily be alarmed by 'gunfire', which is much more likely to be fireworks and bangers, a national pastime, especially early in the morning.

Robberies and serious assaults on tourists are becoming more common. While you can do nothing to counter the bad luck of being in the wrong place at the wrong time, sensible precautions can minimize risks. Single women should be especially careful. Tourist groups are not immune and some excursion companies take precautions. Do not travel at night if at all possible and take care on roads that are more prone to vehicle hijacks – the road between Flores and the Belizean border, the highway between Antigua and Panajachel and the principal highway between the capital and El Salvadorean border. Assaults and robberies on the public (former US) buses have increased. There have been a high number of attacks on private vehicles leaving the airport.

Consult www.fco.gov.uk, http://guatemala.usembassy.gov/recent_incidents.html and http://travel.state.gov.

Asistur, T1500/2421-2810 is a 24-hr, year-round tourist assistance programme for any problem or question. There is also a national tourist police force, **POLITUR**, T5561-2073, or for emergencies: T120/122/123. Other useful numbers include: **national police** T110; and **tourist police** in Antigua T832-7290.

Tax

There is a 17% ticket tax on all international tickets sold in Guatemala. There is also a US$30 or quetzal equivalent international departure tax.

The tourist institute **INGUAT** tax is 10%. Service charge is usually an extra 12%.

Telephone → *Country code T+502, Directory enquiries T+154.*

All phone numbers in the country are on an 8-figure basis. There are 2 main service providers – **Telgua** and **Telefónica**. Telefónica sells cards with access codes, which can be used from any private or public Telefónica phone. Telgua phone booths are ubiquitous and use cards sold in values of 20 and 50 quetzales. From a Telgua phone, dial 147 before making an international call.

Most businesses offering a phone-call service charge a minimum of US$0.13 for a local call, making a phone card a cheaper option.

International calls can be made from phone booths, however, unlike the local calls, it is cheaper to find an internet café or shop, which tend to offer better rates.

Mobile phone sim cards are affordable, with good deals costing around US$10-20 for the card, which includes free calls. Comcel and PCS offer mobile phone services. Rates are around US$0.03 a minute for a national call, US$1.20 for international.

Operator calls are more expensive. For international calls via the operator, dial T147-110. For calling card and credit card call options, you need a fixed line in a hotel or private house. First you dial 9999 plus the following digits: For **Sprint USA**, dial 136; **AT&T Direct**: 190; **Germany**: 049; **Canada**: 198; **UK (BT)**: 044; **Switzerland**: 041; **Spain**: 034, **Italy**: 039.

Collect calls may be made from public Telgua phones by dialling T147-120.

Time
GMT -6 hrs.

Tipping
Tip hotel and restaurant staff 10% in the better places (often added to the bill). Tip airport porters US$0.25 per bag.

Tourist information
The Guatemalan Maya Centre, 94b Wandsworth Bridge Rd, London SW6 2TF, T020-7371-5291, www.maya.org.uk, has information on Guatemala, the Maya, a library, video archive and a textile collection; visits by prior appointment.
Instituto Guatemalteco de Turismo (**INGUAT**), 7 Av, 1-17, Zona 4, Centro Cívico, Guatemala City, T2421-2800, www.visit guatemala.com. INGUAT provides bus times, hotel lists and road maps. Staff are helpful. Open Mon-Fri 0800-1600. Also office at the airport, open for all arrivals. The INGUAT airport office is open daily 0600-2400.

INGUAT offices outside Guatemala
See also Embassies and consulates, page 14.
Germany, Joachim Karntaz-Alle 45-47, 10557, Berline Tiergarten.
Italy, Viale Prassilla 152, 00124, Rome, T390-6-5091-6626.
Mexico, T00-52-5202-1457, turismoembagua@prodigy.net.mx.

Spain, Calle Rafael Salgado 9, 4th Izquierda, 28036 Madrid, T/F34-91-457-3424.
USA, T001-202-518-5514.

Useful websites
Regional websites covering some of the more popular areas include **www.atitlan.com**, **www.mayaparadise.com** (Río Dulce/Lívingston), **www.cobanav.net** (Cobán) and **www.xelapages.com** (Quetzaltenango). **Posada Belén** in Guatemala City run a very informative site packed with information, www.guatemalaweb.com.

Of the several publications with websites, the *Revue*, **www.revuemag.com**, is probably the most useful to the visitor.

Visas and immigration
Only a valid passport is required for citizens of all Western European countries; USA, Canada, Mexico, all Central American countries, Australia, Israel, Japan and New Zealand. The majority of visitors get 90 days on arrival.

Visa renewal must be done in Guatemala City after 90 days, or on expiry. Passport stamp renewal on expiry for those citizens only requiring a valid passport to enter Guatemala must also be done at the immigration office at **Dirección General de Migración**, 6 Av, 3-11, Zona 4, Guatemala City, T2411-2411, Mon-Fri 0800-1600 (0800-1230 for payments). This office extends visas and passport stamps only once for a further period of time, depending on the original time awarded (maximum 90 days). Since 2006, when Guatemala signed a Central America-4 (CA-4) Border Control Agreement with El Salvador, Honduras, and Nicaragua you will have to visit a country outside of these 3 to re-enter and gain 90 days. These rules have been introduced to stop people leaving the country for 72 hrs (which is the legal requirement) every 6 months and returning, effectively making them permanent residents.

Working and volunteering

If you would like to volunteer, it is best to try and make contact before arriving, if only by a few days. Such is the demand for positions that unskilled volunteers very often have to pay for board and lodgings. Work needs to be planned and, although there is always work to do, your time will be used most efficiently if your arrival is expected and planned for.

Asociación de Rescate y Conservación de Vida Silvestre (**ARCAS**), T2478-4096, www.arcasguatemala.com. Runs projects involving working with nature and wildlife, returning wild animals to their natural habitat.

Casa Alianza, 13 Av, 0-37, Zona 2 de Mixco, Col la Escuadrilla Mixco, Guatemala City, T2250-4964, www.casa-alianza.org. A project that helps street kids.

Casa Guatemala, 14 C, 10-63, Zona 1, Guatemala City, T2331-9408, www.casa-guatemala.org. Runs a project for abandoned and malnourished children at Río Dulce.

Comité Campesino del Altiplano, on Lake Atitlán, 10 mins from San Lucas, T5804-9451, www.ccda.galeon.com. This Campesino Cooperative now produces Fair Trade organic coffee buying from small farmers in the region; long-term volunteers are welcome but Spanish is required.

Fundación Mario Dary, Diagonal 6, 17-19, Zona 10, Guatemala City, T2333-4957, fundary@intelnet.net.gt. Operates conservation, health and education projects on the Punta de Manabique and welcomes volunteers.

Proyecto Ak' Tenamit, 11 Av 'A', 9-39, Zona 2, Guatemala City, T2254-1560, www.aktenamit.org, based at Clínica Lámpara, 15 mins upriver from Lívingston. This project was set up to help 7000 civil-war-displaced Q'eqchi' Maya who now live in the region in 30 communities.

Proyecto Mosaico Guatemala, 3 Av Norte 3, Antigua. T7832-0955, www.promosaico.org. An information centre and clearing house for volunteers, with access to opportunities all over the country.

Quetzaltrekkers, Casa Argentina, 12 Diagonal, 8-37, Zona 1, Quetzaltenango, T7765-5895, www.quetzaltrekkers.com. Volunteer opportunities for hiking guides and office workers, minimum 3-month commitment.

UPAVIM, C Principal, Sector D-1, Col La Esperanza, Zona 12, Guatemala City, T2479-9061, www.upavim.org. This project helps poor families, providing social services and education for the workers using fair-trade principles.

There are also opportunites to work in children's homes in Quetzaltenango (Xela). 2 organizations are **Casa Hogar de Niños** and the **Asociación Hogar Nuevos Horizontes**. See page 107. Also check out Xela-based volunteering information organization www.entremundos.org. Several language schools in Xela fund community development projects and seek volunteers. Make enquiries in town or via www.xelapages.com.

The London-based **Guatemala Solidarity Network**, www.guatemalasolidarity.org.uk, can assist with finding projects that look at human rights issues.

Contents

Guatemala

Footprint features

At a glance

◉ **Getting around** Bus and the odd flight for long distances, minibus shuttles for shorter distances. Boats to Belize on the Caribbean coast.

⏱ **Time required** 3-4 weeks; any less and you'll have to rush around.

☁ **Weather** Mid-20°Cs, but chilly at higher altitudes. Wet season is May-Oct.

✖ **When not to go** Lowlands in the wet season, if you don't like rain.

Guatemala City

Smog-bound and crowded, Guatemala City is the commercial and administrative centre of the country. It is a sprawl of industrial activity lightly sprinkled with architectural treasures and out-of-place tributes to urban sculpture. Rarely rated by visitors, this is the beating heart of Guatemala and is worth a couple of days if you have time and can bear the noise and pollution in Zona 1. Guatemala City is surrounded by active and dormant volcanoes easily visited on day trips.

Ins and outs → *Altitude: 1500 m.*

Getting there
The airport is in the south part of the city at La Aurora, 4 km from the Plaza Central, T2331-8392. It has banks, ATMs, internet, bars and restaurants. A taxi to Zona 10 is US$8, Zona 1, US$10 and from Antigua, US$25-30. Shuttles from outside airport to Antigua meet all arriving flights, US$10. The Zona 4 chicken bus terminal between 1-4 Avenida and 7-9 Calle serves the Occidente (west), the Costa Sur (Pacific coastal plain) and El Salvador. The area of southern Zona 1 contains many bus offices and is the departure point for the Oriente (east), the Caribbean zone, Pacific coast area towards the Mexican border and the north, to Flores and Tikal. First-class buses often depart from company offices in Zona 1 (see map, page 22). Note that some companies have been moved from Zona 1 and Zona 4 out to Zona 7 and 12. ▶▶ *See Transport, page 30.*

Getting around
Any address not in Zona 1 – and it is absolutely essential to quote zone numbers in addresses – is probably some way from the centre. Addresses themselves, being purely numerical, are usually easy to find. For example, 19 Calle, 4-83 is on 19 Calle between 4 Avenida and 5 Avenida at No 83.

If driving, *Avenidas* have priority over *calles* (except in Zona 10, where this rule varies).

Tourist information
INGUAT ① *7 Av, 1-17, Zona 4 (Centro Cívico), 24 hrs T1801-464-8281, T2421-2800, www.visitguatemala.com, Mon-Fri 0800-1600, English is sometimes spoken.* They are very friendly and provide a hotel list, a map of the city, and general information on buses, market days, museums, etc. They also have an office in the **airport arrivals hall** ① *T2331-4256, 0600-2100,* where staff are exceptionally helpful and on the ball.

Background

Guatemala City was founded by decree of Carlos III of Spain in 1776 to serve as capital after earthquake damage to the earlier capital, Antigua, in 1773. Almost completely destroyed by earthquakes in 1917-1918, it was rebuilt in modern fashion, or in copied colonial, only to be further damaged by earthquake in 1976. Most of the affected buildings have been restored.

Sights → See listings, pages 26-34.

The old centre of the city is Zona 1. It is still a busy shopping and commercial area, with some good hotels and restaurants, and many of the cheaper places to stay. However, the main activity of the city has been moving south, first to Zona 4, now to Zonas 9, 10 and 14. With the move have gone commerce, banks, embassies, museums and the best hotels and restaurants. The best residential areas are in the hills to the east, southeast and west.

① **Guatemala City orientation**

N

1 km
1 mile

→ **Guatemala City maps**
1 Orientation, page 21
2 Zona 1, page 22
3 Zona 9, 10 & 13, page 24

Around Zona 1

At the city's heart lies the **Parque Central**. It is intersected by the north-to-south-running 6 Avenida, the main shopping street. The eastern half has a floodlit fountain; on the west side is **Parque Centenario**, with an acoustic shell in cement used for open-air concerts and public meetings. The Parque Central is popular on Sunday with many *indígenas* selling textiles.

To the east of the plaza is the **cathedral** (www.catedral.org.gt). It was begun in 1782 and finished in 1815 in classical style with notable blue cupolas and dome. Inside are paintings and statues from ruined Antigua. Solid silver and sacramental reliquary are in the east side chapel of the Sagrario. Next to the cathedral is the colonial mansion of the Archbishop. Aside from the cathedral, the most notable public buildings constructed between 1920 and 1944, after the 1917 earthquake, are the **Palacio Nacional** ① *visits every 15 mins Mon-Fri 0900-1645; every 30 mins Sat and Sun 0900-1630*, built

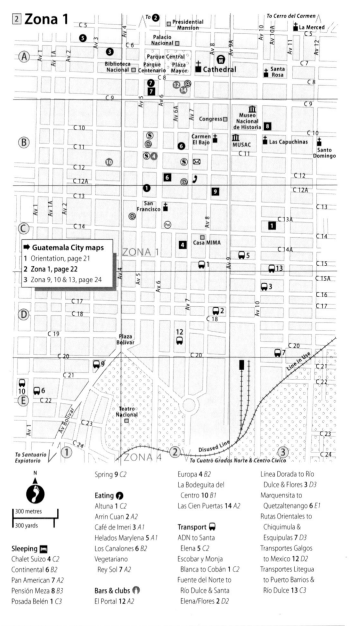

② Zona 1

To ② — Presidential Mansion

To Cerro del Carmen

La Merced

Palacio Nacional

A — Biblioteca Nacional — Parque Centenario — Plaza Mayor — Cathedral — Santa Rosa

Parque Central

B — Congress — Museo Nacional de Historia — Carmen El Bajo — MUSAC — Las Capuchinas — Santo Domingo

C — San Francisco — Casa MIMA

➡ **Guatemala City maps**
1 Orientation, page 21
2 Zona 1, page 22
3 Zona 9, 10 & 13, page 24

ZONA 1

D — Plaza Bolívar

E — Teatro Nacional

To Santuario Expiatorio

ZONA 4 — Disused Line — To Cuatro Grados Norte & Centro Cívico

Line In Use

N

300 metres
300 yards

Sleeping ▦
Chalet Suizo **4** C2
Continental **6** B2
Pan American **7** A2
Pensión Meza **8** B3
Posada Belén **1** C3

Spring **9** C2

Eating ☻
Altuna **1** C2
Arrin Cuan **2** A2
Café de Imeri **3** A1
Helados Marylena **5** A1
Los Canalones **6** B2
Vegetariano
Rey Sol **7** A2

Bars & clubs ☻
El Portal **12** A2

Europa **4** B2
La Bodeguita del
Centro **10** B1
Las Cien Puertas **14** A2

Transport ☻
ADN to Santa
Elena **5** C2
Escobar y Monja
Blanca to Cobán **1** C2
Fuente del Norte to
Río Dulce & Santa
Elena/Flores **2** D2

Línea Dorada to Río
Dulce & Flores **3** D3
Marquensita to
Quetzaltenango **6** E1
Rutas Orientales to
Chiquimula &
Esquipulas **7** D3
Transportes Galgos
to Mexico **12** D2
Transportes Litegua
to Puerto Barrios &
Río Dulce **13** C3

of light green stone, the Police Headquarters, the Chamber of Deputies and the Post Office. To the west of the cathedral are the Biblioteca Nacional and the Banco del Ejército. Behind the Palacio Nacional is the Presidential Mansion.

Museums in Zona 1 include the **Museo Nacional de Historia** ① *9 Calle, 9-70, T2253-6149, Mon-Fri 0900-1600, Sat-Sun 0900-1200 and 13001600, US$6*, which has historical documents and objects from Independence onward. **Museo de la Universidad de San Carlos de Guatemala (MUSAC)** ① *9 Av, 9-79, T2232-0721, www.musacenlinea.org, Mon, Wed-Fri 0930-1730, Sat 0930-1700, closed Tue and Sun, US$1; guided tours at 1000 and 1400*, charts the history of the university. The Salón Mayor is where Guatemala signed its Independence from Mexico in 1823, and in 1826, the Central American Federation, with Guatemala as the seat of power, abolished slavery in the union. Also, Doctor Mariano Gálvez, the country's president from 1831-1838, is buried behind part of the salon wall and a marble bust of him sits outside the door. The Universidad de San Carlos was the first university in Guatemala City. **Casa MIMA** ① *8 Av, 14-12, T2253-6657, casamima@hotmail.com, Mon-Sat 0900-1230, 1400-1500, US$1, no photography,* is the only authentic turn-of-the-19th-century family home open to the public, once owned by the family Ricardo Escobar Vega and Mercedes Fernández Padilla y Abella. It is furnished in European-influenced style with 15th- to mid-20th-century furniture and ornaments.

Most of the churches worth visiting are in Zona 1. **Cerro del Carmen** ① *11 Av y 1 Calle A,* was built as a copy of a hermitage destroyed in 1917-1918, containing a famous image of the Virgen del Carmen. Situated on a hill with good views of the city, it was severely damaged in the earthquake of 1976 and remains in poor shape. **La Merced** ① *11 Av y 5 Calle,* dedicated in 1813, has beautiful altars, organ and pulpit from Antigua as well as jewellery, art treasures and fine statues. **Santo Domingo** ① *12 Av y 10 Calle,* built between 1782 and 1807, is a striking yellow colour, reconstructed after 1917, with an image of Nuestra Señora del Rosario and sculptures. **Sagrado Corazón de Jesús,** or **Santuario Expiatorio** ① *26 Calle y 2 Av,* holds 3000 people; the colourful, exciting modern architecture was by a young Salvadorean architect who had not qualified when he built it. Part of the complex, built in 1963 (church, school and auditorium) is in the shape of a fish. The entrance is a giant arch of multicoloured stained glass, wonderfully illuminated at night. The walls are lined with glass confessionals. **Las Capuchinas** ① *10 Av y 10 Calle,* has a very fine St Anthony altarpiece, and other pieces from Antigua. **Santa Rosa** ① *10 Av y 8 Calle,* was used for 26 years as the cathedral until the present building was ready. The altarpieces are from Antigua (except above the main altar). **San Francisco** ① *6 Av y 13 Calle,* a large yellow and white church that shows earthquake damage outside (1976), has a sculpture of the Sacred Head, originally from Extremadura, in Spain. **Carmen El Bajo** ① *8 Av y 10 Calle,* was built in the late 18th century; again the façade was severely damaged in 1976.

North of the centre

Parque Minerva ① *Av Simeón Cañas, Zona 2, 0900-1700, US$1.50,* has a huge relief map of the country made in 1905 to a horizontal scale of 1:10,000 and a vertical scale of 1:2,000. The park has basketball and baseball courts, bar and restaurant and a children's playground (unsafe at night). To get there, take bus V21 from 7 Avenida, Zona 4. Just beyond is a popular park, the **Hipódromo** which is packed on Sundays with bumper cars and mechanical games, and a great little train for kids.

South of the centre: Avenida La Reforma

The modern **Centro Cívico**, which links Zona 1 with Zona 4, includes the Municipalidad, the Palacio de Justicia, the Ministerio de Finanzas Públicas, the Banco de Guatemala, the mortgage bank, the social-security commission and the tourist board. The curious **Teatro Nacional** ① *Mon-Fri 0800-1630 for tours, US$4*, with its blue and white mosaic, dominates the hilltop of the west side of the Centro Cívico. There is an excellent view of the city and surrounding mountains from the roof. An old Spanish fortress provides a backdrop to the open-air theatre adjoining the Teatro Nacional.

Cuatro Grados Norte, located on Vía 5 between Ruta 1 and Ruta 2, is a pedestrianized area that has grown up around the IGA theatre and bookshop (a cultural centre, which sometimes has interesting concerts and exhibitions). Cafés and bars have tables on the street and it's safe and fun to wander around at night. The **Centro Cultural de España** is located here with live music, films, exhibitions and conferences, there is also a branch of

3 Zona 9, 10 & 13

➡ Guatemala City maps
1 Orientation, page 21
2 Zona 1, page 22
3 Zona 9, 10 & 13, page 24

600 metres
600 yards

Sleeping 🛏
Aeropuerto Guest House 2
Dos Lunas Guest House 1
Hincapié Guest House 3
Otelito 8
San Carlos 5
Residencial Reforma
  La Casa Grande 5

Westin Camino Real 6

Eating 🍴
Casa Chapina 7
Hacienda de los Sánchez 1
Hacienda Real 2
Inca Grill 3
Kacao 5

Los Alpes 6
Tamarindos 12
Tre Fratelli 8

Bars & clubs 🍸
Cheers 9
Kalua 10
Shakespeare's Pub 11

Sophos, an excellent bookshop. On Saturdays there is a street market with craft and jewellery stalls, often cultural events in the street. On Sundays there are clowns and events for children. It's a strange mix of wealthy Guatemalans strolling with their poodles and alternative street-market types; sit back and enjoy watching the people.

To see the finest residential district go south down 7 Avenida to Ruta 6, which runs diagonally in front of Edificio El Triángulo, past the orange **Capilla de Yurrita** (Ruta 6 y Vía 8). Built as a private chapel in 1928 on the lines of a Russian Orthodox church, it has been described as an example of "opulent 19th-century bizarreness and over-ripe extravagance". There are many woodcarvings, slender white pillars, brown/gold ornamentation and an unusual blue sky window over the altar. Ruta 6 runs into the wide tree-lined Avenida La Reforma.

To the east, in Zona 10, are some excellent museums. **Museo Ixchel del Traje Indígena** ① *Campus of Universidad Francisco Marroquín, 6 Calle Final, T2331-3623, www.museoixchel.org, Mon-Fri 0900-1700, Sat 0900-1300, US$4*, has a collection of indigenous dress. In addition to the clothes there are photos from the early 20th century, paintings and very interesting videos. A shop sells beautiful textiles that aren't available on the tourist market, prices are fixed, and quality costs. **Museo Popol Vuh de Arqueología** ① *6 Calle Final, T2338-7896, www.popolvuh.ufm.edu.gt, Mon-Fri 0900-1700, Sat 0900-1300, US$5.50, US$3 charge to take photographs*, has an extensive collection of pre-Columbian and colonial artefacts, as well as a replica of the Dresden Codex, one of the only Maya parchment manuscripts in existence. **Museo de Historia Natural de la USAC y Jardín Botánico** ① *Calle Mcal Cruz 1-56, T2334-6065, Mon-Fri 0800-1600, Sat 0830-1230, US$1.30*, has gardens, stuffed animals and live snakes.

In **Parque Aurora**, Zona 13, in the southern part of the city, are La Aurora International Airport, the Observatory, racetrack and **Parque Zoológico La Aurora** ① *T2472-0507, Tue-Sun 0900-1700, US$1.10*. The newer areas show greater concern for the animals' well-being. There are also several museums: **Museo Nacional de Antropología y Etnología** ① *Salón 5, Parque Aurora, Zona 13, T2475-4406, Tue-Fri 0900-1600, Sat-Sun 0900-1200, 1330-1600, US$5, no photos*. Outstanding Maya pieces including stelae from Piedras Negras and typical Guatemalan dress, as well as good models of Tikal, Quiriguá and Zaculeu. There are sculptures, murals, ceramics, textiles, a collection of masks and an excellent jade collection. Around the corner is the **Museo Nacional de Historia Natural** ① *6 Calle, 7-30, Zona 13, T2472-0468, Mon-Fri 0900-1600, Sat-Sun 0900-1200, 1400-1600, US$5*, which houses a collection of national fauna, including stuffed birds, animals, butterflies, geological specimens, etc. Opposite the archaeology museum, the **Museo de Arte Moderno** ① *Salón 6, Parque Aurora, Zona 13, T2472-0467, US$5, Tue-Fri 0900-1600*, has a modest but enjoyable collection. Next door is the **Museo de los Niños** ① *T2475-5076, Tue-Fri 0830-1200, 1300-1630, US$4*, an interactive museum with a gallery of Maya history and the Gallery of Peace which houses the world's largest single standing artificial tree – a *ceiba*.

Guatemala City listings

For Sleeping and Eating price codes and other relevant information, see pages 12-13.

⊙ Sleeping

You can get better prices in the more expensive hotels by booking corporate rates through a travel agent or simply asking at the desk if any lower prices are available. Hotels are often full at holiday times, eg Easter and Christmas. At the cheaper hotels, single rooms are not always available. There are many cheap *pensiones* near bus and railway stations and markets; those between Calle 14 and Calle 18 are not very salubrious.

Hoteles Villas de Guatemala, reservations 8 Calle 1-75 Zona 10, T2223-5000, www.villasdeguatemala.com, rents luxury villas throughout Guatemala.

Zona 1 *p21, map p22*
$$$ Pan American, 9 Calle, 5-63, T2232-6807, www.hotelpanamerican.com.gt. Quiet and comfortable rooms with TV, but try to avoid rooms on the main-road side. Parking, and breakfast included. Restaurant with good food in the mid-range price bracket.
$$ Continental, 12 Calle, 6-10, T2251-8237. 2 floors up with a very secure street entrance. It has vast, comfortable rooms, but they're spartan; some quadruples available. All are very clean with private bath. Credit cards accepted.
$$ Posada Belén, 13 Calle "A", 10-30, T2232-9226, www.posadabelen.com. A colonial-style house run by the friendly Francesca and René Sanchinelli, who speak English. Quiet, comfy rooms with good hot showers. Laundry, email service, luggage store and good meals. Parking. Tours available. A lovely place to stay, highly recommended.
$$ Spring, 8 Av, 12-65, T2230-2858. Bright rooms with TV in this quiet haven of tranquillity and flowers amid the pollution of Zona 1. Rooms without private shower are cheaper. Patio garden, good breakfasts, and

parking near by. Free coffee, email service, phone calls, luggage store. Probably the best choice in Zona 1 at this price.
$$-$ Chalet Suizo, 7a Calle, 14-34, T2251-3786, chaletsuizo@gmail.com. In a good central position with constant hot-water showers (cheaper with shared bathroom). It is popular, so often crowded. There is a locked luggage store, safety box, and the rooms are secure. Those rooms facing the main street are noisy. Avoid rooms 9-12 as a noisy pump will disturb sleep and 19-21 have very thin walls. Free parking.
$ Pensión Meza, 10 Calle, 10-17, T2232-3177. A large ramshackle place with beds in dorms. It's popular with helpful staff and English is spoken. It's sometimes noisy and some rooms are damp. Other rooms are darker than a prison cell, but cheered by graffiti, poetry and paintings. There is a ping-pong table, book exchange, internet at US$80 per hr, or free Wi-Fi.

South of the centre: Avenida La Reforma *p24, map p24*
$$$$ Westin Camino Real, Av La Reforma y 14 Calle, Zona 10, T2333-3000, www.starwoodhotels.com. Excellent value, good restaurants open 0600-2330, gym, pool, spa, airport shuttle, piano bar and live Cuban music Fri and Sat at 2100.
$$$ Otelito, 12 Calle, 4-51, T2339-1811, Zona 10, www.otelito.com. 12 lovely rooms in this small boutique hotel. Includes breakfast, shuttle to hotel and internet. Restaurant open Mon-Wed 0630-2100, Thu-Sat 0630-2230, Sun 0630-2030.
$$$ Residencial Reforma La Casa Grande, Av La Reforma, 7-67, Zona 10, T2332-0914, www.casagrande-gua.com. Near US Embassy, with nicer rooms than the next door **San Carlos**. Colonial style, all rooms come with TV. Good, small restaurant, open 0630-2100, a bar and internet service. Good value.

$$$ San Carlos, Av La Reforma, 7-89, Zona 10, T2362-9076, www.hsancarlos.com. A small, charming hotel, with pool and plant-filled patio. Includes breakfast and free airport transfer.

$$ Hincapié Guest House, Av Hincapié, 18-77, Zona 13, T2332-7771, ruedapinillos@yahoo.com. On the far side of the airport runway. Continental breakfast included and free airport transport. Cable TV in the rooms.

$$ Hotel Aeropuerto Guest House, 5 mins' walk from the airport at 15 Calle "A", 7-32, Col Aurora 1, Zona 13, T2332-3086, www.aeropuertoguesthouse.com. Free transport to and from the airport. With or without bath, and is clean and safe, breakfast included. Free internet.

$ Dos Lunas Guest House, 21 Calle, 10-92, Zona 13, T2261-4248, www.hoteldoslunas.com. Private rooms and dorms in a comfy B&B. Very close to the airport with free transport to or from the airport. Storage service, free breakfast and water and tourist information. Lorena, the landlady, also organizes shuttles and taxis and tours. English spoken. Reservations advisable as often full.

🍴 Eating

Zona 1 *p21, map p22*

There are all kinds of food available in the capital, from the simple national cuisine to French, Chinese and Italian food. There is a plethora of fast-food restaurants and traditional *comedores* where you will get good value for money; a reasonable set meal will cost no more than US$3. The cheapest places to eat are at street stalls and the various markets – take the normal precautions.

$$$ Altuna, 5 Av, 12-31. Serves tasty Spanish food in huge portions. Lobster available but expensive. Delicious coffee. This hotel has a beautiful traditional Spanish bar interior. There is a branch in Zona 10 at 10 Calle, 0-45.

$$$ Hotel Pan American, 9 Calle, 5-63 (see Sleeping). Best lunchtime menu.

$$ Arrin Cuan, 5 Av, 3-27. A famous local institution specializing in traditional food from Cobán (*subanik*, *gallo en chicha* and *kak ik*). The restaurant is centred around a small courtyard with a little fountain and live lunchtime marimba music. Breakfast available. Also on 16 Calle, 4-32, Zona 10.

$$ Los Canalones – Parrillada Argentina, 6 Av A, 10-39. Mon-Sat 1200-1630. Barbecue on the street outside, for serious meat eaters. Alejandro *El Argentino* does tasty chunks of meat and chorizo served with excellent salad, get there early. Meals include soup, endless tortillas and *refresco*.

$$-$ Café de Imeri, 6 Calle, 3-34. Closed Sun. Sandwiches, salads, soups and pastries in a patio garden. Set lunch and excellent cakes. It's popular with young professional Guatemalans. Try the *pay de queso de elote* (maize cheesecake). Its bakery next door has a rare selection of granary breads, birthday cakes, etc.

$ Restaurante Vegetariano Rey Sol, 8 Calle, 5-36. Closed Sun. A prize vegetarian find – wholesome food and ambience oasis amid the fumes of Zona 1, and popular with the locals. Delicious veggie concoctions at excellent prices served canteen-style by friendly staff. Breakfasts and *licuados* also available. Newer, larger and brighter branch at 11 Calle, 5-51.

Ice cream parlours

Helados Marylena, 6 Calle, 2-49. Open daily 1000-2200. Not quite a meal but almost. This establishment has been serving up the weirdest concoctions for 90 years. From the probably vile – fish, chilli, yucca and cauliflower ice cream – to the heavenly – beer and sputnik (coconut, raisins and pineapple). The *elote* (maize) is good too. This city institution is credited with making children eat their vegetables! Anyone travelling with fussy eaters should stop by here.

South of the centre: Avenida La Reforma *p24, map p24*

Most of the best restaurants are in the 'Zona Viva', within 10 blocks of the Av La Reforma on the east side, between 6 Calle and 16 Calle in Zona 10. Zona 9 is just across the other side of Av La Reforma.

There are several options in the area around Cuatro Grados Norte providing tapas, sushi, *churros* and chocolate. Lively, especially on Fri and Sat nights.

$$$ Café Rouge, Cuatro Grados Norte, Vía 5 between Ruta 1 and Ruta 2. Good cappuccinos, chocolate things and apple pie.

$$$ Hacienda de los Sánchez, 12 Calle, 2-25, Zona 10. Good steaks and local dishes, but seriously crowded at weekends, and so not the most pleasant of settings compared with other steakhouses in the vicinity.

$$$ Hacienda Real, 15 Calle, 15, Zona 10. An excellent steak selection. Candles and palms create a garden-like atmosphere. Nice little bar with Mexican leather chairs on one side.

$$$ Inca Grill, 2 Av 14-32, Zona 10. Tasty Peruvian food, live Andean music.

$$$ Kacao, 2 Av, 13-44, Zona 10. A large variety of delicious local and national dishes, which are attractively prepared and served in ample portions. The setting is fantastic – a giant thatched room, *huípiles* for tablecloths, beautiful candle decorations; some options are expensive.

$$$ L'Ostería, Cuatro Grados Norte, Vía 5 between Ruta 1 and Ruta 2. Popular Italian on the corner with leafy terrace; brick pizza oven.

$$$ Tamarindos, 11 Calle, 2-19A, Zona 10, T2360-2815. Mixed Asian, sushi, Vietnamese rolls, mushrooms stuffed with almonds and crab are some of the tantalizing options at this very smart Asian restaurant with spiral shades and soothing bamboo greens.

$$$ Tre Fratelli, 2 Av 13-25, Zona 10. Good Italian food; tasty bread and parmesan cheese; very lively and popular, some outside tables.

$$ Arguileh, Cuatro Grados Norte, Vía 5 between Ruta 1 and Ruta 2. Eastern-style kebabs and *pan árabe*, wooden decor, looks good.

$$ Café Vienés, in the Westin Camino Real (see Sleeping). One of the best places for German-style coffee and cakes, your chance to try a chocolate fondu.

$$ Casa Chapina, 1a Av, 13-42, Zona 10, T4212-2746. Near the quality hotels, friendly service, reasonable prices and a wide range of traditional and international dishes to choose from.

$$ Los Alpes, 10 Calle, 1-09, Zona 10. Closed Mon. A Swiss/Austrian place with light meals, which also offers a smorgasbord of excellent cakes and chocolates. Popular with Guatemalan families.

$$ Tarboosh, Cuatro Grados Norte, Vía 5 between Ruta 1 and Ruta 2, not far from L'Ostería. Mediterranean cuisine in a funky upstairs setting with loud live music acts.

$$-$ Cafesa, 6 Av, 11-64, Zona 9. 24-hr diner serving Western and Guatemalan food with some seriously cheap options.

🎭 Entertainment

Guatemala City *p20, maps p21, p22 and p24*

Bars and clubs

Cheers, 13 Calle, 0-40, Zona 10. A basement sports bar with pool tables, darts and large cable TV. Mon-Sat 0900-0100, Sun 1300-2400ish. Happy hour until 1800.

El Portal, Portal del Comercio, 8 Calle, 6-30, Zona 1. Mon-Sat 1000-2200. This was a favourite spot of Che Guevara and you can imagine him sitting here holding court at the long wooden bar. A stuffed bull's head now keeps watch over drinkers. To get there, enter the labyrinths of passageways facing the main plaza at No 6-30 where there is a Coke stand. At the first junction bear round to the left and up on the left you will see its sign. *Comida típica* and marimba music, beer from the barrel.

Europa, 11 Calle, 5-16, Zona 1. Mon-Sat 0800-0100. Popular peace-corps/travellers' hangout, sports bar, shows videos, books for sale.
Kalua, 1 Av, 15-06. Huge club, 3 floors with different tunes, stylish.
La Bodeguita del Centro, 12 Calle, 3-55, Zona 1, T2239-2976. The walls of this hip place in an old stockhouse are adorned with posters of Che Guevara, Bob Marley and murdered Salvadorean Archbishop Romero. There's live music Thu-Sat at 2100, talks, plays, films, exhibitions upstairs. Wooden tables are spread over 2 floors; seriously cheap nachos and soup on the menu. It's an atmospheric place to spend an evening. Call in to get their **Calendario Cultural** leaflet.
Las Cien Puertas, Pasaje Aycinea, 7 Av, 8-44, just south of Plaza Mayor, Zona 1. Daily 1600-2400. Has a wonderful atmosphere with political, satirical and love missives covering its walls. There's excellent food and outdoor seating and it's friendly.
Sabor Latino, 1 Av, 13 Calle, Zona 10. A club that's under **Rock and Salambo** on the same block as **Mi Guajira**. The night begins with salsa and graduates to a more hip-hop beat.
Shakespeare's Pub, 13 Calle, 1-51, Zona 10. Mon-Fri 1100-0100, Sat and Sun 1400-0100. English-style basement bar with a good atmosphere, American owner, a favourite with ex-pats and locals, safe for women to drink.

Cinema and theatre
There are numerous cinemas and they often show films in English with Spanish subtitles.
Teatro Nacional, Centro Cívico. Most programmes are Thu-Sun.

◔ Shopping

Guatemala City *p20, maps p21, p22 and p24*
Bookshops
Museo Ixchel, page 25, has a bookshop.
Museo Popol Vuh bookshop, page 25, has a good selection of books on pre-Columbian art, crafts and natural history.

Maps
Maps can be bought from the **Instituto Geográfico Nacional** (IGN), Av Las Américas, 5-76, Zona 13, T2332-2611. Mon-Fri 0900-1730. The whole country is covered by about 200 1:50,000 maps available in colour or photocopies of out of print sections. None is very up to date. There is, however, an excellent 1996, 1:15,000 map of Guatemala City in 4 sheets. A general *Mapa Turístico* of the country is available here, also at INGUAT.

Markets and supermarkets
The **Central Market** operates underground behind the cathedral, from 7 to 9 Av, 8 Calle, Zona 1. One floor is dedicated to textiles and crafts, and there is a large, cheap basketware section on the lower floor. Silverware is cheaper at the market than elsewhere in Guatemala City. Other markets include the **Mercado Terminal** in Zona 4, and the **Mercado de Artesanía** in the Parque Aurora, near the airport, which is for tourists. Large shopping centres are good for a wide selection of local crafts, artworks, funky shoes, and clothes. Don't miss the *dulces*, candied fruits and confectionery.

The best shopping centres are **Centro Comercial Los Próceres**, 18 Calle and 3 Av, Zona 10, the **Centro Comercial La Pradera**, Carretera Roosevelt and Av 26, Zona 10. There is a large **Paiz** supermarket on 18 Calle and 8 Av and a vast shopping mall **Tikal Futura** at Calzada Roosevelt and 22 Av, Zona 11. *Artesanías* for those who shop with a conscience at the fair-trade outlet **UPAVIM**, Calle Principal, Col La Esperanza, Mesquital Zona 12, T2479-9061, www.upavim.org, Mon-Fri 0800-1800, Sat 0800-1200.

▲ Activities and tours

Guatemala City *p20, maps p21, p22 and p24*

Aire, Mar y Tierra, Plaza Marítima, 6 Av, 20-25, Zona 10, T2337-0149. Recommended.
Clark Tours, Plaza Clark, 7 Av 14-76, Zona 9, T2412-4700, www.clarktours.com.gt, and several other locations. Long-established, very helpful, tours to Copán, Quiriguá, etc.
Four Directions, 1 Calle, 30-65, Zona 7, T2439-7715, www.fourdirections.com.gt. Recommended for Maya archaeology tours. English spoken.
Maya Expeditions, 15 Calle "A", 14-07, Zona 10, T2363-4955, www.mayaexpeditions.com. Very experienced and helpful, with varied selection of short and longer river/hiking tours, whitewater rafting, bungee jumping, cultural tours, tours to Piedras Negras.
Setsa Travel, 8 Av, 14-11, Zona 1, T2230-4726, karlasetsa@intelnet.net.gt, very helpful, tours arranged to Tikal, Copán, car hire.
Tourama, Av La Reforma, 15-25, Zona 10, T2368-1820, turama@intelnet.net.gt. English spoken. Recommended.
Trolley Tour, T5907-0913, Tue-Sat 1000-1300, Sun 1000. Pickups from Zona 10 hotels for 3-hr city tours, US$20, children US$10.
Turismo Ek Chuah, 3 Calle 6-24, Zona 2, T2220-1491, www.ekchuah.com. Nationwide tours as well as some specialist and tailor-made tours on bicycle and horseback.

⊖ Transport

Guatemala City *p20, maps p21, p22 and p24*
Air
Flights to **Flores** with **Grupo Taca** 0820, 1605 and 1850, and **TAG** at 1630 daily.

Charter airlines Aero Ruta Maya, Av Hincapié and 18 Calle, Zona 13, T2339-0502.

Domestic airlines Aerocharter, 18 Calle and Av Hincapié, Zona 13, T5401-5893, to **Puerto Barrios**. Phone for schedule. **Aeródromo**, Av Hincapié and 18 Calle, Zona 13, T5539-9364, to **Huehuetenango**. Phone for schedule. Aerolucía, 18 Calle and Av Hincapié, T5959-7008 to **Quetzaltenango**. Phone for schedule. Grupo Taca at the airport and Av Hincapié, 12-22, Zona 13, T2470-8222, www.taca.com. **Tag**, Av Hincapié y 18 Calle, Zona 13, T2361-1180, www.tag.com.gt.

International airlines American Airlines, Hotel Marriot, 7 Av, 15-45, Zona 9, T2422-0000. **Continental Airlines**, 18 Calle, 5-56, Zona 10, Edif Unicentro, T2385-9610. **Copa**, 1 Av, 10-17, Zona 10, T2385-5555. Cubana de Aviación, Edificio Atlántis, 13 Calle, 3-40, Zona 10, T2361-0857. **Delta Airlines**, 15 Calle, 3-20, Zona 10, Edif Centro Ejecutivo, T2263-0600. Iberia, Av La Reforma, 8-60, Zona 9, Edif Galerías Reforma, T2332-7471/ 2332-0911, www.iberia.com. Inter Jet, T1-800-835-0271, www.interjet.mx. Mexicana,13 Calle, 8-44, Zona 10, Edif Plaza Edyma, T2333-6001. Spirit Air, www.spiritair.com. Taca (includes Aviateca, Lacsa, Nica and Inter), see above. United, Av La Reforma, 1-50, Zona 9, Edif La Reformador, 2nd floor, T1-800-835-0100.

Bus
Local
Buses operate between 0600-2000, after which you will have to rely on taxis.

In town, US$0.13 per journey on regular buses and on the larger red buses known as *gusanos* (worms) except on Sun and public holidays when they charge US$0.16.) One of the most useful bus services is the **101**, which travels down 10 Av, Zona 1, and then cuts across to the 6 Av, Zona 4, and then across Vía 8 and all the way down the Av La Reforma, Zona 10. The **82** also travels from Zona 1 to 10 and can be picked up on the 10 Av, Zona 1 and the 6 Av, Zona 4. Bus **85**, with the same pickup points, goes to the cluster of museums in Zona 13. Buses **37**, **35**, **32** all head for the INGUAT building, which is the large blue and white building in the Centro Cívico complex. **R40** goes from the 6 Av, Zona 4, to the Tikal Futura shopping complex – a good spot to catch the Antigua bus, which pulls up by the bridge to the complex. Buses leaving the 7 Av, Zona 4, just 4 blocks from the Zona 4 bus terminal, for the Plaza Mayor, Zona 1, are *gusano* **V21**, **35**, **36**, **82**, and **101**.

Long distance

Watch your bags everywhere, but like a hawk in the Zona 4 terminal.

There are numerous bus terminals in Guatemala City. The majority of 1st-class buses have their own offices and departure points around Zona 1. Hundreds of chicken buses for the south and west of Guatemala leave from the Zona 4 terminal, as well as local city buses. However, there was a plan, at the time of writing, to redirect all buses for the southern region to leave from Central Sur, Col Villalobos. International buses (see below) have their offices scattered about the city. (The cheaper Salvador buses leave from near the Zona 4 terminal.) The Zona 4 bus terminal has to be the dirtiest and grimmest public area in the whole of the city.

The main destinations with companies operating from Guatemala City are:

Antigua, every 15 mins, 1 hr, US$1, until 2000 from Av 23 and 3 Calle, Zona 3. To **Chimaltenango** and **Los Encuentros**, from 1 Av between 3 y 4. Calle, Zona 7. **Chichicastenango** hourly from 0500-1800, 3 hrs, US$2.20 with **Veloz Quichelense**. **Huehuetenango**, with Los Halcones, Calzada Roosevelt, 37-47, Zona 11, T2439-2780, 0700, 1400, 1700, US$7, 5 hrs, and **Transportes Velásquez**, Calzada Roosevelt 9-56, Zona 7, T2440-3316, 0800-1630, every 30 mins, 5 hrs, US$7.

Panajachel, with Transportes Rebulí, 41 Calle, between 6 y 7 Av, Zona 8, T2230-2748, hourly from 0530-1530, 3 hrs, US$2.20; also to **San Lucas Tolimán** 0530-1530, 3 hrs US$2.10 **San Pedro La Laguna** with Transportes Méndez, 41 C, between 6 y and Av, Zona 8, 1300, 4 hrs. **Santiago Atitlán**, with various companies, from 4 C, between 3 y 4 Av, Zona 12, 0400-1700, every 30 mins, 4 hrs, US$4.

Quetzaltenango (Xela) and **San Marcos**. 1st-class bus to Xela with **Transportes Alamo**, 12 Av "A", 0-65, Zona 7, T2471-8626, from 0800-1730, 6 daily 4 hrs, US$7. **Líneas Américas**, 2 Av, 18-47, Zona 1, T2232-1432, 0500-1930, 7 daily, US$7. **Galgos**, 7 Av, 19-44, Zona 1, T2232-3661, between 0530-1700, 5 daily, 4 hrs, US$7 to **Tapachula** in Mexico through the El Carmen border. **Marquensita**, 1 Av, 21-31, Zona 1, T2230-0067. From 0600-1700, 8 a day, US$6.10, to Xela and on to San Marcos. To **Tecpán**, with Transportes Poaquileña, 1 Av corner of 3 and 4 Calle, Zona 7, 0530-1900, every 15 mins, 2 hrs, US$1.20.

To **Santa Cruz del Quiché**, Sololá and Totonicapán, buses depart from 41 Calle between 6 and 7 Av, Zona 8.

To **Biotopo del Quetzal** and **Cobán**, 3½ hrs and 4½ hrs respectively, hourly from 0400-1700, US$6 and US$7.50, with **Escobar y Monja Blanca**, 8 Av, 15-16, Zona 1, T2238-1409. **Zacapa**, **Chiquimula** (for **El Florido**, Honduran border) and **Esquipulas** with **Rutas Orientales**, 19 Calle, 8-18, Zona 1, T2253-7282, every 30 mins 0430-1800. To **Zacapa**, 3¼ hrs, to **Chiquimula**, 3½ hrs, to **Esquipulas**, 4½ hrs, US$6.

Puerto Barrios, with Transportes Litegua, 15 Calle, 10-40, Zona 1, T2220-8840, www.litegua.com, 0430-1900, 31 a day, 5 hrs, US$6.80, 1st class US$12 and **Río Dulce**, 0600, 0900, 1130, 5 hrs, US$6.20.

El Petén with Fuente del Norte (same company as Líneas Máxima de Petén), 17 Calle, 8-46, Zona 1, T2251-3817, going

to **Río Dulce** and **Santa Elena/Flores**.
There are numerous departures 24 hrs; 5 hrs
to Río Dulce, US$6.50; to Santa Elena,
9-10 hrs, US$12; buses vary in quality and
price, breakdowns not unknown. The 1000
and 2130 departures are a luxury bus **Maya
del Oro** with snacks, US$18, the advantage
being it doesn't stop at every tree to pick
up passengers. **Línea Dorada**, 16 Calle,
10-03, Zona 1, T2220-7990, www.tikalmayan
world.com, at 1000, US$16 to **Flores**, 8 hrs
and on to **Melchor de Mencos**, 10 hrs.
To **Santa Elena** ADN, 8 Av, 16-41, Zona 1,
T2251-0050, www.adnautobuses
delnorte.com, luxury service, 2100
and 2200, returns at 2100 and 2300,
US$19, toilets, TV and snacks.

To **Jalapa** with **Unidos Jalapanecos**,
22 Calle 1-20, Zona 1, T2251-4760,
0430-1830, every 30 mins, 3 hrs, US$2.50
and with **Transportes Melva Nacional**,
T2332-6081, 0415-1715, every 30 mins,
3 hrs 30 mins, US$2.50. Buses also from
the Zona 4 terminal. To **San Pedro Pinula**
between 0500-1800.

To **Chatia Gomerana**, 4 Calle y 8 Av,
Zona 12, to **La Democracia**, every 30 mins
from 0600-1630 via Escuintla and Siquinala,
2 hrs. **Transportes Cubanita** to **Reserva
Natural de Monterrico** (La Avellana),
4 Calle y 8 Av, Zona 12, at 1030, 1230, 1420,
3 hrs, US$2.50. To **Puerto San José** and
Iztapa, from the same address, 0430-1645
every 15 mins, 1 hr. To **Retalhuleu** (Reu on
bus signs) with **Transportes Fortaleza del
Sur**, Calzada Aguilar Batres, 4-15, Zona 12,
T22230-3390, between 0010-1910 every
30 mins via Escuintla, Cocales and
Mazatenango, 3 hrs, US$6.80. Numerous
buses to **Santa Lucía Cotzumalguapa**
go from the Zona 4 bus terminal.

International buses
Reserve the day before if you can. Taking
a bus from Guatemala City as far as, say,
San José, is tiring and tiresome (the bus

company's bureaucracy and the hassle
from border officials all take their toll).

To **Honduras** avoiding El Salvador, take
a bus to **Esquipulas**, then a minibus to the
border. **Hedman Alas**, 2 Av, 8-73, Zona 10,
T2362-5072, www.hedmanalas.com, to
Copán via El Florido, at 0500 and 0900,
5 hrs, US$30. Also goes on to **San Pedro
Sulas**, US$45, and **La Ceiba**, US$52.
Pullmantur to **Tegucigalpa** daily at
0700 via San Salvador, US$66 and US$94.
Ticabus to **San Pedro Sula**, US$34 and
Tegucigalpa, US$34 via San Salvador.
Rutas Orientales, 19 C, 8-18, T2253-7282
goes to **Honduras** at 0530 via Agua
Caliente, 8 hrs, US$28.

To **Mexico** with **Trans Galgos Inter**,
7 Av, 19-44, Zona 1, T2223-3661,
www.transgalgosinter.com.gt to **Tapachula**
via **El Carmen**, 0730, 1330, and 1500, 7 hrs.
Línea Dorada, address above, to **Tapachula**
at 0800, US$24. **Transportes Velásquez**,
20 Calle, 1-37, Zona 1, T2221-1084,
0800-1100, hourly to **La Mesilla**, 7 hrs,
US$5. **Transportes Fortaleza del Sur**,
Calzada Aguilar Batres, 4-15, Zona 12,
T2230-3390 to **Ciudad Tecún Umán**, 0130,
0300, 0330, 0530 via **Retalhuleu**, 5 hrs.

To **Chetumal** via **Belize City**, with **Línea
Dorada** change to a minibus in Flores.
Leaves 1000, 2100, 2200 and 2230, 2 days,
US$42. Journey often takes longer than
advertised due to Guatemala–Belize and
Belize–Mexico border crossings.

To **El Salvador** via **Valle Nuevo**, border
crossing, with **Ticabus**, 0600 and 1300 daily
to San Salvador, US$17 1st class, 5 hrs. From
Ticabus terminal, Calzada Aguilar Batres
22-25, T2473-0633, www.ticabus.com,
clean, safe, with waiting area, café, toilets,
no luggage deposit.

Shuttles
Shuttles are possible between Guatemala
City and all other destinations, but it's a
case of reserving them first. Contact shuttle

operators in Antigua (see Antigua Transport, page 49). Guatemala City to **Antigua**, US$15, **Panajachel** US$30, Chichicastenango US$30, **Copán Ruinas**, US$40, **Cobán**, US$30 and **Quetzaltenango**, US$25.

Car

Car hire companies Hertz, at the airport, T2470-3800, www.hertz.com. **Budget**, at the airport; also at 6 Av, 11-24, Zona 9, www.budget.co.uk. **Tabarini**, 2 Calle "A", 7-30, Zona 10, T2331-2643, airport T2331-4755, www.tabarini.com. **Tally**, 7 Av, 14-60, Zona 1, T2232-0421, very competitive, have pickups. Recommended.

Car and motorcycle repairs Mike and Andy Young, 27 Calle, 13-73, Zona 5, T2331-9263, Mon-Fri 0700-1600. Excellent mechanics for all vehicles, extremely helpful. Honda motorcycle parts from **FA Honda**, Av Bolívar, 31-00, Zona 3, T2471-5232. Some staff speak English. Car and motorcycle parts from **FPK**, 5 Calle, 6-75, Zona 9, T2331-9777. **David González**, 32 Calle, 6-31, Zona 11, T5797-2486, for car, bike and bicycle repairs. Recommended.

Taxi

If possible call a taxi from your hotel or get someone to recommend a reliable driver; there are hundreds of illegal taxis in the city that should be avoided.

There are 3 types of taxis – Rotativos, **Estacionarios** and the ones that are metered, called **Taxis Amarillos**. *Rotativos* are everywhere in the city cruising the length and breadth of all zones. You will not wait more than a few mins for one to come along. They are numbered on their sides and on their back windscreen will be written TR (*Taxi Rotativo*) followed by 4 numbers. Most of them have a company logo stamped on the side as well. *Estacionarios* also have numbers on the sides but are without logo. On their back windscreen they have the letters TE (*Taxi Estacionario*) followed by 4 numbers. They are to be found at bus terminals and outside hotels or in other important places. They will always return to these same waiting points (good to know if you leave something in a taxi). Do not get in a taxi that does not have either of these labels on its back windscreen. *Rotativos* and *Estacionarios* are unmetered, but *Estacionarios* will always charge less than *Rotativos*. The fact that both are unmetered will nearly always work to your advantage because of traffic delays. You will be quoted an inflated price by *Rotativos* by virtue of being a foreigner. *Estacionarios* are fairer. It is about US$8 from the airport to Zona 1. From Zona 1 to 4 is about US$4. The metered *Taxi Amarillo* also moves around but less so than the *Rotativos*, as they are more on call by phone. They only take a couple of minutes to come. **Amarillo Express**, T2332-1515, are 24 hr.

6 Directory

Guatemala City *p20, maps p21, p22 and p24*
Banks
The legal street exchange for cash may be found on 7 Av, between 12 and 14 Calle, near the post office (Zona 1), but be careful; don't go alone. Banks change US dollars into quetzales at the free rate, but actual rates and commission charges vary; if you have time, shop around. **Banco Industrial**, Av 7, opposite the central post office, Visa cards only, Mon-Fri 0900-1530. **Bancared**, near Parque Centanario on 6 Calle and 4 Av has 24-hr ATM for Visa/Cirrus. **Lloyds Bank plc**, 6 Av, 9-51, Zona 9, Edif Gran Vía, also at 14 Calle and 4 Av, Zona 10, with ATM. Mon-Fri 0900-1500. **Banco Uno**, 10 Calle, 5-40, Visa and ATM. Mon-Fri 0930-1730, Sat 1000-1300. Quetzales may be bought with MasterCard at **Credomatic**, beneath the Bar Europa, at 11 Calle, 5-6 Av, Zona 1. Mon-Sat 0800-1900.

MasterCard ATM also at **Banco Internacional**, Av La Reforma and 16 Calle, Zona 10. **Western Union**, T2360-1737, collect T1-800-360-1737.

Embassies and consulates

Australia, Australians should report loss or theft of passports at the Canadian Embassy. Nearest Australian embassy is in Mexico. **Austria**, in Mexico (T+52) 55 52 510806, www.embajadadeaustria.com.mx. **Belgium**, in Costa Rica, T(+506) 225 6633. **Belize**, 5 Av 5-55, Zona 14, Europlaza Torre II, office 1502, T2367-3883. Mon-Fri 0900-1200, 1400-1600. **Canada**, 13 Calle, 8-44, Zona 10, T2363-4348. Mon-Thu, 0800-1700, Fri 0800-1330. **Costa Rica**, 15 C 7-59, Zona 10, T2366-9918. Mon-Fri 0900-1400. **El Salvador**, Av de las Américas 16-46, Zona 13, T2360-7670. Mon-Fri 0800-1500. **France**, 5 Av, 8-59, Zona 14, Edif Cogefar, T2421-7370. Mon-Fri 0900-1200. **Germany**, 20 Calle, 6-20, Zona 10, T2364-6700. Mon-Fri 0900-1200. **Honduras**, 19 Av "A", 20-19, Zona 10, T2363-5495. Mon-Fri 0900-1700. **Israel**, 13 Av, 14-07, Zona 10, T2333-6951. Mon-Fri 0800-1600. **Japan**, Av La Reforma, 16-85, Zona 10, Edif Torre Internacional, T2367-2244. Mon-Fri 0930-1230, 1400-1630. **Mexico**, 2 Av, 7-57, Zona 10, T2420-3430. Mon-Fri 0900-1300, 1400-1700. **Netherlands** 16 Calle, 0-55, Zona 10, T2381-4300. Mon-Fri 0800-1700. **Nicaragua**, 10 Av, 14-72, Zona 10, T2368-0785. Mon-Fri 0900-1300. **Panama**, 12 Av, 2-65, Zona 14, T2366-3331. Mon-Fri 0900-1400. **Spain**, 6 Calle, 6-48, Zona 9, T2379-3530. Mon-Fri 0800-1400. **Switzerland**, 16 Calle, 0-55, Zona 10, Edif Torre Internacional, 14th floor, T2367-5520. Mon-Fri 0900-1130. **UK**, 16 Calle, 0-55, Zona 10, T2367-5425-29. Embassy open Mon-Thu 0800-1230, 1330-1700, Fri 0800-1200. Consulate Mon-Thu 0830-1200, Fri 0830-1100. **USA**, Av La Reforma, 7-01, Zona 10, T2326-4000, http://guatemala.usembassy.gov, Mon-Fri 0800-1700.

Emergency
T128 for ambulance, T122 for the fire brigade (*bomberos*) who also get called to accidents.

Immigration
Immigration office Dirección General de Migración, 6 Av, 3-11, Zona 4, T2411-2411. For extensions of visas. If you need new entry stamps in a replacement passport (ie if one was stolen), a police report is required, plus a photocopy and a photocopy of your passport. They also need to know your date and point of entry to check their records.

Internet
There's an internet café in **Edificio Geminis** in Zona 10.

Medical services
Doctors Dr Boris Castillo Camino, 6 Av, 7-55, Zona 10, Of 17, T2334-5932. 0900-1230, 1430-1800. Recommended. **Dentists** Centro Médico, 6 Av, 3-47, Zona 10, T2332-3555, English spoken by some staff. **Hospitals** Hospital de las Américas, 10a. Calle 2-31, Zona 14, T2384-3535, info@hospitalesdeguatemala.com. Private hospital, must be able to demonstrate you have funds for treatment. **Roosevelt Hospital**, Calzada Roosevelt, Zona 11, T2471-1441. Public hospital affiliated with University San Carlos School of Medicine. **Opticians** Optico Popular, 11 Av, 13-75, Zona 1, T2238-3143, excellent for repairs.

Post
The main post office is at 7 Av and 12 Calle, Zona 1. Mon-Fri 0830-1700.

Antigua and around

*Antigua is rightly one of Guatemala's most popular destinations.
It overflows with colonial architecture and fine churches on streets
that are linked by squat houses, painted in ochre shades and topped
with terracotta tiles, basking in the fractured light of the setting sun.
Antigua is a very attractive city and is the cultural centre of Guatemala;
arts flourish here. Maya women sit in their colourful clothes amid the
ruins and in the Parque Central. In the late-afternoon light, buildings
such as Las Capuchinas are beautiful, and in the evening the
cathedral is wonderfully illuminated as if by candlelight. Around
Antigua are a cluster of archaeological sites, highland villages and
volcanoes to explore.*

Ins and outs

Getting around *Avenidas* run north to south and *calles* run from east to west. House numbers do not give any clue about how far from the Parque Central a particular place is. ▶▶ *See Transport, page 49.*

Tourist information INGUAT office ① *2a Calle Ote,11 (between Av 2 and Av 3 Norte), Mon-Fri 0800-1700, Sat and Sun 0900-1700, T7832-3782, info-antigua@inguat.gob.gt, www.visit guatemala.com,* is very helpful, with maps and information; occasional exhibitions in rooms around courtyard behind office. Information available about volunteer work. English, Italian and a little German spoken. The monthly magazine *The Revue* is a useful source of tourist information in English with articles, maps, events and advertisements; it's free and widely available in hotels and restaurants.

Safety Unfortunately, despite its air of tranquillity, Antigua is not without unpleasant incidents. Take care and advice from the tourist office on where to go or not to go. There are numerous tourist police (green uniforms) who are helpful and conspicuous; their office is at 4 Avenida Norte at the side of the Municipal Palace. If you wish to go to Cerro de la Cruz (see page 40), or the cemetery, they will escort you, leaving 1000 and 1500 daily. Antigua is generally safe at night, but it's best to keep to the well-lit area near the centre. Report incidents to police and the tourist office. Tourist assistance 24 hours, T2421-2810. ▶▶ *See also page 16.*

Background

Until it was heavily damaged by an earthquake in 1773, Antigua was the capital city. Founded in 1543, after the destruction of an even earlier capital, Ciudad Vieja, it grew to

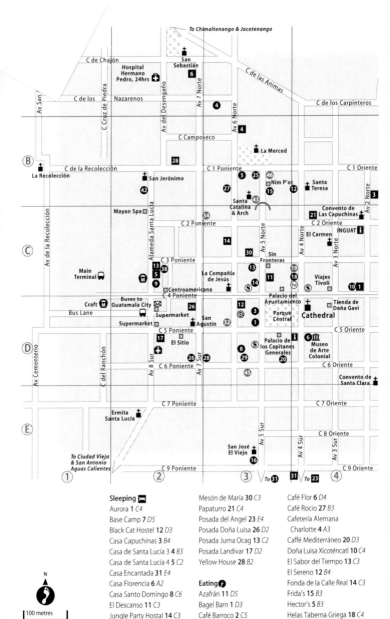

Sleeping 🛏

Aurora **1** *C4*
Base Camp **7** *D5*
Black Cat Hostel **12** *D3*
Casa Capuchinas **3** *B4*
Casa de Santa Lucía 3 **4** *B3*
Casa de Santa Lucía 4 **5** *C2*
Casa Encantada **31** *E4*
Casa Florencia **6** *A2*
Casa Santo Domingo **8** *C6*
El Descanso **11** *C3*
Jungle Party Hostal **14** *C3*
Las Camelias Inn **2** *C5*

Mesón de María **30** *C3*
Papaturro **21** *C4*
Posada del Angel **23** *E4*
Posada Doña Luisa **26** *D2*
Posada Juma Ocag **13** *C2*
Posada Landivar **17** *D2*
Yellow House **28** *B2*

Eating 🍴

Azafrán **11** *D5*
Bagel Barn **1** *D3*
Café Barroco **2** *C5*
Café Condesa **3** *D3*

Café Flor **6** *D4*
Café Rocio **27** *B3*
Cafetería Alemana
   Charlotte **4** *A3*
Caffé Mediterráneo **20** *D3*
Doña Luisa Xicoténcatl **10** *C4*
El Sabor del Tiempo **13** *C3*
El Sereno **12** *B4*
Fonda de la Calle Real **14** *C3*
Frida's **15** *B3*
Hector's **5** *B3*
Helas Taberna Griega **18** *C4*
La Antigua Viñería **16** *E3*

To Cerro de la Cruz   To Guatemala City

C de la Candelaria

La Candelaria

Santa Rosa

Plazuela
Santa Rosa

C de la Beatas Indias

C de los Duelos

Santo Domingo

Av 1 Norte

C 3 Oriente

8

2

2

41

1

C 4 Oriente

La Concepción

11

C del Hermano Pedro

7

Av 1 Sur

C de los Pasos

San
Francisco

C del Hermano Pedro

Santa Cruz

C de la
To Escuela
de Cristo &
El Calvario

To Santa Isabel, San Juan
del Obispo & Santa María
de Jesús

5   6

be the finest city in Central America, with numerous great churches, a university (1676), a printing press (founded 1660), and a population of around 50,000, including many famous sculptors, painters, writers and craftsmen.

Antigua has consistently been damaged by earthquakes. Even when it was the capital, buildings were frequently destroyed and rebuilt, usually in a grander style, until the final cataclysm in 1773. For many years it was abandoned, and most of the accumulated treasures were moved to Guatemala City. Although it slowly repopulated in the 19th century, little was done to prevent further collapse of the main buildings until late in the 20th century when the value of the remaining monuments was finally appreciated. Since 1972, efforts to preserve what was left have gained momentum, and it is now a UNESCO World Heritage Site. The major earthquake of 1976 was a further setback, but you will see many sites that are busy with restoration, preservation or simple clearing. If the city was not treasure enough, the setting is truly memorable. Volcán Agua (3766 m) is due south and the market is to the west, behind which hang the imposing peaks of Volcán Acatenango (3976 m) and Volcán Fuego (3763 m), which still emits the occasional column of ash as a warning of the latent power within.

Sights → *See listings, pages 43-52.*

In the centre of the city is the **Parque Central**, the old Plaza Real, where bullfights and markets were held in the early days. The present park was constructed in the 20th century though the fountain dates back to the 18th century. The **cathedral** ① *US$0.40*, to the east, dates from 1680 (the first cathedral was demolished in 1669). Much has been destroyed since then and only two of the many original chapels are now in use. The remainder can be visited. The **Palacio de los Capitanes Generales** is to the south. The original building dates from 1558, was virtually destroyed in 1773, was partly restored in the 20th century, and now houses police and government offices. The **Cabildo**, or **Municipal Palace**, is to the north and an arcade of shops to the west. You can climb to the second floor for a great view of the volcanoes (Monday to Friday 0800-1600). The **Museo de Santiago** ① *Tue-Fri 0900-1600, Sat-Sun 0900-1200, 1400-1600, US$4*, is in the municipal offices to the north of the plaza, as is the **Museo del Libro Antiguo** ① *same hours and price*, which contains a replica of a 1660 printing press (the original is in Guatemala City), old documents and a collection of 16th- to 18th-century books (1500 volumes in the library). The **Museo de Arte Colonial** ① *Tue-Fri 0900-1600, Sat-Sun 0900-1200, 1400-1600, US$4*, is half a block from Parque Central at Calle 5 Oriente, in the building where the San Carlos University was first housed. It now has mostly 17th- to 18th-century religious art, well laid out in large airy rooms around a colonial patio.

Hotel Casa Santo Domingo is one of Antigua's most beautiful sights – a converted old Dominican church and also monastery property. Archaeological excavations have turned up some unexpected finds at the site. During the cleaning out of a burial vault in September 1996, one of the greatest finds in Antigua's history was unearthed. The vault had been filled with rubble, but care had been taken in placing stones a few feet away from the painted walls. The scene is in the pristine colours of natural red and blue, and depicts Christ, the Virgin Mary, Mary Magdalene and John the Apostle. It was painted in 1683, and was only discovered with the help of ultraviolet light. Within the monastery grounds are the **Colonial Art Museum**, with displays of Guatemalan baroque imagery and silverware and the **Pre-Columbian Art Museum**, **Glass Museum**, **Museum of Guatemalan Apothecary** and the **Popular Art and Handicrafts of Sacatepequez Museum** ① *3 Calle Ote 28, 0900-1700, US$5 for each museum*.

There are many fine colonial religious buildings: 22 churches, 14 convents and 11 monasteries, most ruined by earthquakes and in various stages of restoration. Top of the list are the cloisters of the convent of **Las Capuchinas** ① *2 Av Norte y 2 Calle Ote, 0900-1700, US$3.90*, with immensely thick round pillars (1736) adorned with bougainvillea. The church and convent of **San Francisco** ① *1 Av Sur y 7 Calle Ote, 0800-1200, 1400-1700, US$0.40*, with the tomb of Hermano Pedro, is much revered by all the local communities. He was canonized in 2002. The church has been restored and now includes the **Museo de Hermano Pedro** ① *Tue-Sun 0900-1200, 1300-1630, US$0.40*. The convent of **Santa Clara** ① *6 Calle Ote y 2 Av Sur, 0900-1700, US$3.90*, was founded in about 1700 and became one of the biggest in Antigua, until the nuns were forced to move to Guatemala City. The adjoining garden is an oasis of peace. **El Carmen** ① *3 Calle Ote y 3 Av Norte*, has a beautiful façade with strikingly ornate columns, tastefully illuminated at night, but the rest of the complex is in ruins. Likewise **San Agustín** ① *5 Calle Pte y 7 Av Norte*, was once a fine building, but only survived intact from 1761 to 1773; earthquake destruction continued until the final portion of the vault collapsed in 1976, leaving an impressive ruin. **La Compañía de Jesús** ① *3 Calle Pte y 6 Av Norte, 0930-1700*, at one time covered the whole block. The church is closed for restoration but you can access the rest of the ruins from 6 Avenida Norte. The church and cloisters of **Escuela de Cristo** ① *Calle de los Pasos y de la Cruz*, a small independent monastery (1720-1730), have survived and were restored between 1940 and 1960. The church is simple and has some interesting original artwork. **La Recolección** ① *Calle de la Recolección, 0900-1700, US$3.90*, despite

Semana Santa

This week-long event in Antigua is a spectacular display of religious ritual and floral design. Through billowing clouds of incense, accompanied by music, processions of floats carried by purple-robed men make their way through the town. The cobbled stones are covered in *alfombras* (carpets) of coloured sawdust and flowers.

The day before the processions leave from each church, Holy Vigils (*velaciones*) are held, and the sculpture to be carried is placed before the altar (*retablo*), with a backdrop covering the altar. Floats (*andas*) are topped by colonial sculptures of the cross-carrying Christ. He wears velvet robes of deep blue or green, embroidered with gold and silver threads, and the float is carried on the shoulders by a team of 80 men (*cucuruchos*), who heave and sway their way through the streets for as long as 12 hours. The processions, arranged by a religious brotherhood (*cofradía*), are accompanied by banner and incense carriers, centurions, and a loud brass band.

The largest processions with some of the finest carpets are on **Palm Sunday** and **Good Friday**. Not to be missed are:

the procession leaving from **La Merced** on **Palm Sunday** at 1200-1300; the procession leaving the church of **San Francisco** on **Maundy Thursday**; the 0200 sentencing of Jesus and 0600 processions from **La Merced** on **Good Friday**; the crucifixion of Christ in front of the **cathedral** at noon on **Good Friday**; and the beautiful, candlelit procession of the crucified Christ which passes the **Parque Central** between 2300 and midnight on **Good Friday**.

This is the biggest Easter attraction in Latin America so accommodation is booked far ahead. If you plan to be here and haven't reserved a room, arrive a few days before Palm Sunday. If unsuccessful, commuting from Guatemala City is an option. Don't rush; each procession lasts up to 12 hours. The whole week is a fantastic opportunity for photographs – and if you want a decent picture remember the Christ figure always faces right. Arm yourself with a map (available in kiosks in the Parque Central) and follow the processional route before the procession to see all the carpets while they are still intact. (There are also processions into Antigua from surrounding towns every Sunday in Lent.)

being a late starter (1700), became one of the biggest and finest of Antigua's religious institutions. It is now the most awe-inspiring ruin in the city. **San Jerónimo** ① *Calle de la Recolección, 0900-1700, US$3.90*, was a school (early 1600s) for La Merced, three blocks away, but later became the local customs house. There is an impressive fountain in the courtyard. **La Merced** ① *1 Calle Pte y 6 Av Norte, 0800-1700*, with its white and yellow façade dominates the surrounding plaza. The church (1767) and cloisters were built with earthquakes in mind and survived better than most. The church remains in use and the **cloisters** ① *US$0.80*, are being further restored. Antigua's finest fountain is in the courtyard. **Santa Teresa** ① *4 Av Norte*, was a modest convent, but the church walls and the lovely west front have survived. It is now the city's men's prison.

Other ruins including **Santa Isabel**, **Santa Cruz**, **La Candelaria**, **San José El Viejo** and **San Sebastián** are to be found round the edges of the city, and there is an interesting set of the Stations of the Cross, each a small chapel, from San Francisco to **El Calvario** church, which was where Pedro de Betancourt (Hermano Pedro) worked as a gardener and planted an esquisuchil tree. He was also the founder of the **Belén Hospital** in 1661, which was destroyed in 1773. However, some years later, his name was given to the **San Pedro Hospital**, which is one block south of the Parque Central.

There is a fabulous panorama from the **Cerro de la Cruz**, which is 15 minutes' walk from the northern end of town along 1 Avenida Norte.

Around Antigua → *For listings, see pages 43-52.*

Ciudad Vieja – the former capital – is 5.5 km southwest of Antigua at the foot of Volcán Agua. In 1527, Pedro de Alvarado moved his capital, known then as Santiago de Los Caballeros, from Iximché to San Miguel Escobar, now a suburb of Ciudad Vieja. On 11 September 1541, after days of torrential rain, an immense mudslide came down the mountain and swallowed up the city. Alvarado's widow, Doña Beatriz de la Cueva, newly elected governor after his death, was among those drowned. Today Ciudad Vieja is itself a suburb of Antigua, but with a handsome church, founded in 1534, and one of the oldest in Central America. There's a fiesta on December 8. Between Ciudad Vieja and San Miguel de las Dueñas is the **Valhalla macadamia nut farm** ① *T7831-5799, www.exvalhalla.net, free visits and nut tasting, 0800-1700.*

About 3 km northwest of Ciudad Vieja is **San Antonio Aguas Calientes**. The hot springs unfortunately disappeared with recent earthquakes, but the village has many small shops selling locally made textiles. **Carolina's Textiles** is recommended for a fine selection, while on the exit road **Alida** has a shop. You can watch the weavers in their homes by the roadside. Local fiestas are 16-21 January, Corpus Christi (a moveable feast celebtrated around June) and 1 November.

Beyond San Juan del Obispo, beside Volcán Agua, is the charming village of **Santa María de Jesús**, with its beautiful view of Antigua. In the early morning there are good views of all three volcanoes from 2 km back down the road towards Antigua. Colourful *huípiles* are worn, made and sold from a couple of stalls, or ask at the shops on the plaza. The local fiesta is on 10 January.

Just north of Antigua is **Jocotenango**. The music museum, **Casa K'ojom** ① *Mon-Fri 0830-1630, Sat 0830-1600, US$4,* is in the **Central Cultural La Azotea**, with displays of traditional Maya and colonial-era instruments. The village also has public saunas at the **Fraternidad Naturista Antigua**.

Five kilometres beyond San Lucas Sacatepéquez, at Km 29.5, Carretera Roosevelt (the Pan-American Highway), is **Santiago Sacatepéquez**, whose fiesta on 1 November, *Día de los Muertos* (All Souls' Day), is characterized by colourful kite-flying (*barriletes*). They also celebrate 25 July. Market days are Wednesday and Friday.

Visiting a **coffee farm** is an interesting short excursion. **Tour Finca Los Nietos** ① *on the outskirts of Antigua, near the Iglesia San Felipe de Jesús, T7728-0812, www.filadelfiaresort. com,* runs two-hour tours (US$18) three times a day. They are very informative and interesting with expert multilingual guides, in beautiful manicured grounds and restored colonial buildings; also with restaurant and shop.

North of Guatemala City is **Mixco Viejo**, the excavated site of a post-Classic Maya fortress, which spans 14 hilltops, including 12 groups of pyramids. Despite earthquake damage it is worth a visit and is recommended. It was the 16th-century capital of the Pokomam Maya.

Volcanoes → *For listings, see pages 43-52.*

Each of the four volcanoes that are immediately accessible from Antigua provides a unique set of challenges and rewards. Agua, Fuego and Acatenango volcanoes directly overlook Antigua whilst Volcan Pacaya is about an hour's drive away. All of these volcanoes can be experienced either as part of a day trip (a cheaper and faster option that requires only lightweight packs) or with an overnight excursion (heavier packs making climbing times longer, but with better light conditions for lava viewing and enhancing already spectacular views with beautiful sunset and sunrises). Whatever option you choose, it is important to prepare properly for the unique features of each volcano (Pacaya is a relatively quick climb in a secure national park, while the three volcanoes on Antigua's perimeter are longer climbs with much greater risk of robberies and attacks). At a minimum, ensure that you have appropriate clothing and footwear (as summits are cold and volcanic ash is sharp bring fleeces and ideally use climbing boots), enough water (very important) and snacks for the trip and make informed decisions about safety (although you can climb each of these volcanoes independently, you will significantly decrease your risks of getting lost, attacked or not finding shelter by using a professional guiding service – **Outdoor Excursions** (OX), which runs trips with expert guides and armed security, is particularly recommended). Remember that altitude takes its toll and for the longer hikes it is important to start early in the morning to allow enough time to ascend and descend in daylight. As a general rule, descents take from a third to a half of the ascent time.

Volcán Pacaya

ⓘ *Tours are available for US$6 upwards and are sold in most tour companies in Antigua. The popular and best time for organized trips is to leave Antigua at 1300 and return at 2100. Departures also 0600 returning 1300. There is also a US$3.50 fee to be paid at the entrance to the Volcán Pacaya National Park in San Francisco de Sales (toilets available).*

At 2552 m, the still-active Volcán Pacaya can't be missed and is the most exciting volcano to climb. Pacaya has erupted about 20 times since 1565, but since the mid-1960s it has been continuously active, meaning it can reward climbers with some spectacular lava flows. The cone – now split in two since the most recent eruption, in 2010 – is covered in black basaltic rock, shed from the crater. The rocks get warm and are lethally sharp. One of the results of the eruption is that shallow tunnels have formed, creating natural open-air saunas. They offer quite a spectacular experience, though for obvious safety reasons you should only enter these at the advice of an experience guide.Take torch/flashlight refreshments and water and – it may sound obvious – wear boots or trainers, not sandals. Walking sticks are also offered at the park entrance – don't be too proud, on the steeper slopes, the crumbly lava screes can be very tricky to climb up or down. If you bring marshmallows to toast on the lava, make sure you have a long stick – lava is (rather unsurprisingly) very hot! Security officers go with the trips and police escorts ensure everyone leaves the area after dark. Check the situation in advance for **camping** (well below the crater lip). Sunrise comes with awesome views over the desolate black lava field to the distant Pacific (airborne dust permitting) and the peaks of Fuego, Acatenango and Agua. And as the sun sets on the horizon, Agua is silhouetted in the distance, a weak orange line streaked behind it.

Volcán Agua

ⓘ *Most organized tours with Antigua tour operators are during the day – you should enure that costs include both a guide and security. Trips normally leave Antigua about 0500.*

At 3760 m, Agua is the easiest but least scenic of the three volcanoes overlooking Antiqua. The trail, which can be quite littered, begins at **Santa María de Jesús**. Speak to Aurelio Cuy Chávez at the **Posada El Oasis**, who offers a guide service or take a tour with a reputable agency. You have to register first at the Municipalidad; guides are also available in the main square, about US$50 a day per guide. For Agua's history, see Ciudad Vieja. The crater has a small shelter (none too clean), which was a shrine, and about 10 antennae. There are great views of Volcán Fuego. It's a three- to five-hour climb if you are fit, and at least two hours down. To get the best views before the clouds cover the summit, it is best to stay at the radio station at the top. Agua can also be climbed from **Alotenango**, a village between Agua and Fuego, south of Ciudad Vieja. It's 9 km from Antigua and its name means 'place surrounded by corn'. Alotenango has a fiesta from 18-20 January.

Volcán Acatenango

ⓘ *If you do this climb independently of a tour agency, ask for a guide in La Soledad. However, it is strongly recommended that you use a professional guiding service, ideally with security.*

Acatenango is classified as a dormant volcano and is the third tallest in the country (3975 m) with two peaks to its name. Its first recorded eruption was in 1924. Two other eruptions were reported in 1924-1927 and 1972. The best trail heads south at **La Soledad**, 2300 m (15 km west of Ciudad Vieja), which is 300 m before the road (Route 5) turns right to Acatenango (see Sleeping). A small plateau, La Meseta on maps, known locally as **El Conejón**, provides a good camping site half way up (three or four hours). From here it is a further three or four hours' harder going to the top. The views of the nearby (lower) active crater of Fuego are excellent.

Volcán Fuego

ⓘ *This is an active volcano with trails that are easy to lose – it is recommended that you use a guiding service and do not venture up to the crater.*

This volcano (3763 m) can be climbed via Volcán Acatenango, sleeping between the two volcanoes, then climbing for a further two to three hours before stopping a safe distance from the crater. This one is for experienced hikers only. Do not underestimate the amount of water needed for the climb. It is a seven-hour ascent with a significant elevation gain – it's a very hard walk, both up and down. There are steep, loose cinder slopes, which are very tedious, in many places. It is possible to camp about three-quarters of the way up in a clearing. Fuego has regular eruptions that shoot massive boulders from its crater – often without warning. Check in Antigua before attempting to climb. If driving down towards the south coast you can see the red volcanic rock it has thrown up.

Antigua and around listings

For Sleeping and Eating price codes and other relevant information, see pages 12-13.

☐ Sleeping

Antigua *p35, map p36*

In the better hotels, advance reservations are advised for weekends and Dec-Apr. During Holy Week, hotel prices are significantly higher, sometimes double for the more expensive hotels. In the Jul-Aug period, find your accommodation early in the day.

$$$$ Posada del Angel, 4 Av Sur 24-A, T7832-5303, www.posadadelangel.com. Breakfast included, dining room, exercise pool, fireplaces, 5 suites individually decorated, roof terrace, romantic, exclusive and private. Bill Clinton once stayed here.

$$$$-$$$ Casa Capuchinas, 2 Av Norte 7, T7832-0121, www.casacapuchinas.com. 5 large, colonially furnished rooms, with fireplaces and massive beds, adjoining beautiful tiled bathrooms and special touches. A continental breakfast is included.

$$$$-$$$ Casa Encantada, 9 Calle Pte1, esq Av 4 Sur, T7832-7903, www.casa encantada-antigua.com. This sweet colonial boutique hotel with 10 rooms is a perfect retreat from the centre of Antigua. It has a small rooftop terrace where breakfast is served and a comfortable sitting room with open fire, books, lilies and textile-lined walls. 2 rooms are accessed by stepping stones in a pond. The suite, with jacuzzi, enjoys views of the 3 volcanoes.

$$$$-$$$ Casa Florencia, 7 Av Norte 100, T7832-0261, www.cflorencia.net. A sweet little hotel enjoying views towards Volcán Agua. 11 rooms with all the usuals including safety box and kitchen for guests. The balcony has *cola de quetzal* plants lining it. Staff are very welcoming. Recommended.

$$$$-$$$ Casa Santo Domingo, 3 Calle Ote 28, T7820-1220, www.casasanto domingo.com.gt. This is a beautifully designed hotel with 126 rooms in the ruins of a 17th-century convent with prehispanic archaeological finds, with good service, beautiful gardens, a magical pool, good restaurant with breakfast included. Worth seeing just to dream. See Sights, page 38.

$$$$-$$$ Hotel Mesón de María, 3 Calle Pte 8, T7832-6068, www.hotelmesonde maria.com. Great little place with a wonderful roof terrace. 20 stylish rooms are decorated with local textiles. Free internet and breakfast included at a local restaurant. Friendly and attentive service. Showers have large skylights.

$$$$-$$$ Las Camelias Inn, 3 Calle Ote 19, T/F7832-5780, www.cameliasinn.com. 16 rooms, some with bath. There's a small patio and balconies to hang out on. There are also 3 apartments for rent. Parking.

$$$ Aurora, 4 Calle Ote 16, T7832-0217, www.hotelauroraantigua.com. The oldest hotel in the city with old plumbing (but it works) and 1970s features. Quieter rooms face a patio overflowing with beautiful flowers. Continental breakfast included, English spoken.

$$ El Descanso, 5 Av Norte 9, T7832-0142. Rents 4 clean rooms on the 2nd floor, with private bath. There's a family atmosphere here and the place is extremely friendly and welcoming.

$$ Papaturro, 2 Calle Ote 14, T7832-0445. Family atmosphere, rooms around attractive restaurant/bar area, run by a Salvadorean couple, 5 rooms, 1 with bath and mini kitchen, breakfast included, full board available, good deals for longer stays.

$$ Posada Doña Luisa, 7 Av Norte 4, T7832-3414, posadadoluisa@hotmail.com. Near San Agustín church, good view of romantically lit ruins at night, a clean and very friendly place with a family atmosphere. It has 8 rooms with private bath and a small cafetería. Parking.

$$ Posada Landivar, 5 Calle Pte 23, close to the bus station, T7832-2962. Rooms with private bathroom and a/c. It's safe and in a good position. Discounts for longer stays. Parking. Recommended.

$ Base Camp, 1 Av 4b, T7832-0074, www.basecamphostel.com. 6 dorm beds and 2 double rooms with lots of shared space. Runs adventure tours through **Outdoor Excursions** (see page 49).

$ Black Cat Hostel, 6 Av Norte 1, T7832-1229. A hostel with dorm rooms. Services include a bar, free breakfasts and DVD screenings. There's also an upmarket option at 9 Calle Ote 5, T7832-2187 with private rooms, free breakfast and a terrace bar.

$ Casa de Santa Lucía No 3, 6 Av Norte, T7832-3302. There are 20 standard clean rooms here all with private bathrooms, towels, soap, hot water and free drinking water. Beautiful views of La Merced and Volcán de Fuego. Parking.

$ Casa de Santa Lucía No 4, Alameda Sta Lucía Norte 5, T7832-3302. Way more attractive than Nos 2 and 3, with 30 rooms for the same price. Only 14 years old, it has been built in a colonial style, with dark wood columns and is decorated with large clay bowls in the patio. Parking.

$ Jungle Party Hostal and Café, 6 Av Norte 20, T7832-0463, www.junglepartyhostal.com. Price per person. 33 beds spread across 6 rooms and 3 shared showers. Friendly management. Hot water, lockers, small patio, TV, free breakfast and movies. BBQ on Sat.

$ Posada Juma Ocag, 8 Av Norte 13 (Alameda Santa Lucía), T7832-3109. A small, but clean and nicely decorated hotel, using local textiles as bedspreads. It has an enclosed roof terrace, is quiet and friendly, shared bathrooms.

$ Yellow House, 1 Calle Pte 24, T7832-6646. 8 clean rooms in this hostel run by the welcoming Ceci. Breakfast included. Colonial style, laundry service, free internet. 3 rooms with bath, kitchen, patio, parking. Recommended.

Apartments

Look on the notice boards in town. Rooms and apartments are available from about US$25 a week up to US$500 per month. One recommended family is **Estella López**, 1 Calle Pte 41A, T7832-1324, who offer board and lodging on a weekly basis. The house is clean, and the family friendly.

Around Antigua *p40*
$ Pensión, Volcán Acatenango. Basic, with good cheap meals.

🍴 Eating

Antigua *p35, map p36*
For the cheapest of the cheap go to the stalls on the corner of 4 Calle Pte and 7 Av Norte, and those at the corner of 5 Calle Pte and 4 Av Sur. During the Easter period, the plaza in front of La Merced is transformed into a food market. At all these places you can pick up *elote, tortillas, tostadas* and *enchiladas*.

$$$ Azafrán, La Casa de los Sueños, 1 Av Norte 1, T7832-5215. Tue-Sun 1200-1500, 1900-2200. Serves international cuisine with tables on the patio. Recommended.

$$$ El Sereno, 4 Av Norte 16, T7832-0501. Open 1200-1500, 1800-2300. International/ Italian cuisine. Grand entrance with massive heliconia plants in the courtyard. It has a lovely terrace bar up some stone steps and a cave for romantic dining; it's popular at weekends.

$$$ La Casserole, Callejón de Concepción 7, T7832-0219 close to **Casa Santo Domingo**. Tue-Sat 1200-1500, 1900-2200, Sun 1200-1500, closed Mon. Sophisticated French cooking with fresh fish daily served at tables set in a beautiful courtyard, exclusive. Rigoberta Menchú dined with Jacques Chirac here.

$$$-$$ Caffé Mediterráneo, 6 Calle Pte 6A, T7832-7180. Wed-Mon 1200-1500, 1830-2200. 1 block south of the plaza. Mouth-watering Italian cuisine with great candlelit ambience. Recommended.

$$$-$$ Fonda de la Calle Real, 5 Av Norte 5 and No 12, T7832 0507, also at 3 Calle Pte 7 (which wins over the others for the setting). Its speciality is *queso fundido*. It also serves local dishes including *pepián* (and a vegetarian version) and *Kak-ik*, a Verapaz speciality.

$$ El Sabor del Tiempo, Calle del Arco and 3 Calle Poniente, T7832 0516. Good steaks, burgers, seafood and pasta in tastefully converted former warehouse, with polished wood and glass cabinets. A bit pricey but full of antiquey character.

$$ Frida's, 5 Av Norte 29, Calle del Arco, T7832-0504. Daily 1200-0100. Ochre and French navy colours decorate this restaurant's tribute to Mexico's famous female artist. It is quite dark inside but Frida memorabilia and colander-like lampshades lighten the interior. Efficient service. 2nd-floor pool table, Wed and Thu ladies' night.

$$ Hector's, 1 Calle Poniente No 9, T7832-9867. Small, busy and welcoming restaurant that serves wonderful food at good prices. Highly recommended.

$$ La Antigua Viñería, 5 Av Sur 34A, T7832-7370. Mon-Thu 1800-0100, Fri-Sun 1300-0100. Owned by Beppe Dángella, next door to San José ruins. Amazing photo-graphic collection of clients in various stages of inebriation, excellent selection of wines and grappa, you name it. Very romantic, feel free to write your comments on the walls, very good food, pop in for a reasonably priced *queso fundido* and glass of wine if you can't afford the whole hog.

$$ Quesos y Vinos, Calle Poniente 1, T7832-7785. Wed-Mon 1200-1600, 1800-2200. Authentic Italian food and owners, good selection of wines, wood-fired pizza oven, sandwiches, popular.

$$ Sabe Rico, 6 Av Sur No 7, 7832-0648. Herb garden restaurant and fine-food deli that serves healthy, organic food in tranquil surroundings.

$$-$ Café Flor, 4 Av Sur 1, T7832-5274. Full-on delicious Thai/Guatemalan-style and Tandoori food, delivered up between 1100-2300. The stir-fries are delicious, but a little overpriced. Discounts sometimes available. Friendly staff.

$$-$ Café Rocio, 6 Av Norte 34. This is a palace of Asian food delight. Virtually everything on the menu is mouth-wateringly delicious. Don't leave without indulging in the *mora crisp*: hot blackberry sauce sandwiched between slices of vanilla ice cream! Highly recommended.

$$-$ Helas Taberna Griega, 4 Av Norte 4, inside **La Escudilla**. Open 1800-0100, from 1300 weekends, closed Wed. Delicious food including pitta bread stuffed with goodies, Greek olives, tzatsiki, all surrounded by a Greek ruin and sea mural, fishing net and shells.

$$-$ Rainbow Café, 7 Av Sur, on the corner of 6 Calle Pte. Consistently delicious vegetarian food served in a pleasant courtyard surrounded by hanging plants, good filling breakfasts, indulgent crêpes, popular, live music evenings, good book exchange. Bar at night with happy hour and ladies' nights. Recommended.

$ In front of La Merced, in the back of the shop opposite La Merced. Open until about 1900. Where local people eat it's ridiculously cheap, large proportions. Arrive respectfully and enjoy a real Guatemalan experience.

$ La Casa de los Mixtas, 3 Calle Pte 3 Callejón 2A. Mon-Sat 0900-1900. Cheap Guatemalan fodder with a few tables on the pavement next to **Casa de Don Ismael**, good breakfasts, set lunch way above average, friendly family. Recommended.

$ Típico Antigüeño, Alameda Sta Lucía 4, near the PO, T7832-5995. This locally run place offers an absolute bargain of a *menú del día* (fish, chicken), which includes soup and sometimes a drink. It is extremely popular and can get ridiculously busy, so best to turn up before 1300 for lunch. Recommended.

$ Travel Menu, 6 Calle Pte 14. Big fat juicy sandwiches and tofu stir-fry, in candlelit place, friendly.

Cafés and delis

Bagel Barn, 5 Calle Pte 2. Open 0600-2200. Popular, breakfast, snack deals with bagels and smoothies, videos shown nightly, free.

Café Barroco, Callejón de la Concepción 2, T7832-0781. Peaceful garden, stylish, delicious cakes, coffees, huge selection of English teas for the deprived.

Café Condesa, 5 Av Norte 4. Open 0700-2100. West side of the main plaza in a pretty courtyard, popular, a little pricey for the portions, breakfast with free coffee fill-ups, desserts, popular Sun brunches.

Cafetería Alemana Charlotte, Callejón de los Nazarenos 9, between 6 and 7 Av Norte. Good breakfasts, cakes, good coffee, German books, newspapers, and films.

Doña Luisa Xicoténcatl, 4 Calle Ote 12, 1½ blocks east of the plaza. Open 0700-2130 daily. Popular meeting place with an excellent bulletin board, serving breakfasts, tasty ice cream, good coffee, burgers, large menu, big portions. Good views of Volcán Agua upstairs. Shop sells good selection of wholemeal, banana bread, yogurts, etc; don't miss the chocolate and orange loaf if you can get it.

Peroleto, Alameda Sta Lucía 36. Run by a Nicaraguan, next to San Jerónimo church, stop by here for the wickedest *licuados* in town and you probably won't be able to bypass the cake cabinet either. It has a *ceviche* restaurant next door open until 1800.

Tostaduría Antigua, 6 Calle Pte/Av Sur Esquina. 0900-1300,1430-1800. Roasts and brews good Antiguan coffee, many say the best in town. You can smell the coffee half a block away in each direction.

Vivero y Café de La Escalonia, 5 Av Sur Final 36 Calle, T7832-7074. Open daily 0900-1800. This delightful place is well worth the walk – a café amid a garden centre with luscious flowers everywhere, pergola, classical music, *postres*, herb breads, salads andcold drinks. Bird of paradise flowers and tumbergia.

Antigua *p35, map p36*
Bars and clubs

Café 2000, 6 Av Norte 8, between 4 and 5 Calle Pte. Daily 0800-0100. Happy hour Tue-Sat 1930-2300. Kicking most nights with indie music, and hard, cool lines in decor, but the free films or sports events shown on a giant screen can alter the balance in the bar between those on a bender and those glued to the screen. Good salads.

Casbah, 5 Av Norte 30. Mon-Sat 1800-0100. Cover charge includes a drink. Gay night Thu. Has a medium-sized dance floor with a podium and plays a mix of good dance and Latin music, the closest place to a nightclub atmosphere in Antigua.

La Chimenea, 7 Av Norte 18. Mon-Sat 1700-2430. Happy hour every day, seriously cheap, relaxed atmosphere, mixed young crowd, dance floor, salsa, rock.

La Sala, 6 Calle Pte, T5671-3008. One of the most popular salsa dancing and watering holes in town.

Reilly's Irish Pub, 5 Av Norte 32. Daily 1400-0100, happy hour 1600-2000. Guinness and other other imported beers available, very popular with sports fans for its international games shown on big TV screens; reasonably priced food.

Riki's Bar, 4 Av Norte 4, inside **La Escudilla**. Usually packed with gringos, but attracts a young Guatemalan crowd as well, and popular with the gay fraternity. Good place to meet people. A good mix of music, including jazz.

Cinemas

Antigua must be the home of the lounge cinema. All show films or videos in English, or with subtitles.

Café 2000, 6 Av Sur. Free films daily and the most popular spot in town to watch movies.

Cine Sin Ventura, 5 Av Sur 8. The only real screen in town, auditorium can get cold, and they need to hit the brightness button.

Antigua *p35, map p36*
Feb International Culture Festival: dance, music and other top-quality performers from around the globe come to Antigua.
Mar/Apr Semana Santa: see box, page 39.
21-26 Jul The feast of **San Santiago**.
31 Oct-2 Nov All Saints and All Souls, in and around Antigua.
7 Dec Quema del Diablo (burning of the Devil) by lighting fires in front of their houses and burning an effigy of the Devil in the Plazuela de La Concepción at night, thereby starting the Christmas festivities.
8 Dec Fiesta in Ciudad Vieja
15 Dec The start of what's known as the **Posadas**, where a group of people leave from each church, dressed as Mary and Joseph, and seek refuge in hotels. They are symbolically refused lodging several times, but are eventually allowed in.

⊙ Shopping

Antigua *p35, map p36*
Antigua is a shopper's paradise, with textiles, furniture, candles, fabrics, clothes, sculpture, candies, glass, jade and ceramics on sale. The **main municipal market** is on Alameda Santa Lucía next to the bus station, where you can buy fruit, clothes and shoes. The *artesanía* market is opposite, next to the bus lane.

Art
Galería de Arte Antigua, 4 Calle Ote 27 y 1 Av. Tue-Sat. Large art gallery.

Bookshops
Numerous bookshops sell books in English and Spanish, postcards, posters, maps and guides, including **Footprint Handbooks**. **Un Poco de Todo**, near Casa del Conde on the plaza. **Casa del Conde**, 5 Av Norte 4; has a full range of books from beautifully illustrated coffee-table books to guides and

history books. **Rainbow Cafe**, 7 Av Sur 18, second-hand books. **Hamlin and White**, 4 Calle Ote 12A. Books on Guatemala are cheaper here than at Casa del Conde.

Crafts, textiles, clothes and jewellery
Many other stores sell textiles, handicrafts, antiques, silver and jade on 5 Av Norte between 1 and 4 Calle Pte and 4 Calle Ote.
Casa Chicob, Callejón de la Concepción 2, www.casachicob.com. Beautiful textiles, candles and ceramics for sale.
Casa de Artes, 4 Av Sur 11, www.casade artes.com.gt, for traditional textiles and handicrafts, jewellery, etc. Very expensive.
Casa de los Gigantes, 7 Calle Ote 18, for textiles and handicrafts.
Diva, at 5 Av Norte 16. For Western-style clothes and jewellery.
El Telar, Loom Tree, 5 Av Sur 7, all sorts of coloured tablecloths, napkins, cushion covers and bedspreads are sold here.
Huipil market, held in the courtyard of La Fuente every Sat 0900-1400. The display is very colourful and if the sun is out this is an excellent place for photos.
Mercado de Artesanías, next to the main market at the end of 4 Calle Pte.
Nativo's, 5 Av Norte, 25 "B", T7832-6556. Sells some beautiful textiles from such places as Aguacatán.
Nim P'ot, 5 Av Norte 29, T7832-2681, www.nimpot.com, a mega-warehouse of traditional textiles and crafts brought from around the country. Excellent prices.
Textura, 5 Av Norte 33, T7832-5067 for lots of bedroom accessories.

Food
Doña María Gordillo, 4 Calle Ote 11. Famous throughout the country. It is impossible to get in the door most days but, if you can, take a peek, to see the *dulces*, as well as the row upon row of yellow wooden owls keeping their beady eyes on the customers.

La Bodegona, 5 Calle Pte 32, opposite **Posada La Quinta**, on 5 Calle Pte and with another entrance on 4 Calle Pte, large supermarket.

Tienda de Doña Gavi, 3 Av Norte 2, behind the cathedral, sells all sorts of lovely potions and herbs, candles and home-made biscuits. Doña Gaviota also sells Guatemala City's most famous ice creams in all sorts of weird and wonderful flavours (see **Helados Marylena**, page 27).

▲ Activities and tours

Antigua *p35, map p36*
Spas
Antigua Spa Resort, San Pedro El Panorama, lote 9 and 10 G, T7832-3960. Daily 0900-2100. Swimming pool, steam baths, sauna, gym, jacuzzi, beauty salon. Reservations advised.

Mayan Spa, Alameda Sta Lucía Norte 20, T7832-3537. Mon-Sat 0900-1800. Massages and pampering packages, including sauna, steam baths and jacuzzi, are available.

Riding
Ravenscroft Riding Stables, 2 Av Sur 3, San Juan del Obispo, T7830-6669. You can also hire horses in Santa María de Jesús.

Swimming
Porta Hotel Antigua, non-residents may use the pool for a charge.

Villas de Antigua (Ciudad Vieja exit), T7832-0011-15. For buffet lunch, swimming and marimba band.

Tour operators
Adrenalina Tours, 3a Calle Poniente, T7882 4147, www.adrenalinatours.com. Xela's respected tour operator has opened up in **Antigua** too. As well as shuttles all around Guatemala, there are minibuses to San Cristóbal de las Casas, Mexico, US$55. Also customized packages, weekend trips to Xela and discounted Tikal trips. Recommended.

Adventure Travel Center Viareal, 5 Av Norte 25B, T7832-0162. Daily trips to Guatemalan destinations (including Río Dulce sailing, river and volcano trips), Monterrico, Quiriguá, El Salvador and Honduras.

Antigua Tours, Casa Santo Domingo, 3 Calle Ote 22, T7832-5821, www.antiguatours.net. Run by Elizabeth Bell, author of 4 books on Antigua. She offers walking tours of the city (US$20 per person), book in advance, Mon, Thu 1400-1700, Tue, Wed, Fri, Sat 0930-1230. During Lent and Holy Week there are extra tours, giving insight into the processions and carpet making. Highly recommended.

Aventuras Naturales, Col El Naranjo No 53, Antigua, T5381-6615, http://aventuras naturales.tripod.com. Specialized trips including guided birding tours.

Aventuras Vacacionales, T5306-3584, www.sailing-diving-guatemala.com. Highly recommended sailing trips on *Las Sirenas* owned by Captain John Clark and sailed by Captain Raúl Hernández (see also under Río Dulce, page 128).

CA Tours, 6 Calle Oriente Casa 14, T7832-9638, www.catours.co.uk. British-run motorbike tour company. Recommended.

Eco-Tour Chejo's, 3 Calle Pte 24, T7832-5464, ecotourchejos@hotmail.com. Well-guarded walks up volcanoes. Interesting tours also available to coffee *fincas*, flower plantations, etc, shuttle service, horse riding, very helpful.

Gran Jaguar, 4 Calle Pte 30, T7832-2712, www.guacalling.com/jaguar/. Well-organized fun volcano tours with official security. Also shuttles and trips to Tikal and Río Dulce. Very highly recommended for the Pacaya trip.

Guatemala Reservations.com, 3 Av Norte 3, T7832-3293, www.guatemala reservations.com. Closed Sun. A wide range of tours and transport services. Frequently recommended. Also has guidebooks for reference or to buy, along with a water bottle-filling service to encourage recycling. Cheap phone call service. Shuttles and tours.

Old Town Outfitters, 5 Av Sur 12 "C", T7832-4171, www.adventureguatemala.com. Action adventure specialists, with mountain-bike tours (½-day tour, US$39), kayak tours hiking and climbing, outdoor equipment on sale, maps, very helpful.

Outdoor Excursions, 1 Av Sur 4b, T7832-0074, www.guatemalavolcano.com. Professional, knowledgeable and fun Volcano tour company with private security. Overnight tours to Fuego (US$79), Acatenango (US$79) and Pacaya (US$59).

Rainbow Travel Center, 7 Av Sur 8, T7931-7878, www.rainbowtravelcenter.com. Full local travel service, specialists in student flights and bargain international flights, they will attempt to match any quote. It also sells ISIC, Go25 and teachers' cards. English, French, German and Japanese spoken.

Sin Fronteras, 5a Av Norte 15 "A", T7720-4400, www.sinfront.com. Local tours, shuttles, horse riding, bicycle tours, canopy tours, national and international air tickets including discounts with ISIC and Go25 cards. Also sells travel insurance. Agents for rafting experts **Maya Expeditions**. Reliable and highly recommended.

Tivoli Travel, 4 Calle Ote 10, T7832-4274, antigua@tivoli.com.gt. Closed Sun. Helpful with any travel problem, English, French, Spanish, German, Italian spoken, reconfirm tickets, shuttles, hotel bookings, good-value tours. Useful for organizing independent travel as well as tours.

ViaVenture, 2 Calle Ote 2, T7832-2509, www.viaventure.com. Professional tour operator offering special interest and tailor-made tours.

⊙ Transport

Antigua *p35, map p36*
Bus
To **Guatemala City**: buses leave when full between 0530 and 1830, US$1, 1-1½ hrs, depending on the time of day, from the Alameda Santa Lucía near the market, from an exit next to **Pollo Campero** (not from behind the market). All other buses leave from behind the market. To **Chimaltenango**, on the Pan-American Hwy, from 0600-1600, every 15 mins, US$0.65, for connections to **Los Encuentros** (for **Lake Atitlán** and **Chichicastenango**), **Cuatro Caminos** (for **Quetzaltenango**) and **Huehuetenango** (for the Mexican border). It is possible to get to Chichicastenango and back by bus in a day, especially on Thu and Sun, for the market. Get the bus to Chimaltenango and then change. It's best to leave early. See Chimaltenango for connections. The only direct bus to **Panajachel** is Rebuli, leaving at 0700, from 4 Calle Pte, in front of **La Bodegona** supermarket, US$5, 2½ hrs, returning 1100. Other buses to **Pana** via Chimaltenango with **Rebuli** and **Carrillo y Gonzalez**, 0600-1645, US$2.50. To **Escuintla**, 0530-1600, 1 hr, US$1.25.

International To **Copán** and other cities in Honduras, including **Tegucigalpa**, with **Hedman Alas**, www.hedmanalas.com, from Posada de Don Rodrigo to its terminal in Guatemala City for a connection to Copán. Leaves at 0330 and 0630 from Antigua, US$41, US$77 return and 0500 and 0900 from Guatemala City, US$35, US$65 return. Return times are 1330 and 1800 to Guatemala City; the earlier bus continues to Antigua.

Shuttles Hotels and travel agents run frequent shuttle services to and from **Guatemala City** and the **airport** (1 hr) from 0400 to about 2000 daily, US$10-15 depending on the time of day: details from any agency in town. There are also shuttles to **Chichicastenango**, US$5-18, **Panajachel**, US$5-12, **Quetzaltenango**, US$16, **Monterrico**, US$15, **Flores**, US$20-40, **Copán**, US$8-25 and other destinations, but check for prices and days of travel. **Plus Travel** (www.plustravelguate.com) has some of the best prices and range of

destinations, with offices in Antigua
(6a Calle Pte No 19, T7832-3147) and
Copán Ruinas. Recommended.

Around Antigua *p40*
Bus To **Ciudad Vieja**, US$0.30, every
30 mins, 20 mins. **San Miguel de las
Dueñas**. Take a bus marked 'Dueñas', every
30 mins, 20 mins, US$0.30. To **San Antonio
Aguas Calientes**, every 30 mins, 30 mins,
US$0.30. To **Santa María de Jesús** every
30 mins, 45 mins, US$0.50. There are a few
buses a day between **Mixco Viejo** and the
Zona 4 terminal, Guatemala City. The bus
goes to Pachalum; ask to be dropped at
ruins entrance.

Volcán Agua *p42*
Bus From Antigua to **Alotenango** from
0700-1800, 40 mins.

Volcán Acatenango *p42*
Bus To reach **La Soledad**, take a bus
heading for Yepocapa or Acatenango
village and get off at La Soledad.

Car Tabarini, 6 Av Sur 22, T7832-8107,
also at the **Hotel Radisson Villa Antigua**,
T7832-7460, www.tabarini.com.

Motorcycle hire La Ceiba, 6 Calle
Pte 15, T7832-0077.

Taxi Servicio de Taxi 'Antigua',
Manuel Enrique Gómez, T5417-2180,
has been recommended.

Horse-drawn carriage Available at
weekends and during fiestas around the plaza.

Tuk-tuk Motorbike taxis with a seat for
2 will whizz you around town for US$1.50.

Antigua *p35, map p36*
Banks Banks are closed Wed-Sun of Holy
Week and none change money between
Christmas and New Year. Most banks are
open Mon-Fri 0900-1800, some until 1900
and Sat 0900-1300. **Banco de América
Central**, on the plaza, Visa and MasterCard
ATM (Cirrus and Plus), but bank hours only.
Banco Industrial, 5 Av Sur 4, near plaza, gives
cash on Visa ATM (24 hr) and Visa credit card
at normal rates, no commission. Extremely
quick service. **Banco Industrial** on plaza,
good rates, no commission, MasterCard
(Cirrus) ATM. **Internet** Some internet cafés
offer discount cards, which are worth buying
if you are in town for any length of time.
The following are recommended: **Enlaces**,
6 Av Norte 1. **Funky Monkey**, Paseo de
los Corregidores, 5 Av Sur 6. **Language
schools** Footprint has received favourable
reports from students for the following
language schools: **Academia Antigüeña
de Español**, 1 Pte 10, T7832-7241,
www.spanishacademy antiguena.com.
Alianza Lingüística 'Cano', Av El Desengaño
21A, T7832-0370. Private classes are also
available. **Amerispan**, 6 Av Norte 40 and 7
Calle Ote, T7832-0164, www.amerispan.com.
In the US, 1334 Walnut St, 6th floor,
Philadelphia PA 19107. **Centro Lingüístico
Maya**, 5 Calle Pte 20, T7832-1342,
www.clmmaya.com. **CSA** (Christian Spanish
Academy), 6 Av Norte 15, Aptdo Postal 320,
T7832-3922, www.learncsa.com. **Don Pedro
de Alvarado**, 6 Av Norte 39, T5872-2469,
www.donpedrospanishschool.com. 25 years'
experience. **Proyecto Bibliotecas Guatemala**
(**PROBIGUA**), 6 Av Norte 41B, T7832-2998,
www.probigua.org. Gives a percentage of
profits towards founding and maintaining
public libraries in rural towns; frequently
recommended. **Proyecto Lingüístico
Francisco Marroquín**, 6 Av Norte, www.plfm-
antigua.org. **Sevilla Academia de Español**,

Learning the lingo

Antigua is overrun with language students and so some say it is not the most ideal environment in which to learn Spanish. There are about 70-plus schools, open year round. At any one time there may be 300-600 overseas students in Antigua. Not all schools are officially authorized by INGUAT and the Ministry of Education. INGUAT has a list of authorized schools in its office. Rates depend on the number of hours of tuition per week, and vary from school to school. As a rough guide, the average fee for four hours a day, five days a week is US$120-200, at a reputable school, with homestay, though many are less and some schools offer cheaper classes in the afternoon. You will benefit more from the classes if you have done a bit of study of the basics before you arrive. There are guides who take students around the schools and charge a high commission (make sure this is not added to your account). They may approach tourists arriving on the bus from the capital.

All schools offer one-to-one tuition; if you can meet the teachers in advance, so much the better, but don't let the director's waffle distract you from asking pertinent questions. Paying more does not mean you get better teaching and the standard of teacher varies within schools as well as between schools. Beware of 'hidden extras' and be clear on arrangements for study books. Some schools have an inscription fee. Several schools use a portion of their income to fund social projects and some offer a programme of activities for students such as dance classes, Latin American film, tours, weaving and football. Before making any commitment, find somewhere to stay for a couple of nights and shop around at your leisure. Schools also offer accommodation with local families, but check the place out if possible before you pay a week in advance. Average accommodation rates with a family with three meals a day are US$75-100 per week. In some cases the schools organize group accommodation; if you prefer single, ask for it.

1 Av Sur 8, T7832-5101, www.sevillantigua. com. **Tecún Umán**, 6 Calle Pte 34A, T7832-2792, www.tecunuman.centramerica. com. **Private lessons** Check ads in **Doña Luisa's** and others around town and the tourist office. Recommended: **Julia Solís**, 5 Calle Pte 36, T7832-5497, julisar@hotmail. com (she lives behind the tailor's shop). **Armalia Jarquín**, Av El Desengaño 11, T7832-2377. There are, unbelievably, numerous No 11s on this road. Armalia's has a sign up and is opposite No 75, which has a tiled plaque. **Laundry** All charge about US$1 per kg and most close Sun and half-day Sat. **Delilah** in La Unión on 1 Av Sur provides an excellent service. **Lavandería Gilda**, 5 Calle Pte between 6 and 7 Av, very

good and can do a wash and dry in 2 hrs. **Central**, 5 Calle Pte 7B. **Medical services Casa de Salud Santa Lucía**, Alameda Sta Lucía Sur 7, T7832-3122. Open 24 hrs, good and efficient service. Consultation prices vary. **Hospital Privado Hermano Pedro**, Av El Desengaño 12A, T7832-6419. **Optica Santa Lucía**, 5 Calle Pte 28, T7832-0384. Opticians selling contact-lens solution and accessories. **Police** Tourism police, Rancho Nimejay, 6 Calle, between 8 Av and 4 Calle del Ranchón, T7832-7290. The office is open 24 hrs. Just knock on the door or ring their number. **National Police** are based in Antigua, in the Palacio de los Capitanes General, on the south side of the plaza. **Post** Post office at Alameda Sta Lucía

and 4 Calle Pte, near the market. Mon-Fri 0800-1730, Sat 0900-1430. The only place in town to buy stamps. Large parcels, up to 4.5 kg, cost approx US$60 to UK and rest of Europe; take about a week to arrive. If you get a cardboard box for your parcel from nearby supermarket, the post office will wrap it up in brown paper and tape it up for you.
Courier services There are several in town, including **DHL**, 6 Calle Pte and 6 Av Sur.

Quicker and maybe more reliable than regular post but nearly 3 times the cost.
Telephone Telgua, 5 Av Sur, corner of the plaza for international and local calls. There are public phone boxes inside the **Telgua** building, which are quieter to use than the couple under the arches on the west side of the square. Mon-Fri 0800-1800, Sat 0800-1200. Try **Funky Monkey** for internet calls.

Lake Atitlán and around

Beautiful scenery stretches west of the capital through the Central Highlands. Here, volcano landscapes are dotted with colourful markets and the Maya wearing traditional clothes in the towns and villages. Aldous Huxley called Lake Atitlán "the most beautiful lake in the world" and attractive villages flank its shores. Further north you can explore the streets of Chichicastenango as the town fills with hawkers and vendors at the weekly markets serving tourists and locals alike. North of Chichicastenango, the Quiché and Ixil Triangle regions have small, very traditional, hamlets set in beautiful countryside that are easily explored by bus.

Ins and outs
The easiest way to get to the Lake Atitlán area is by the numerous buses that ply the Pan-American Highway, changing at Los Encuentros or El Cuchillo junctions. Alternatively, shuttles go to Panajachel from most big tourist centres. Villages around the lake are connected to Panajachel by boat services. Some are served by buses. Some Hurricane Stan damage from October 2005 is still visible and some small roads remain unrepaired. Access is not affected, though. Panabaj, the village that was completely destroyed behind Santiago Atitlán, was declared a mass graveyard. Tropical Storm Agatha caused further destruction in 2010, with roads all around the lake badly affected and slowing down transport access. ▸▸ *See Transport, page 78.*

Towards Lake Atitlán
The Pan-American Highway heads west out of the capital passing through Chimaltenango and on to Los Encuentros where it turns north for Chichicastenango, Santa Cruz del Quiché, Nebaj and the Ixil Triangle, and south for Sololá and the Lake Atitlán region. It continues to the western highland region of Quetzaltenango (see page 94), Totonicapán, Huehuetenango and the Cuchumatanes Mountains (see pages 86 and 88).

Chimaltenango and around
Chimaltenango is busy with traffic. Here, another road runs south for 20 km to Antigua. This tree-lined road leads to Parramos where it turns sharp left. Straight on through the village, in 1.5 km, is a well known inn and restaurant (see Sleeping, page 69). This road continues through mountains to Pastores, Jocotenango and finally to Antigua. Some 6 km south of Chimaltenango, **San Andrés Itzapa** is well worth a visit; there is a very interesting **chapel to Maximón** ① *open till 1800 daily.* Shops by the chapel sell prayer pamphlets and pre-packaged offerings. Beyond Chimaltenango is **Zaragoza**, a former Spanish penal settlement, and beyond that a road leads 13 km north to the interesting village of **Comalapa**. This is the best place to see *naíf* painting and there are plenty of

galleries. The **tourist information office** ① *Av 3-76, T5766-3874*, is in the house of Andrés Curuchich, a popular artist). There's a colourful market on Monday and Tuesday.

Routes west: Tecpán and Los Encuentros

Returning to the Pan-American Highway the road divides 6 km past Zaragoza. The southern branch, the old Pan-American Highway, goes through Patzicía and Patzún (see

Lake Atitlán

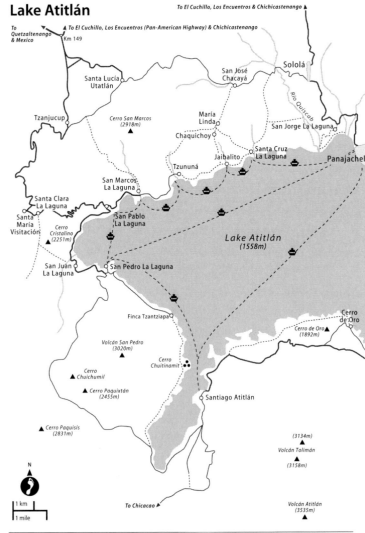

below) to Lake Atitlán, then north to Los Encuentros. The northern branch, the new Pan-American Highway, which is used by all public transport, goes past Tecpán (see below) and then to Los Encuentros. From Los Encuentros there is only the one road west to San Cristóbal Totonicapán, where it swings northwest to La Mesilla/Ciudad Cuauhtémoc, at the Mexican border.

To Las Trampas, Guatemala City & Zaragoza

Río Panajachel

San Andrés Semetabaj

Las Canoas

Santa Catarina Palopó

Godínez

To Patzún

San Antonio Palopó

Tzampetey

Agua Escondida

Pachitulúl

Panaranjo

San Lucas Tolimán

San Gabriel

To Cocales & Pacific Highway

From Zaragoza the Pan-American Highway runs 19 km to near **Tecpán**, which is slightly off the road at 2287 m. It has a particularly fine church with silver altars, carved wooden pillars, odd images and a wonderful ceiling that was severely damaged by the 1976 earthquake. There is accommodation, restaurants and banks. Near Tecpán are the important Maya ruins of **Iximché** ⓘ *5 km of paved road south of Tecpán, 0800-1700, US$3.25*, once capital and court of the Cakchiqueles. The first capital of Guatemala after its conquest was founded near Iximché; followed in turn by Ciudad Vieja, Antigua and Guatemala City. The ruins are well presented with three plazas, a palace and two ball courts on a promontory surrounded on three sides by steep slopes.

The old and new Pan-American highways rejoin 11 km from Sololá at the **El Cuchillo** junction. About 2 km east is **Los Encuentros**, the junction of the Pan-American Highway and the paved road 18 km northeast to Chichicastenango, see page 64.

To Lake Atitlán along the old Pan-American Highway

With amazing views of Lake Atitlán and the surrounding volcanoes, travellers of the southern road from Zaragoza to Lake Atitlán encounter a much more difficult route than the northern option, with several steep hills and many hairpin bends. Nevertheless, if you have both the time and a sturdy vehicle, it is an extremely rewarding trip. Note that there is no police presence whatsoever along the old Pan-American Highway.

The route goes through **Patzicía**, a small Maya village founded in 1545 (no accommodation). Market days are Wednesday and Saturday and the local fiesta is 22-27 July. The famous church, which had a fine altar and beautiful silver, was destroyed by the 1976 earthquake. Beyond is the small town of **Patzún**; its church, dating from 1570, is severely damaged and is not open to the public. There is a Sunday market, which is famous for the silk (and wool) embroidered napkins and for woven *fajas* and striped red cotton cloth; other markets are on Tuesday and Friday and the town fiesta is 17-21 May. For accommodation, ask at the *tiendas*.

The road leaves Patzún and goes south to Xepatán and on to **Godínez**, the highest community overlooking the lake. From Godínez, a good paved road turns off south to the village of San Lucas Tolimán and continues to Santiago Atitlán.

The main (steep, paved) road continues straight on for Panajachel. The high plateau, with vast wheat and maize fields, now breaks off suddenly as though pared by a knife. From a viewpoint here, there is an incomparable view of Lake Atitlán, 600 m below. The very picturesque village of **San Antonio Palopó** is right underneath you, on slopes leading to the water. It is about 12 km from the viewpoint to Panajachel. For the first 6 km you are close to the rim of the old crater and, at the point where the road plunges down to the lakeside, is **San Andrés Semetabaj** which has a beautiful ruined early 17th-century church. Market day is Tuesday. Buses go to Panajachel.

Sololá → *Altitude: 2113 m.*

On the road down to Panajachel is Sololá, which has superb views across Lake Atitlán. Outside the world of the tourist, this is the most important town in the area. A fine, modern, white church, with bright stained-glass windows and an attractive clocktower dominates the west side of the plaza. Sololá is even more special for the bustling market that brings the town to life every Tuesday and Friday, when the Maya gather from surrounding commuities to buy and sell local produce. Women and particularly men wear traditional dress. While it is primarily a produce market, there is also a good selection of used *huípiles*. Even if you're not in the market to buy, it is a colourful sight. Markets are mornings only; Friday market gets underway on Thursday. There's a fiesta 11-17 August.

From Sololá the old Pan-American Highway weaves and twists through a 550-m drop in 8 km to Panajachel. The views are impressive at all times of day, but particularly in the morning. Time allowing, it is quite easy to walk down direct by the road (two hours); you also miss the unnerving bus ride down (US$0.40).

Panajachel → *For listings, see pages 69-83.*

The old town of Panajachel is charming and quiet but the newer development, strung along a main road, is a tucker and trinket emporium. It's busy and stacked cheek by jowl with hundreds of stalls and shops along the main road. Some of the best bargains are here and textiles and crafts from across the country can be found. Panajachel is a gringo magnet, and if you want to fill up on international cuisine and drink then it's a good place to stay for a few days. There are also stunning views from the lakeshore.

Ins and outs
Getting there and around Good connections from most large town in the highlands, including Antigua, Chichicastenango and Quetzaltenango. The town centre is the

junction of Calle Principal and Calle (or Avenida) Santander. The main bus stop is here, stretching south back down Calle Real, and it marks the junction between the old and the modern towns. It takes about 10 minutes to walk from the junction to the lake shore. Calle

Panajachel

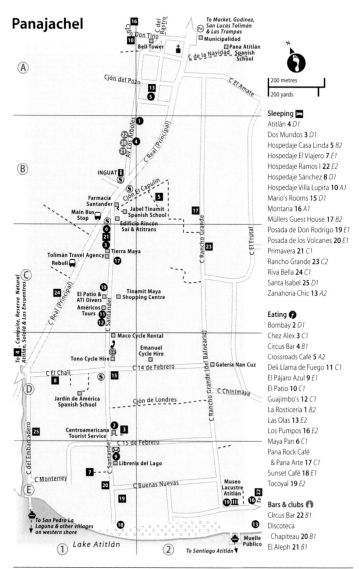

Sleeping
Atitlán **4** *D1*
Dos Mundos **3** *D1*
Hospedaje Casa Linda **5** *B2*
Hospedaje El Viajero **7** *E1*
Hospedaje Ramos I **22** *E2*
Hospedaje Sánchez **8** *D1*
Hospedaje Villa Lupita **10** *A1*
Mario's Rooms **15** *D1*
Montana **16** *A1*
Müllers Guest House **17** *B2*
Posada de Don Rodrigo **19** *E1*
Posada de los Volcanes **20** *E1*
Primavera **21** *C1*
Rancho Grande **23** *C2*
Riva Bella **24** *C1*
Santa Isabel **25** *D1*
Zanahoria Chic **13** *A2*

Eating
Bombay **2** *D1*
Chez Alex **3** *C1*
Circus Bar **4** *B1*
Crossroads Café **5** *A2*
Deli Llama de Fuego **11** *C1*
El Pájaro Azul **9** *E1*
El Patio **10** *C1*
Guajimbo's **12** *C1*
La Rostícería **1** *B2*
Las Olas **13** *E2*
Los Pumpos **16** *E2*
Maya Pan **6** *C1*
Pana Rock Café
& Pana Arte **17** *C1*
Sunset Café **18** *E1*
Tocoyal **19** *E2*

Bars & clubs
Circus Bar **22** *B1*
Discoteca
Chapiteau **20** *B1*
El Aleph **21** *B1*

Rancho Grande is sometimes called Calle del Balneario and other streets have variants. ►► *See Transport, page 79.*

Tourist information **INGUAT** ① *Calle Real Principal and Av Los Arboles, T7762-1106, daily 0900-1300 and 1400-1700.* Helpful with information about buses, boats and good local knowledge. Also see www.atitlan.com.

Safety There have been reports from travellers who have suffered **robbery** walking around the lake between San Juan and San Pablo and between San Marcos and Tzununá. Seek local advice from **INGUAT**, other travellers and local hotels/hostels before planning a trip.

Background

The original settlement of Panajachel was tucked up against the steep cliffs to the north of the present town, about 1 km from the lake. Virtually all traces of the original Kaqchikel village have disappeared, but the early Spanish impact is evident with the narrow streets, public buildings, plaza and church. The original Franciscan church was founded in 1567 and used as the base for the Christianization of the lake area. Later, the fertile area of the river delta was used for coffee production, orchards and many other crops, some of which are still grown today and can be seen round the back of the tourist streets or incorporated into the gardens of the hotels. Tourism began here in the early 20th century with several hotels on the waterfront, notably the **Tzanjuyú** and the **Monterrey**, the latter originally a wooden building dating from about 1910, rebuilt in 1975. In the 1970s came an influx of young travellers, quite a few of whom stayed on to enjoy the climate and the easy life. Drugs and the hippy element eventually gave Panajachel a bad name, but rising prices and other pressures have encouraged this group to move on – some to San Pedro across the lake. Others joined the commercial scene and still run services today.

Sights

The old town is 1 km from the lake and dominated by the **church**, originally built in 1567, but now restored. It has a fine decorated wooden roof and a mixture of Catholic statues and Maya paintings in the nave. A block up the hill is the daily market, worth a visit on Sunday mornings especially for embroideries. The local fiesta runs from 1-7 October, the main days are at the weekend and on 4 October.

In contrast, the modern town, almost entirely devoted to tourism, spreads out towards the lake. Calle Santander is the principal street, leading directly to the short but attractive **promenade** and boat docks. The section between Calle Santander and Calle Rancho Grande has been turned into a park, which delightfully frames the traditional view across the lake to the volcanoes. Near the promenade, at the **Hotel Posada de Don Rodrigo**, is the **Museo Lacustre Atitlán** ① *daily 0900-1200, 1400-1800, US$4.40,* created by Roberto Samayoa, a prominent local diver and archaeologist, to house some of the many items found in the lake. The geological history is explained and there is a fine display of Maya classical pottery and ceremonial artefacts classified by period. A submerged village has been found at a depth of 20 m, which is being investigated. It has been named **Samabaj** in honour of Don Roberto. For those interested in local art, visit **La Galería** (near **Rancho Grande Hotel**), where Nan Cuz, an indigenous painter, sells her pictures evoking the spirit of village life. She has been painting since 1958 and has achieved international recognition. On the road past the entrance to Hotel Atitlán is the **Reserva Natural Atitlán** ① *T7762-2565, www.atitlanreserva.com, daily 0800-1800, US$5.50*, a reserve with a bird refuge, butterfly collection, monkeys and native mammals in natural surroundings, with a picnic area, herb garden, waterfall, visitor centre, café, zip-lines and access to the lakeside beach. Camping and lodging are available.

Around Lake Atitlán → *For listings, see pages 69-83.*

Getting around Travelling round the lake is the best way to enjoy the stunning scenery and the effect of changing light and wind on the mood of the area. The slower you travel the better, and walking round the lake gives some fantastic views (but take advice on safety). With accommodation at towns and villages on the way, there is no problem finding somewhere to bed down for the night if you want to make a complete circuit. The lake is 50 km in circumference and you can walk on or near the shore for most of it. Here and there the cliffs are too steep to allow for easy walking and private properties elsewhere force you to move up 'inland'. For boat information see Transport, Panajachel. At almost any time of year, but especially between January and March, strong winds (*El Xocomil*) occasionally blow up quickly across the lake. This can be dangerous for small boats. ▶▶ *See Transport, page 78.*

Santa Catarina Palopó
The town, within easy walking distance (4 km) of Panajachel, has an attractive adobe church. Reed mats are made here, and you can buy *huípiles* (beautiful, green, blue and yellow) and men's shirts. Watch weaving at **Artesanías Carolina** on the way out towards San Antonio. Bargaining is normal. There are hot springs close to the town and an art gallery. Houses can be rented and there is at least one superb hotel (see Sleeping, page 70). The town fiesta is 25 November.

San Antonio Palopó
Six kilometres beyond Santa Catarina, San Antonio Palopó has another fine 16th-century church. Climbing the hill from the dock, it lies in an amphitheatre created by the mountains behind. Up above there are hot springs and a cave in the rocks used for local ceremonies. The village is noted for the clothes and head dresses of the men, and *huípiles* and shirts are cheaper than in Santa Catarina. A good hike is to take the bus from Panajachel to Godínez, take the path toward the lake 500 m south along the road to Cocales, walk on down from there to San Antonio Palopó (one hour) and then along the road back to Panajachel via Santa Catarina Palopó (three hours). You can walk on round the lake from San Antonio, but you must eventually climb steeply up to the road at Agua Escondida. The local fiesta is 12-14 June.

San Lucas Tolimán
San Lucas is at the southeastern tip of the lake and is not so attractive as other towns. It is known for its fiestas and markets especially Holy Week with processions, arches and carpets on the Thursday and Friday, and 15-20 October. Market days are Tuesday, Friday and Sunday (the best). There are two banks and an internet centre. **Comité Campesino del Altiplano** ① *T5804-9451, www.ccda.galeon.com*, is based in the small village of

Quixaya, 10 minutes from San Lucas. This Campesino Cooperative now produces fair trade organic coffee buying from small farmers. You can visit its organic processing plant on a small coffee *finca* and learn about its *café justicia,* and political work. Long-term volunteers welcome, Spanish required.

Volcán Atitlán and Volcán Tolimán

ⓘ *Ask Father Gregorio at the Parroquia church, 2 blocks from the Central Plaza, or at the Municipalidad for information and for available guides in San Lucas. Father Greg has worked in the area for more than 40 years so has a vested interest in recommending safe and good guides. One such is Carlos Huberto Alinan Chicoj, leaving at 2400 with torches to arrive at the summit by 0630 to avoid early cloud cover.*

From San Lucas the cones of **Atitlán**, 3535 m, and **Tolimán**, 3158 m, can be climbed. The route leaves from the south end of town and makes for the saddle (known as Los Planes, or Chanán) between the two volcanoes. From there it is south to Atitlán and north to the double cone (they are 1 km apart) and crater of Tolimán. Though straightforward, each climb is complicated by many working paths and thick cover above 2600 m. If you are fit, either can be climbed in seven hours, five hours down. Cloud on the volcano is common, but least likely from November to March. There have been reports of robbery so consider taking a guide, and ask local advice before setting out.

Santiago Atitlán

Santiago is a fascinating town, as much for the stunningly beautiful embroidered clothing of the locals, as for the history and character of the place with its mix of Roman Catholic, evangelical and Maximón worship. There are 35 evangelical temples in town as well as the house of the revered idol Maximón. The Easter celebrations here rival Antigua's for interest and colour. These are some of the most curious and reverential ceremonies in the world. If you only visit Guatemala once in your lifetime and it's at Easter and you can't bear to leave Antigua, come to Santiago at least for Good Friday. Commemorative events last all week and include Maximón as well as Christ.

You will be taken to the house of Maximón for a small fee. The fine church, with a wide nave decorated with colourful statues, was founded in 1547. The original roof was lost to earthquakes. There is a plaque dedicated to priest Father Francis Aplas Rother who was assassinated by the government in the church on 28 August 1981. At certain times of the year, the square is decked with streamers gently flapping in the breeze. The Tz'utujil women wear fine clothes and the men wear striped, half-length embroidered trousers (the most beautiful in Guatemala). There is a daily market, best on Friday and all sorts of art work and crafts can be bought. **Asociación Cojol ya weaving centre** ⓘ *T5499-5717, Mon-Fri 0900-1600, Sat 0900-1300, free, weaving tours also.* As well as Holy Week, the local fiesta takes place 23-27 July.

Near town is the hill, **Cerro de Oro**, with a small village of that name on the lake. The summit (1892 m) can be reached from the village in 45 minutes.

For more information on the **Lake Atitlán Medical project** and volunteer opportunities, see www.puebloapueblo.org.

San Pedro La Laguna

San Pedro is a small town set on a tiny promontory with coffee bushes threaded around tracks lined with hostels and restaurants on the lakeside fringes. The tourists and long-term

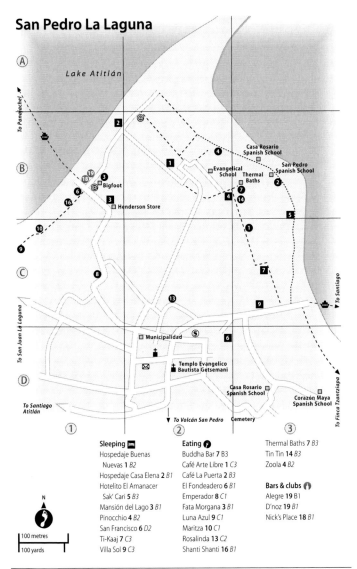

San Pedro La Laguna

Lake Atitlán

To Panajachel

Casa Rosario Spanish School

Evangelical School

Thermal Baths

San Pedro Spanish School

Bigfoot

Henderson Store

To San Juan La Laguna

Municipalidad

Templo Evangelico Bautista Getsemani

Casa Rosario Spanish School

Corazón Maya Spanish School

To Santiago Atitlán

To Volcán San Pedro   Cemetery

To Santiago

To Finca Tzantziapa

N

100 metres
100 yards

Sleeping 🛏
Hospedaje Buenas
  Nuevas **1** *B2*
Hospedaje Casa Elena **2** *B1*
Hotelito El Amanacer
  Sak' Cari **5** *B3*
Mansión del Lago **3** *B1*
Pinocchio **4** *B2*
San Francisco **6** *D2*
Ti-Kaaj **7** *C3*
Villa Sol **9** *C3*

Eating 🍴
Buddha Bar **7** *B3*
Café Arte Libre **1** *C3*
Café La Puerta **2** *B3*
El Fondeadero **6** *B1*
Emperador **8** *C1*
Fata Morgana **3** *B1*
Luna Azul **9** *C1*
Maritza **10** *C1*
Rosalinda **13** *C2*
Shanti Shanti **16** *B1*

Thermal Baths **7** *B3*
Tin Tin **14** *B3*
Zoola **4** *B2*

Bars & clubs 🍸
Alegre **19** B1
D'noz **19** B1
Nick's Place **18** B1

gringos have colonized the lakeside while the **Tz'utujil Maya** dominate the main part of the town up a very steep hill behind. San Pedro is now the favourite spot to hang out in for a couple of days or longer. It's a place to relax, to soak in hot baths, learn a bit of Spanish, horse ride and trek up Nariz de Maya. Some of the semi-permanent gringo inhabitants now run bars and cafés or sell home-made jewellery and the like. The cobbled road from the dock facing Panajachel (known as the *muelle*) climbs up to the centre and another goes down, more or less at right angles, to the other dock (known as the *playa* – beach) facing Santiago with the town arranged around. There's a mazy network of *callejones* and paths that fringe the shoreline between the two ferries. Market days are Thursday and Sunday (better) and there's a fiesta 27-30 June with traditional dances.

The town lies at the foot of the **Volcán San Pedro** (3020 m), which can be climbed in four to five hours, three hours down. It is now in the Parque Ecológico Volcán San Pedro, and the US$15 entrances includes a guide. **Politur** also work in the park and there have been no incidents of robbery since the park's inauguration. Camping is possible. Go early (0530) for the view, because after 1000 the top is usually smothered in cloud; also you will be in the shade all the way up and part of the way down.

Descubre San Pedro has set up a museum of local culture and coffee, with natural medicine and Maya cosmovision tours.

Evangelical churches are well represented in San Pedro, and you can hardly miss the yellow and white **Templo Evangélico Bautista Getsemaní** in the centre. A visit to the rug-making cooperative on the beach is of interest and backstrap weaving is taught at some places. A session at the **thermal baths** ① *about US$10, Mon-Sat 0800-1900*, is a relaxing experience. Note that the water is solar heated, not chemical hot springs. Best to reserve in advance. Massage is also available, US$10.

For general local information ask at **Bigfoot**, page 78, who will advise you on horse riding to neighbouring villages, guides for climbing Volcán San Pedro and whatever else you have in mind. Canoes are made in San Pedro and hire is possible.

San Juan La Laguna and Santa Clara La Laguna

The road north from San Pedro passes around a headland to San Juan La Laguna (2 km), a traditional lakeside town. Look for **Los Artesanos de San Juan** ① *8 Av, 6-20, Zona 2, T5963-9803*, and another image of Maximón displayed in the house opposite the Municipalidad. **Rupalaj Kistalin** ① *close to the textile store, LEMA, T5964-0040, daily 0800-1700*, is a highly recommended organization run by local guides. **LEMA** ① *T2425-9441, lema@sanjuanlalaguna.com*, the women weavers' association that uses natural dyes in their textiles, is also in town. Weaving classes are also possible (T7759-9126). On the road towards San Pablo there's a good viewpoint from the hilltop with the cross; a popular walk. A more substantial walk, about three hours, is up behind the village to Santa Clara La Laguna, 2100 m, passing the village of **Cerro Cristalino** with its attractive, white church with images of saints around the walls.

Santa María Visitación and San Pablo La Laguna

A short distance (500 m) to the west, separated by a gully, is a smaller village, Santa María Visitación. As with Santa Clara La Laguna, this is a typical highland village, and unspoilt by tourism. San Juan is connected to San Pablo by the lakeshore road, an attractive 4-km stretch mainly through coffee plantations. San Pablo, a busy village set 80 m above the lake, is known for rope making from *cantala* (maguey) fibres, which are also used for bags and fabric weaving.

San Marcos La Laguna

San Marcos' location is deceptive with the main part of the community 'hidden' up the hill. The quiet village centre is set at the upper end of a gentle slope that runs 300 m through coffee and fruit trees down to the lake, reached by two paved walkways. If arriving by boat and staying in San Marcos, ask to be dropped at the Schumann or the Pirámides dock. The village has grown rapidly in the last few years with a focus on the spiritual and energy – there is lots of massage, yoga, and all sorts of other therapies. It is the ideal place to be pampered. Beyond the centre, 300 m to the east is the main dock of the village down a cobbled road. Down the two main pathways are the hotels; some with waterfront sites have their own docks. There is a slanting trail leaving the village up through dramatic scenery over to Santa Lucía Utatlán, passing close to Cerro San Marcos, 2918 m, the highest point in the region apart from the volcanoes.

San Marcos to Santa Cruz

From the end of San Marcos where the stone track goes down to the dock, a rough track leads to **Tzununá**, passable for small trucks and 4WD vehicles, with views across the lake all the way. The village of Tzununá is along the tree-lined road through coffee plantations with a few houses up the valley behind. There is also a hotel with wonderful views (see Sleeping). There is a dock on the lakeside but no facilities. From here to Panajachel there are no roads or vehicular tracks and the villages can only be reached by boat, on horse or on foot. Also from here are some of the most spectacular views of the lake and the southern volcanoes. **Jaibalito** is smaller still than Tzununá, and hemmed in by the mountains with wonderful accommodation (see Sleeping, page 72). Arguably the best walk in the Atitlán area is from Jaibalito to Santa Cruz.

Santa Cruz La Laguna

Santa Cruz village is set in the most dramatic scenery of the lake. Three deep ravines come down to the bay separating two spurs. A stone roadway climbs up the left-hand spur, picks up the main walking route from Jaibalito and crosses over a deep ravine (unfortunately used as a garbage tip) to the plaza, on the only flat section of the right spur, about 120 m above the lake. The communal life of the village centres on the plaza. The hotels, one of them overflowing with flowers, are on the lake shore. Behind the village are steep, rocky forested peaks, many too steep even for the locals to cultivate. The fiesta takes place 7-11 May.

There is good walking here. Apart from the lake route, strenuous hikes inland eventually lead to the Santa Lucía Utatlán–Sololá road. From the left-hand (west) ravine reached from the path that runs behind the lake shore section, a trail goes through fields to an impossible looking gorge, eventually climbing up to Chaquijchoy, **Finca María Linda** and a trail to San José Chacayá (about four hours). In the reverse direction, the path southwest from San José leads to the Finca María Linda, which is close to the crater rim from where due south is a track to Jaibalito, to the left (east) round to the trail to Santa Cruz. Others follow the ridges towards San José and the road. These are for experienced hikers, and a compass (you are travelling due north) is essential if the cloud descends and there is no one to ask. From Santa Cruz to Panajachel along the coast is difficult, steep and unconsolidated, with few definitive paths. If you do get to the delta of the Río Quiscab, you may find private land is barred. The alternatives are either to go up to Sololá, about 6 km and 800 m up, or get a boat.

Chichicastenango → *For listings, see pages 69-83. Altitude: 2071 m.*

Chichicastenango is a curious blend of mysticism and commercialism. It is famous for its market where hundreds come for a bargain. On market mornings the steps of the church are blanketed in flowers as the women, in traditional dress, fluff up their skirts, amid baskets of lilies, roses and blackberries. But, with its mixture of Catholic and indigenous religion readily visible, it is more than just a shopping trolley stop. On a hilltop peppered with pine, villagers worship at a Maya shrine; in town, a time-honoured tradition of brotherhoods focuses on saint worship. Coupled with the mist that encircles the valley in the late afternoon, you can sense an air of intrigue. The **tourist office** ① *5 Av and Teatro Municipalidad, 1 block from church, daily 0800-2000, T7756-2022*, is helpful and provides a free leaflet with map, and local tour information.

Ins and outs
Getting there Chichicastenango is served by numerous chicken buses that head north from Los Encuentros or south from Santa Cruz del Quiché. There are direct buses from Xela and Guatemala City and shuttles from Antigua, the city and Pana. ▶▶ *See Transport, page 81.*

Background
Often called 'Chichi' but also known as Santo Tomás, Chichicastenango is the hub of the Maya-K'iche' highlands. The name derives from the *chichicaste*, a prickly purple plant-like a nettle, which grows profusely, and *tenango*, meaning 'place of'. Today the locals call the town 'Siguan Tinamit' meaning 'place surrounded by ravines'. The townsfolk are also known as *Masheños,* which comes from the word *Max*, also meaning Tomás. About 1000 *ladinos* live in the town, but 20,000 Maya live in the hills nearby and flood the town for the Thursday and Sunday markets. The town itself has winding streets of white houses roofed with bright red tiles, which wander over a little knoll in the centre of a cup-shaped valley surrounded by high mountains. The men's traditional outfit is a short-waisted embroidered jacket and knee breeches of black cloth, a woven sash and an embroidered kerchief around the head. The cost of this outfit, now over US$200, means that fewer and fewer men are wearing it. Women wear *huipiles* with red embroidery against black or brown and their *cortes* have dark blue stripes.

Sights
A large plaza is the focus of the town, with two white churches facing one another: **Santo Tomás** the parish church and **Calvario**. Santo Tomás, founded in 1540, is open to visitors, although photography is not allowed, and visitors are asked to be discreet and enter by a side door (through an arch to the right). Next to Santo Tomás are the cloisters of the Dominican monastery (1542). Here the famous *Popol Vuh* manuscript of the Maya creation story was found. A human skull wedged behind a carved stone face, found in Sacapulas, can be seen at the **Museo Arqueológico Regional** ① *main plaza, Tue, Wed, Fri,*

Sat 0800-1200, 1400-1600, Thu 0800-1600, Sun 0800-1400, closed Mon, US$0.70, photographs and video camera not permitted. There's also a jade collection once owned by 1926-1944 parish priest Father Rossbach.

The Sunday and Thursday markets are both very touristy, and bargains are harder to come by once shuttle-loads of people arrive mid-morning. Articles from all over the Highlands are available: rugs, carpets and bedspreads; walk one or two streets away from the main congregation of stalls for more realistic prices, but prices are cheaper in Panajachel for the same items and you won't find anything here that you can't find in Panajachel.

The idol, **Pascual Abaj**, a god of fertility, is a large black stone with human features on a hill overlooking the town. Crosses in the ground surrounding the shrine are prayed in front of for the health of men, women and children, and for the dead. Fires burn and the wax of a thousand candles, flowers and sugar cover the shrine. One ceremony you may see is that of a girl from the town requesting a good and sober husband. If you wish to undergo a ceremony to plead for a partner, or to secure safety from robbery or

Chichicastenango

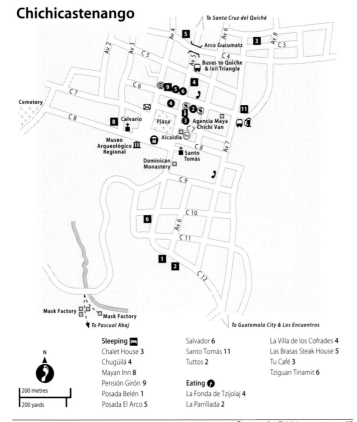

Sleeping	Salvador 6	La Villa de los Cofrades 4
Chalet House 3	Santo Tomás 11	Las Brasas Steak House 5
Chugüilá 4	Tuttos 2	Tu Café 3
Mayan Inn 8		Tziguan Tinamit 6
Pensión Girón 9	Eating	
Posada Belén 1	La Fonda de Tzijolaj 4	
Posada El Arco 5	La Parrillada 2	

N

200 metres
200 yards

misfortune, you may ask the *curandero* (US$7 including photographs). To reach the deity, walk along 5 Avenida, turn right on 9 Calle, down the hill, cross the stream and take the second track from the left going steepest uphill, which passes directly through a farmhouse and buildings. The farm now belongs to a mask-maker whom you can visit and buy masks from. Follow the path to the top of the pine-topped hill where you may well see a Maya ceremony in progress. It's about half an hour's walk. The site can be easily visited independently (in a small group), or an INGUAT-approved guide arranged through the local tourist committee can take you there and explain its history and significance (US$6.50, one or two hours, identified by a license in town).

Santa Cruz del Quiché and around → *Population: 7750. Altitude: 2000 m.*

Santa Cruz del Quiché, often simply called Quiché, is a quaint, friendly town, with a colourful daily market covering several blocks. There are few tourists here and prices are consequently reasonable. Its main attraction is **Utatlán**, the remains of the Maya K'iche' capital. The large Parque Central has a military garrison on the east side with a jail on the lower floor and a sinister military museum with reminders of recent conflicts above. The date of the town's fiesta varies around the Assumption but is usually held around 14-20 August.

Three kilometres away are the remains of temples and other structures of the former Quiché capital, **Gumarcaj**, sometimes spelt **K'umarkaaj**, and now generally called **Utatlán** ① *0800-1700, US$1.30, from the bus station, walk west along 10 Calle for 40 mins until you reach a small junction with a blue sign (SECP), take the right lane up through gates to the site.* The city was largely destroyed by the Spaniards, but the stonework of the original buildings can be seen in the ruins, which can be reached on foot; the setting is very attractive and well maintained. There are two subterranean burial chambers (take a torch, as there are unexpected drops) still used by the Maya for worship and chicken sacrifices. The seven plazas, many temples, ball court, gladiator's archway and other features are marked.

There is a paved road east from Quiché to (8 km) **Santo Tomás Chiché**, a picturesque village with a fine, rarely visited Saturday market (fiesta 25-28 December). There is also a road to this village from Chichicastenango. Although it is a short-cut, it is rough and virtually impassable in any vehicle. It makes a good, three- to four-hour walk, however. Further east (45 km) from Chiché is **Zacualpa**, where beautiful woollen bags are woven. The church has a remarkably fine façade and there is an unnamed *pensión* near the plaza. Market days are Sunday and Thursday.

At **Joyabaj** women weave fascinating *huípiles* and there is a colourful Sunday market, followed by a procession at about noon from the church led by the elders with drums and pipes. This was a stopping place on the old route from Mexico to Antigua. There is good walking in the wooded hills around, for example north to Chorraxaj (two hours), or across the Río Cocol south to Piedras Blancas to see blankets being woven. During fiesta week (9-15 August) Joyabaj has a *Palo Volador* and other traditional dances. There is a restaurant next to the Esso station on the Santa Cruz end of the plaza with a bank opposite (will change US dollars cash).

The road east to Cobán

The road east from **Sacapulas** is one of the most beautiful mountain roads in all Guatemala, with magnificent scenery in the narrow valleys. There is accommodation in

Uspantán and this is the place to stay for the night enroute to Cobán. The road is not paved beyond Uspantán. ▶▶ *See Transport, page 81.*

It's a five-hour walk from Uspantán south to **Chimul**, the birthplace of **Rigoberta Menchú**, Nobel Peace Prize winner in 1992. The village was virtually wiped out during the 1980s, but the settlement is coming to life again. Only pickups go to the village.

The Ixil Triangle → *For listings, see pages 69-83.*

The Ixil Triangle is made of up of the highland communities of Nebaj, Chajul and Cotzal. The forested mountainous scenery provides great walking opportunities, although sadly, out of local necessity, many of the slopes have been badly deforested and the wood burnt for fires. The traditional dress of the Nebaj women – an explosion of primary colours – is spectacular. Much of this area was decimated during the Civil War and then repopulated with the introduction of 'model villages' established by the government. Evidence of wartime activities can still be seen and more remote Maya Ixil-speaking villages are gradually opening up to visitors with the introduction of hostel and trekking facilities.

Nebaj and around

The town of Nebaj is high in the Cuchumatanes Mountains and its green slopes are often layered with mist. It is coloured by the beautiful dress worn by the local women, in an extravaganza of predominantly green, with red, yellow, orange, white and purple. The *corte* is mainly maroon with vertical stripes of black and yellow; some are bright red, and the *huipil* is of a geometric design. The women also wear a headdress with colourful bushy pom-poms on them. The men hardly ever wear the traditional costume; their jacket is red and embroidered in black designs. The main plaza is dominated by a large, simple white church. At the edge of the plaza there are weaving cooperatives selling *cortes, huípiles* and handicrafts from the town and the surrounding area – bargaining is possible. When you arrive, boys will meet you from incoming buses and will guide you to a *hospedaje* – they expect a tip. Nebaj has Sunday and Thursday markets and a fiesta on 12-15 August with traditional dancing. There is an excellent website for Nebaj, www.nebaj.com, run by **Solidaridad Internacional**, with useful phrases in Ixil and your daily Maya horoscope. There's a **tourist office** ⓘ *6a Av and 8a Calle Cantón Vitzal, T7755-8337.*

La tumba de la Indígena Maya is a shrine just outside Nebaj (15 minutes) where some of those massacred during the war were buried. Take the same route as to Ak'Tzumbal, but at the bottom of the very steep hill, immediately after the bridge over the river, take a left, walk straight on over a paved road, then you come to a small junction – carry straight on until you see a minor crossroads on a path with an orange house gate to your left. Look up and you will see a small building. This is the shrine. Walk to your right where you will see a steep set of stairs leading to the shrine.

There is a walk to **Ak'Tzumbal**, through fields with rabbits, and through long, thin earth tunnels used by the military and guerrillas during the war. You need a guide to walk this cross-country route. Alternatively you can take the road to Ak'Tzumbal, where the new houses still display signs warning of the danger of land mines. Walk down 15 Avenida de Septiembre away from the church, and take a left just before **El Triangulo** gas station past **El Viajero Hospedaje**, then left and then right down a very steep hill and keep walking (1½ hours). When you reach a small yellow tower just before a fork – take the right (the left goes to Salquil Grande) to reach the 'model village'. Above the village of Ak'Tzumbal is **La Pista**, an airstrip used during the war. Next to it bomb craters scar the landscape. Only a few avocado trees, between the bomb holes, survive, and the *gasolinera* to refuel planes, is still there, although it is now covered in corrugated iron. Ask around for directions.

Chajul and Cotzal

Chajul, the second largest village in the Ixil Triangle, is known for its part in the Civil War, where Rigoberta Menchú's brother was killed in the plaza, as relayed in her book *I, Rigoberta Menchú*. According to the Nobel Peace Prize winner on 9 September 1979, her 16-year-old brother Petrocinio was kidnapped after being turned in for 15 quetzales. He was tortured in the plaza by the army along with numerous others. Villagers were forced to watch the torture under threat of being branded communists. People were set on fire, but the onlookers had weapons and looked ready to fight. This caused the army to withdraw. Chajul's main fiesta is the second Friday in Lent. There is also a pilgrimage to Christ of Golgotha on the second Friday in Lent, beginning the Wednesday before (the image is escorted by 'Romans' in blue police uniforms). Market day is Tuesday and Friday. It is possible to walk from Chajul to Cotzal. It is a six-hour walk from Nebaj to Chajul. A couple of very basic *hospedajes* are in town.

Cotzal is spread over a large area on a number of steep hills. The village's fiesta is 22-25 June, peaking on the day of St John the Baptist (24 June). Market days are Wednesday and Saturday. You can hire bikes from **Maya Tour** on the plaza next to the church. Nebaj to Cotzal is a pleasant four-hour walk. There's no accommodation or restaurants in other small villages and it is difficult to specify what transport is available in this area as trucks and the occasional pickup or commercial van are affected by road and weather conditions. For this reason, be prepared to have to spend the night in villages.

Lake Atitlán and around listings

For Sleeping and Eating price codes and other relevant information, see pages 12-13.

⊜ Sleeping

Chimaltenango and around *p53*
$$ La Posada de Mi Abuelo, Carretera a Yepocapa, Parramos, T7849-5930, www.la posadademiabuelo.com. A delightful inn formerly a coffee farm, good restaurant. Packages with horse riding, biking and meals are available.
$ Pixcayá, 0 Av, 1-82, Comalapa, T7849-8260. Hot water, parking.

Sololá *p56*
$ Del Viajero, 7 Av, 10-45, on Parque Central (also annexe around the corner on Calle 11) T7762-3683. Rooms with bath, cheaper without, spacious, clean and friendly, good food in restaurant on plaza (**El Cafetín**).
$ El Paisaje, 9 Calle, 5-41, 2 blocks from Parque Central, T7762-3820. Pleasant colonial courtyard, shared baths and toilets, clean, hot water, restaurant, good breakfast, family-run, laundry facilities.

Panajachel *p56, map p57*
$$$ Atitlán, 1 km west of centre on lake, 2nd turning off the road to Sololá, T7762-1441, www.hotelatitlan.com. Full board available, colonial style, excellent rooms and service, beautiful gardens with views across lake, pool, private beach, top-class restaurant.
$$$ Posada de Don Rodrigo, final Calle Santander, overlooks the lake, T7762-2326, www.posadadedonrodrigo.com. Pool, sauna, terrace, gardens, good restaurant, excellent food and service, comfortable and luxurious bathrooms, fireplaces.
$$$ Rancho Grande, Calle Rancho Grande, Centro, T7762-1554, www.ranchogrande inn.com. Cottages in charming setting, 4 blocks from beach, popular for long stay, good, including breakfast with pancakes.

Pool with café in spacious gardens with good children's play equipment. Staff are helpful. Recommended.
$$ Dos Mundos, Calle Santander 4-72, Centro, T7762-2078, www.hoteldosmundos. com. Pool, cable TV, some rooms surround pool, good Italian restaurant (**La Lanterna**). Breakfast included.
$$ Müllers Guest House, Calle Rancho Grande 1-81, Centro, T7762-2442. Comfortable, quiet, good breakfast included. Recommended.
$$ Posada de los Volcanes, Calle Santander, 5-51, Centro, T7762-0244, www.posadade losvolcanes.com. 12 rooms with bath, hot water, clean, comfortable, quiet, friendly owners, Julio and Jeanette Parajón.
$$ Primavera, Calle Santander, Centro, T7762-2052, www.primaveratitlan.com. Clean, bright rooms, with TV, cypress wood furniture, gorgeous showers, washing machine available, friendly. Recommended. **Chez Alex** next door serves French food but lovely patio setting at the back. Don't get a room overlooking the street at weekends.
$ Hospedaje Casa Linda, Callejón El Capulín, Centro, T7762-0386. Hot shower in shared or private bathrooms, garden, friendly, clean and quiet. Good value. Recommended.
$ Hospedaje El Viajero, final Calle Santander, Centro, T7762-0128, www.sleeprentbuy.com/elviajero. With bath, comfortable large, clean rooms, hot water, friendly, laundry facilities, nice flower garden.
$ Hospedaje Ramos I, close to public beach, T7762-0413. Run by Maya family, friendly, safe, with bath, hot water, clean, good value, some rooms have TV. View from 2nd floor.
$ Hospedaje Sánchez, Calle El Chali 3-65, Centro, T7762-2224. Clean, friendly, hot shower, family-run, quiet, comfortable. Recommended.

$ Hospedaje Villa Lupita, Callejón Don Tino, old town, T5054-2447. Pretty courtyard, hot showers, clean, friendly, parking, good value. Recommended.

$ Mario's Rooms, Calle Santander esq Calle 14 Febrero, Centro, T7762-1313. Cheaper without bath, with garden, clean, bright rooms, hot showers, good breakfast, but not included, popular and friendly.

$ Montana, Callejón Don Tino, near bell tower in the old town, T7762-2180, www.hotelmontanapanajachel.com. Comfortable, TV, hot water, parking, Wi-Fi, large patio filled with plants.

$ Riva Bella, Calle Real, 2-21, Centro, T7762-1348. Bungalows with parking, with bath, good, clean, nice garden. Recommended.

$ Santa Isabel, Calle del Embarcadero 8-86, Centro, T7762-1462. 2 rooms in large house, quiet, hot water, with bath, friendly, nice gardens, parking, also fully equipped bungalow for longer rent. Recommended.

$ Zanahoria Chic, 3 Av 0-46, Av de los Arboles, old town, T7762-1249, www.zanahoriachic.com. Restaurant, rooms above, clean, TV, hot water in shared or private bathrooms, colonial style, friendly, coffee, luggage store.

Apartments

Ask around for houses to rent; available from US$125 a month for a basic place, to US$200, but almost impossible to find in Nov and Dec. Break-ins and robberies of tourist houses are not uncommon. Water supply is variable.

Apartamentos Bohemia, Callejón Chinimaya, rents furnished bungalows.

Camping

Possible in the grounds of **Hotel Visión Azul** and **Tzanjuyú**.

Santa Catarina Palopó *p59*

You can stay in private houses (ask around) or rent rooms (take sleeping bag).

$$$$ Casa Palopó, Carretera a San Antonio Palopó, Km 6.8, less than 1 km beyond Santa Catarina, on the left up a steep hill, T5773-7777, www.casapalopo.com. One of the finest hotels in the country, 9 beautiful rooms all richly furnished, flowers on arrival, excellent service, heated pool, spa, gym, top-class restaurant overlooking the lake – reservations necessary.

$$$$ Tzam Poc Resort, Vía Rural Km 6.5, T7762-2680, www.atitlanresort.com. Resort on the slopes above Santa Catarina with an amazing infinity pool. Lovely villas and spa. There's also an archery range.

$$$ Villa Santa Catarina, T7762-1291, www.villasdeguatemala.com. 36 comfortable rooms with balconies around the pool, most with view of the lake. Good restaurant.

$$ Hotel Terrazas del Lago, T7762-0157, www.hotelterrazasdellago.com. On the lake with view, bath, clean, restaurant, a unique hotel built up over the past 30 plus years.

San Lucas Tolimán *p59*

$$$ Toliman, Av 6, 1 block from the lake, T7722-0033. 18 rooms and suites in colonial style washed in terracotta colours with some lovely dark wood furniture. Suite No 1 is very romantic with lit steps to a sunken bath, good but expensive restaurant (reservations), fine gardens, pool, partial lake views. Recommended.

$ Casa Cruz Inn, Av 5 4-78, a couple of blocks from the park. Clean, comfortable beds, run by an elderly couple, garden, quiet, good value.

$ Hotel y Restaurante Don Pedro, Av 6, on lakeside, T7722-0028. Unattractive building – a sort of clumsy rustic, 12 rooms, a little rough around the edges, restaurant, bar.

$ La Cascada de María, Calle 6, 6-80, T7722-0136. With bath, TV, parking, garden, restaurant, good.

Santiago Atitlán p60
Book ahead for Holy Week.
$$$-$$ Posada de Santiago, 1.5 km south of town, T7721-7366, www.posadade santiago.com. Highly recommended relaxing lakeside lodge with comfortable stone cottages (some cheaper accommodation), restaurant with home-grown produce and delicious food, tours and pool. Massage and language classes arranged. Friendly and amusing management – David, Susie and his mum, Bonnie – quite a trio. Has its own dock or walk from town.
$$ Bambú, on the lakeside, 500 m by road towards San Lucas, T7721-7332, www.ecobambu.com. 10 rooms, 2 bungalows and 1 *casita* in an attractive setting with beautifully tended gardens, restaurant, a secluded pool, a few mins by *lancha* from the dock. Kayaks available.
$ Chi-Nim-Ya, walk up from the dock, take the 1st left and walk 50 m and it's there on the left, T7721-7131. Good, clean, comfortable and friendly, cheaper without bath, good value, good café, cheap, large helpings.
$ Tzutuhil, on left up the road from the dock to centre, above **Ferretería La Esquina**, T7721-7174. With bath and TV, cheaper without, restaurant, great views, good.

Camping
Camping is possible near **Bambú**.

San Pedro La Laguna p61, map p61
Accommodation is mostly cheap and laid back; your own sleeping bag, etc, will be useful.
$ Hospedaje Buenas Nuevas.
Small, friendly, with hot shower.
$ Hospedaje Casa Elena, along the path behind **Nick's Place**. With large bathrooms or shared bath (some are nicer than others), clean, excellent views of lake. Recommended.
$ Hotel San Francisco. Rooms with lake view, garden, cooking facilities, cold water, helpful owner, washing facilities, cheaper without bath, good value. Tours offered.

$ Hotelito El Amanacer Sak' Cari, T7721-8096, www.hotelsakcari.com. With bath, hot water, lovely rooms with great garden – get those with fabulous lake views. Extremely good value. Recommended.
$ Mansión del Lago, T7721-8041, www.hotelmansiondellago.com. Up a hill with good views, with bath, hot water, TV costs more, very good value.
$ Pinocchio. Rooms with private bath, nice garden and use of kitchen. Hammocks available.
$ Ti-Kaaj, uphill from Santiago dock, 1st right. Simple rooms, hammock space, popular with backpackers, lovely garden and small pool; basic, but worth it for pool.
$ Villa Sol, T2334-0327. With bath, cheaper shared, but the rooms aren't as nice. The newer part is a lot nicer. There are 2 bungalows with kitchen facilities, friendly staff, nice rooms. Recommended.

San Juan La Laguna p62
$$$-$$ Hotel Uxlabil, T5990-6016/2366-9555 (in Guatemala City), www.uxlabil.com. This is an eco-hotel set up on the hill with its own dock (flooded, like all the village shore, in 2010), a short walk from the town centre. It's run by very friendly people with a small restaurant, and beautiful views from its roof-top terrace. It is a perfect, relaxing getaway, with Maya sauna and tended gardens, in this most unassuming and interesting of towns. It has links with the ecotourism association in town. Recommended.

San Marcos La Laguna p63
$$$-$$ Aaculaax, Las Pirámides dock, on a path from the **Centro Holístico**, T5287-0521, www.aaculaax.com. A Hansel-and-Gretel affair on the lake shore. It is a blend of cave work with Gaudí-type influence from the stained-glass work down to the sculptures and lamp shades. A corner of artistic Nirvana on Lake Atitlán – this place is highly recommended. Each of the 7 rooms with

private bathroom is different, with quirky decor. It is run on an eco-basis, compost toilets and all. It is run by a German, Niels. There is a restaurant, bar, bakery and massage room. Also glass and papier mâché workshops.

$$-$ Posada Schumann, 2nd dock, T5202-2216, www.posadaschumann.com. With waterfront and dock, bungalows in attractive gardens, some with kitchenettes, sauna, restaurant, comfortable.

$ Hotel Jinava, 2nd dock, left at the top of 1st pathway, T5299-3311, www.hoteljinava.com. This is heaven on a hill. With fabulous views, it clings to a steep slope with lovely rooms, restaurants, terraces and a patio. Books and games and solitude if you want it. Close to the lakeshore with its own dock where launches will drop you. Only 5 rooms, breakfast included. German-owned. Recommended.

$ La Paz, 2nd dock, 1st pathway, T5702-9168. Bungalows and 1 dorm, vegetarian restaurant, quiet with nice communal area, popular.

$ Las Pirámides del Ka, Las Pirámides dock, www.laspiramidesdelka.com. A residential, meditation centre. See also page 8.

$ Quetzal, Las Pirámides dock, 2nd pathway, T5306-5039. Price per person. 4 bunk rooms, shared bath, restaurant.

$ Unicornio, Las Pirámides dock, 2nd pathway. With self-catering, bungalows, shared kitchen and bathrooms. Has a little post office.

San Marcos to Santa Cruz *p63*
$$$ Lomas de Tzununá, Tzununá, T7820-4060, www.lomasdetzununa.com. This hotel enjoys a spectacular position high up above the lake. The views from the restaurant terrace are magnificent. The 10 spacious rooms, decorated with local textiles, have 2 beds each with lake views and a balcony. The hotel, run by a friendly Belgian family, offers walking,

biking, kayaking and cultural tours. The restaurant (**$$-$**) uses home-made ingredients, the hotel is run on solar energy and the pool does not use chlorine. Board games, internet, bar and giant chess available. The family are reforesting a hill. Breakfast and taxes included.

$$ La Casa del Mundo, Jaibalito, T5218-5332, www.lacasadelmundo.com. Enjoys one of the most attractive positions on the entire lake. Room No 15 has the best view followed by room No 1. Cheaper rooms have shared bathrooms. Many facilities, standard family-style dinner, lakeside hot tub, a memorable place with fantastic views. Repeatedly recommended.

Santa Cruz La Laguna *p63*
$$$-$$ Villa Sumaya, Paxanax, beyond the dock, about 15 mins' walk, T5810-7199, www.villasumaya.com. Including breakfast, with its own dock, sauna, massage and healing therapies, yoga, comfortable, peaceful.

$$-$ Arca de Noé, to the left of the dock, T5515-3712. Bungalows, cheaper rooms with shared bathrooms, good restaurant, BBQ, lake activities arranged, nice atmosphere, veranda overlooking a really beautiful flower-filled gardens and the lake. Low-voltage solar power.

$$-$ La Casa Rosa, to the right as you face the dock from the water, along a path, T5416-1251, www.atitlanlacasarosa.com. Bungalows and rooms, with bath, cheaper without, home-made meals, attractive garden, sauna. Candlelit dinners at weekends.

$$-$ La Iguana Perdida, opposite dock, T5706-4117, www.laiguanaperdida.com. Rooms with and without bathroom and dorm (**$** per person) with shared bath, lively, especially weekends, delicious vegetarian food, BBQ, popular, friendly, great atmosphere. **ATI Divers** centre (see page 77), waterskiing; kayaks and snorkelling. Bring a torch.

Chichicastenango *p64, map p65*

You won't find accommodation easily on Sat evening, when prices are increased. As soon as you get off the bus, boys will swamp you and insist on taking you to certain hotels.

$$$ Mayan Inn, corner of 8 Calle, 1-91, T7756-1176, www.mayaninn.com.gt. A classic, colonial-style courtyard hotel, filled with plants, polished antique furniture, beautiful dining room and bar with fireplaces. Gas-heated showers and internet The staff are very friendly and wear traditional dress. Secure parking.

$$$ Santo Tomás, 7 Av, 5-32, T7756-1061. A very attractive building with beautiful colonial furnishings and parrots in patios. It is often full at weekends, pool, sauna, good restaurant and bar. Buffet lunch (US$14) on market days in stylish dining room, with attendants in traditional dress.

$$ Posada El Arco, 4 Calle, 4-36, T7756-1255. Clean, very pretty, small, friendly, garden, washing facilities, negotiate lower rates for stays longer than a night, some large rooms, good view, parking, English spoken.

$$-$ Chalet House, 3 Calle, 7-44, T7756-1360, www.chalethotelguatemala.com. A clean, guesthouse with family atmosphere, hot water. Don't be put off by the dingy street.

$ Chugüilá, 5 Av, 5-24, T7756-1134, hotelchuguila@yahoo.com. Some rooms with fireplaces. Avoid the front rooms, which are noisy, restaurant.

$ Pensión Girón, Edif Girón on 6 Calle, 4-52, T7756-1156. Clean rooms with bath, cheaper without, hot water, parking, 17 rooms.

$ Posada Belén, 12 Calle, 5-55, T7756-1244. With bath, cheaper without, hot water, clean, will do laundry, fine views from balconies and hummingbirds in attractive garden, good value. Recommended.

$ Salvador, 10 Calle, 4-47. 55 large rooms with bath, a few with fireplace (wood for sale in market), good views over town, parking. Cheaper, smaller rooms without bath available.

$ Tuttos, 12 Calle, near **Posada Belén**, T7756-7540. Reasonable rooms.

Santa Cruz del Quiché and around *p66*

Several very basic options around the bus arrival/departure area.

$ La Cascada, 10 Av, 10 Calle. Friendly, clean.

$ Maya Quiché, 3 Av 4-19, T7755-1667. With bath, hot water, restaurant.

$ Rey K'iché, 8 Calle, 0-9, 2 blocks from bus terminal. Clean, comfortable, hot water, parking, restaurant, TV.

$ San Pascual, 7 Calle, 0-43, 2 blocks south of the central plaza, T5555-1107. Good location, with bath, cheaper without, quiet, locked parking.

The road east to Cobán *p66*

There are a couple of *hospedajes* in Uspantán.

$ Galindo, 4 blocks east of the Parque Central. Clean, friendly, recommended.

The Ixil Triangle *p67*

$ Solidaridad Internacional supports 6 hostels in the villages of **Xexocom**, **Chortiz**, **Xeo**, **Cocop**, **Cotzol** and **Párramos Grande** where there is room for 5 people. Contact them at the PRODONT-IXIL office, Av 15 de Septiembre, Nebaj.

Nebaj and around *p67*

$$-$ Hotel Turansa, 1 block from plaza down 5 Calle, T7755-8219. Tiny rooms, but very clean, soap, towels, 2nd-floor rooms are nicer, cable TV and parking, little shop in entrance, phone service.

$ Hospedaje Esperanza, 6 Av, 2-36. Very friendly, clean, hot showers in shared bathroom, noisy when evangelical churches nearby have activities, hotel is cleaner than it looks from the outside.

$ Hostal Ixil Don Juan, 0 Av A, 1 Calle B, Canton Simocol. Take Av 15 de Septiembre and take a left at **Comedor Sarita**, opposite grey office of PRODONT-IXIL, then it's 100 m to the right, on the right, T7755-4014/1529.

Part of **Programa Quiché**, run with the support of the EU, there are 6 beds in 2 rooms, each bed with a locked strongbox, and hot showers. The colonial building has a traditional sauna, *chuj*.

$ Hotel Mayan Ixil, on north side of main square, T7755-8168. Just 5 rooms with private bath and gas hot water. Small restaurant overlooking the plaza, internet service downstairs.

$ Ilebal Tenam, Cantón Simecal, bottom of Av 15 de Septiembre, road to Chajul, T7755-8039. Hot water, shared and private bath, very clean, friendly, parking inside, attractive decor.

$ Media Luna MediaSol, T5749-7450, www.nebaj.com/hostel.htm. A backpackers' hostel close to **El Descanso** restaurant with dorms and private rooms. The hostel's also got a little kitchenette, DVD player and Wi-Fi.

Cotzal *p68*

$ Cafetería and Hospedaje Christian, alongside the church. Basic.

$ Hostal Doña Teresa. Has a sauna, patio and honey products for sale.

🍴 Eating

Panajachel *p56, map p57*

$$$ Chez Alex, Calle Santander, centre, T7762-0172. Open 1200-1500 and 1800-2000. French menu, good quality, mainly tourists, credit cards accepted.

$$$ Tocoyal, annexe to **Hotel del Lago**. A/c, groups welcome, buffet on request but tourist prices.

$$ Circus Bar, Av Los Arboles 0-62, T7762-2056. Open 1200-2400. Italian dishes including delicious pasta and pizzas, good coffee, popular. Live music from 2030, excellent atmosphere. Recommended.

$$ Crossroads Café, Calle de Campanario 0-27. Tue-Sat 0900-1300,1500-1900. Global choice of quality coffee, but you can't go wrong with Guatemalan! Excellent cakes.

$$ El Patio, Calle Santander. Good food, very good large breakfasts, quiet atmosphere but perfect for people-watching from the garden. Try the amaretto coffee.

$$ Guajimbo's, Calle Santander. Good atmosphere, excellent steaks, fast service, popular, live music some evenings. Recommended.

$$ La Rostícería, Av Los Arboles 0-42, T7762-2063. Daily 0700-2300. Good food, try eggs 'McChisme' for breakfast, good fresh pasta, excellent banana cake, good atmosphere, popular, a bit pricey. Live piano music at weekends, friendly service.

$$ Los Pumpos, Calle del Lago. Varied menu, bar, good fish and seafood dishes.

$$ Pana Rock Café, with **Pana Arte** upstairs, Calle Santander 3-72. Buzzing around happy hour (2 for 1), salsa music, very popular, international food, pizza.

$$ Sunset Café, superb location on the lake. Open 1100-2400. Excellent for drinks, light meals and main dishes, live music evenings, but you pay for the view.

$$-$ Bombay, Calle Santander near Calle 15 Febrero, T7762-0611. Open 1100-2130. Vegetarian recipes, including spicy curries, German beer, Mexican food, good food and wines, set lunch popular, good service. Very highly recommended.

$$-$ El Pájaro Azul, Calle Santander 2-75, T7762-2596. Café, bar, crêperie with gorgeous stuffed sweet or savoury crêpes, cakes and pies. Vegetarian options available. Reasonable prices, good for late breakfasts. 1000-2200. Recommended.

$ Deli Llama de Fuego, Calle Santander, T7762-2586. Thu-Tue 0700-2200. Sweet little café with a giant cheese plant as its focus. Breakfasts, muffins, bagels, pizzas, pasta, Mexican food and vegetarian sandwiches.

$ Restaurante Las Olas, overlooking the lake at the end of Calle Santander, down by the dock. Serves the absolute best nachos, great for just before catching the boat.

Bakeries
Maya Pan, Calle Santander 1-61. Excellent wholemeal breads and pastries, banana bread comes out of the oven at 0930, wonderful, cinnamon rolls and internet too. Recommended.

San Lucas Tolimán *p59*
$ La Pizza de Sam, Av 7, 1 block down from the plaza towards the lake. Pizzas and spaghetti.
$ Restaurant Jardín, orange building on corner of plaza. *Comida típica* and *licuados*.

Santiago Atitlán *p60*
There are many cheap *comedores* near the centre. The best restaurants are at the hotels.
$$$ El Pescador, on corner 1 block before Tzutuhil. Full menu, good but expensive.
$$$ Posada de Santiago, 1.5 km south of town, T/F7721-7167. Delicious, wholesome food and excellent service in lovely surroundings. Highly recommended.
$ Restaurant Wach'alal, close to Gran Sol. Daily 0800-2000. A small yellow-painted café serving breakfasts, snacks and cakes. Airy and pleasant.

San Pedro La Laguna *p61, map p61*
Be careful of drinking water in San Pedro; both cholera and dysentery exist here.
$$-$ Café Arte Libre, up the hill from Hotel San Pedro. All meals, vegetarian dishes, good value.
$$-$ Luna Azul, along shore. Popular for breakfast and lunch, good omelettes.
$$-$ Restaurant Maritza, with commanding views over lake. Chilled place to hang out with reggae music. Service is slow though. 5 rooms also to rent with shared bath (**$**).
$$-$ Tin Tin. Good value, Thai food, delightful garden. Recommended.
$ Buddha Bar. Shows movies every night and has a rooftop and sports bar.

$ Café La Puerta, on the north shore coastal path. Open daily 0800-1700. Cheap, tasty dishes, with tables in a quirky garden, or looking out over the lake. Beautiful.
$ Comedor Sta Elena, near Nick's Italian. Seriously cheap and filling breakfasts.
$ El Fondeadero. Good food, lovely terraced gardens, reasonable prices.
$ Emperador, up the hill. *Comedor* serving good local dishes.
$ Fata Morgana, near the Panajachel dock, great focaccia bread sandwiches, with pizza and fine coffee too.
$ Rosalinda, near centre of village. Friendly, breakfasts (eg *mosh*), local fish and good for banana and chocolate cakes.
$ Shanti Shanti. Run by Israelis, Italian dishes.
$ Thermal Baths, along shore from *playa*. Good vegetarian food and coffee, expensive.
$ Zoola. Open 0900-2100. Close to the north shore, a quiet, hideaway with pleasant garden. A great spot .

San Marcos La Laguna *p63*
All hotels and hostels offer food.
$$-$ Il Giardino, up the 2nd pathway. Attractive garden, Italian owners, good breakfasts.

Chichicastenango *p64, map p65*
The best food is in the top hotels, but is expensive. On market days there are plenty of good food stalls and *comedores* in the centre of the plaza that offer chicken in different guises or a set lunch for US$1.50. There are several good restaurants in the **Centro Comercial Santo Tomás**, on the north side of the plaza (market).
$$ La Fonda de Tzijolaj, on the plaza. Great view of the market below, good meals, pizza, prompt service, reasonable prices.
$$ Las Brasas Steak House, 6 Calle 4-52, T7756-2226. Nice atmosphere, good steak menu, accepts credit cards.
$$-$ La Villa de los Cofrades, on the plaza. Café downstairs, breakfasts, cappuccinos,

espressos, good value. There is a 2nd restaurant 2 blocks up the street towards Arco Gucumatz, more expensive, great people-watching upstairs location and an escape during market days, popular for breakfast.

$$-$ Tziguan Tinamit, on the corner of 5 Av, esq 6 Calle. Some local dishes, steaks, tasty pizzas, breakfasts, good pies but a little more expensive than most places, good.

$ Caffé Tuttos, see Sleeping. Daily 0700-2200. Good breakfast deals, pizzas, and *menú del día*, reasonable prices.

$ La Parrillada, 6 C 5-37, Interior Comercial Turkaj. Escape the market bustle, courtyard, reasonable prices, breakfast available.

$ Tu Café, 5 Av 6-44, on market place, Santo Tomás side. Open 0730-2000. Snacks, budget breakfast, sandwiches, set lunch, good value.

Santa Cruz del Quiché and around *p66*

Try *sincronizadas*, hot tortillas baked with cubed ham, spiced chicken and cheese.

$ La Cabañita Café, 1 Av, 1-17. Charming, small café with pinewood furniture, home-made pies and cakes, excellent breakfasts (pancakes, cereals, etc), eggs any way you want 'em, great snacks, for example *sincronizadas*.

$ La Toscan, 1 Av just north of the church, same road as **La Cabañita**. A little pizza and *pastelería* with checked cloth-covered tables. Lasagne lunch a bargain with garlic bread and pizza by the slice also.

Nebaj and around *p67*

Boxboles are squash leaves rolled tightly with *masa* and chopped meat or chicken, boiled and served with salsa and fresh orange juice.

$ El Descanso. Popular volunteer hang-out, good food and useful information about their other community-based projects (see www.nebaj.com).

$ Maya Ixil, on the Parque Central. Substantial food, local and international dishes, pleasant family atmosphere.

$ Pizza del César. Daily 0730-2100. Breakfasts, mouth-wateringly good strawberry cake, and hamburgers as well as pizzas.

Cotzal *p68*

$ Comedor and Hospedaje El Maguey. Bland meal, but decent size, plus drink, are served up for for US$1.70. Don't stay here though, unless you're desperate.

☺ Entertainment

Panajachel *p56, map p57*
Circus Bar, Av los Arboles. Open daily 1200-0200. Good live music from 2030.
Discoteca Chapiteau, Av los Arboles 0-69. Nightclub Thu-Sat 1900-0100.
El Aleph, Av los Arboles. Thu-Sat 1900-0300. One of a number of bars.

San Pedro La Laguna *p61, map p61*
Nick's Place, overlooking the main dock, is popular, and well frequented in the evening. Nearby are **Bar Alegre**, a sports bar (www.thealegrepub.com) and **D'noz**. **Ti Kaaj** is another popular spot.

☺ Festivals and events

Chichicastenango *p64, map p65*
1 Jan Padre Eterno.
20 Jan San Sebastián.
19 Mar San José.
Feb/Apr Jesús Nazareno and María de Dolores (both Fri in Lent).
Mar/Apr Semana Santa (Holy Week).
29 Apr San Pedro Mártir.
3 May Santa Cruz.
29 Jun Corpus Christi.
18 Aug Virgen de la Coronación.
14 Sep Santa Cruz.
29 Sep San Miguel.
30 Sep San Jerónimo Doctor.
1st Sun of Oct Virgen del Rosario.
2nd Sun in Oct Virgen de Concepción.
1 Nov San Miguel.

13-22 Dec Santo Tomás, with 21 Dec being the main day. There are processions, traditional dances, the *Palo Volador* (19, 20, 21 Dec) marimba music, well worth a visit – very crowded.

O Shopping

Panajachel *p56, map p57*
Bartering is the norm. There are better bargains here than in Chichicastenango. The main tourist shops are on Calle Santander.
Tinamit Maya Shopping Centre, Calle Santander. Bargain for good prices. Maya sell their wares cheaply on the lakeside; varied selection, bargaining is easy/expected.
Librería del Lago, Calle Santander Local A-8, T7762-2788. Daily 0900-1800. Great bookshop selling a good range of quality English-language and Spanish books.

Chichicastenango *p64, map p65*
Chichicastenango's markets are on Sun and Thu. See page 65.
Ut'z Bat'z, 5a Avenida and 5a Calle, T5008-5193. Women's Fair Trade weaving workshop, with free demonstrations; high-quality clothes and bags for sale.

▲ Activities and tours

Panajachel *p56, map p57*
Diving
ATI Divers, round the back of El Patio, Calle Santander, T5706-4117, www.laiguana perdida.com. A range of options including PADI Open Water US$220, fun dive US$30, 2 for US$50. PADI Rescue and Dive Master also available. Altitude speciality, US$80. Dives are made off Santa Cruz La Laguna and are of special interest to those looking for altitude diving. Here there are spectacular walls that drop off, rock formations you can swim through, trees underwater, and because of its volcanic nature, hot spots, which leaves the lake bottom sediment boiling to touch. Take advice on visibility before you opt for a dive.

Fishing
Lake fishing can be arranged, black bass (*mojarra*) up to 4 kg can be caught. Boats for up to 5 people can be hired for about US$15. Check with INGUAT for latest information.

Hang-gliding
Rogelio, contactable through **Americo's Tours**, Calle Santander, and other agencies will make arrangements, at least 24 hrs' notice is required. Jumps are made from San Jorge La Laguna or from above Santa Catarina, depending on weather conditions.

Kayaking and canoing
Kayak hire is around US$2 per hr. Ask at the hotels, INGUAT and at lakeshore. **Diversiones Acuáticos Balán**, in a small red and white tower on the lakeshore, rent out kayaks. Watch out for strong winds that occasionally blow up quickly across the lake; potentially dangerous in small boats.

Tour operators
All offer shuttle services to Chichicastenango, Antigua, the Mexican borders, etc, and some to San Cristóbal de las Casas (see Transport) and can arrange most activities on and around the lake. There are a number of tour operators on Calle Santander, including those listed below. **Americo's Tours**, T7762-2021. **Centroamericana Tourist Service**, T7832-5032. **Tierra Maya**, T7725-7320. Friendly and reliable tour operator, which runs shuttles to San Cristóbal de las Casas as well as within Guatemala. **Toliman Travel**, T7762-1275. Also **Atitrans** on Edif Rincón Sai, T7762-2336, www.atitrans.com.

Waterskiing
Arrangements can be made with **ATI Divers** at **Iguana Perdida** in Santa Cruz.

Santiago Atitlán p60
Aventura en Atitlán, Jim and Nancy Matison, **Finca San Santiago**, T7811-5516. 10 km outside Santiago. Riding and hiking tours.

Francisco Tizná from the **Asociación de Guías de Turismo**, T7721-7558, is extremely informative. Ask for him at the dock or at any of the hotels. Payment is by way of donation.

San Pedro La Laguna p61, map p61
A growing list of activities from hiking up the Nariz de Maya (5 hrs, US$13) and other local trips, through to local crafts. Yoga for all levels is available down towards the shore (US$5 for 1½ hrs).
Bigfoot, 0800-1900. Run by the super-helpful Juan Baudilio Chipirs, T7721-8203. Also close to the small streets away from the docks.

San Juan La Laguna p62
Rupalaj Kistalin,T5964-0040, rupalajkistalin@ yahoo.es, offers interesting cultural tours of the town visiting painters, weavers, *cofradías* and traditional healers. As well as this cultural circuit there is an adventure circuit taking in Panan forest and a canopy tour at Park Chuiraxamolo' or a nature circuit taking in a climb up the Rostro de Maya and fishing and kayaking. Highly recommended. Some of the local guides speak English.

San Marcos La Laguna p63
Wellbeing
Casa Azul Eco Resort, T5070-7101, www.casa-azul-ecoresort.com, is a gorgeous little place offering yoga and reiki, among other therapies and writers' workshops hosted by Joyce Maynard. There's also a sauna, campfire and café/restaurant serving vegetarian food. You can reach it from the first dock, or from the centre of the village.
Las Pirámides del Ka, www.laspiramides delka.com. The month-long course costs US$420, or US$15 by the day if you stay for

shorter periods, accommodation included. Courses are also available for non-residents. In the grounds are a sauna, a vegetarian restaurant with freshly baked bread and a library. This is a relaxing, peaceful place.
San Marcos Holistic Centre, up the 2nd pathway, beyond **Unicornio**, www.sanm holisticcentre.com. Mon-Sat 1000-1700. Offers iridology, acupuncture, kinesiology, Indian head massage, reflexology and massage. Classes in various techniques can also be taken.

Chichicastenango p64, map p65
Maya Chichi Van, 6 Av, 6-45, T7756-2187, mayachichivan@yahoo.com. Shuttles and tours ranging from US$10-650.

Nebaj and around p67
Guías Ixiles (El Descanso Restaurant), www.nebaj.com ½- to 3-day hikes, bike rental. There's also a 3-day hike to Todos Santos.
Solidaridad Internacional, Av 15 de Septiembre, www.nebaj.org. Inside the PRODONT-IXIL (Proyecto de Promoción de Infraestructuras y Ecoturismo) office, in a grey building on the right 1 block after the **Gasolinera El Triángulo** on the road to Chajul. For further information call in to see the director Pascual, who is very helpful. 2-, 3- and 4-day hikes, horses available. Options to stay in community *posadas*, with packages available, from 1-4 days, full board, from about US$100-200 per person.

Chajul and Cotzal p68
Ask Teresa at **Hostal Doña Teresa** about trips from the Cotzal or ask for Sebastián Xel Rivera who leads 1-day camping trips.

⊖ Transport

Chimaltenango and around p53
Bus
Any bus heading west from Guatemala City stops at Chimaltenango. To **Antigua**

leave from the corner of the main road and the road south to Antigua where there is a lime green and blue shop – **Auto Repuestos y Frenos Nachma**, 45 mins, US$0.34. To **Chichicastenango**, every 30 mins, 0600-1700, 2 hrs, US$2. To **Cuatro Caminos**, 2½ hrs, US$2.50. To **Quetzaltenango**, every 45 mins, 0700-1800, 2½ hrs, US$2.80. To **Tecpán** every 30 mins, 0700-1800, 1 hr.

Routes west: Tecpán and Los Encuentros *p54*
Bus
From Tecpán to **Guatemala City**, 2¼ hrs, buses every hour, US$2.20; easy day trip from Panajachel or Antigua.

To Lake Atitlán along the old Pan-American Highway *p55*
Bus
To and from **Godínez** there are several buses to Panajachel, US$0.45 and 1 bus daily Patzún–Godínez. To **San Andrés Semetabaj**, bus to Panajachel, US$0.40.

Sololá *p56*
Bus
To **Chichicastenango**, US$0.50, 1½ hrs; to **Panajachel**, US$0.38, every 30 mins, 20 mins, or 1½-2 hrs' walk. To **Chimaltenango**, US$1.20. To **Quetzaltenango**, US$1.8. *Colectivo* to **Los Encuentros**, US$0.20. To **Guatemala City** direct US$2.50, 3 hrs.

Panajachel *p56, map p57*
Boat
There are 2 types of transport – the scheduled ferry service to Santiago Atitlán and the *lanchas* to all the other villages. The tourist office has the latest information on boats. The boat service to **Santiago Atitlán** runs from the dock at the end of Calle Rancho Grande (Muelle Público) from 0600-1630, 8 daily, 20 mins in launch, US$3.10, 1 hr in the large **Naviera Santiago** ferry, T7762-0309 or 20-35 mins in the fast *lanchas*. Some

lanchas to all the other villages leave from here, but most from the dock at the end of Calle Embarcadero run by **Tzanjuyú** from 0630-1700 every 45 mins or when full (min 10 people). If you set off from the main dock the *lancha* will pull in at the Calle Embarcadero dock as well. These *lanchas* call in at **Santa Cruz**, **Jaibalito**, **Tzununá**, **San Marcos**, **San Pablo**, **San Juan** and **San Pedro**, US$1.20 to US$2.50 to **San Marcos** and beyond. To **San Pedro** US$3.10. The 1st boat of the day is at 0700. If there is a demand, there will almost always be a boatman willing to run a service but non-official boats can charge what they like. Virtually all the dozen or so communities round the lake have docks, and you can take a regular boat to any of those round the western side. Note that, officially, locals pay less. The only reliable services back to Panajachel are from **Santiago** or **San Pedro** up to about 1600. If you wait on the smaller docks round the western side up to this time, you can get a ride back to Panajachel, flag them down in case they don't see you, but they usually pull in if it's the last service of the day. Only buy tickets on the boat – if you buy them from the numerous ticket touts on the dockside, you will be overcharged. There are no regular boats to Santa Catarina, San Antonio or San Lucas: pickups and buses serve these communities, or charter a *lancha*, US$30 return to Santa Catarina and San Antonio. Bad weather can, of course, affect the boat services. Crossings are generally rougher in the afternoons, worth bearing in mind if you suffer from sea-sickness.

Boat hire and tours *Lanchas* can be hired to go anywhere round the lake, about US$100 for 5 people for a full day. For round trips to **San Pedro** and **Santiago** and possibly **San Antonio Palopó**, with stopovers, go early to the lakefront and bargain. Trip takes a full day, eg 0830-1530, with stops of 1 hr or so at each, around US$6-7, if the boat is full. If on a tour, be careful not to miss the boat at each stage – if you do, you will have to pay again.

Bus
Rebuli buses leave from opposite Hotel Fonda del Sol on Calle Real, otherwise, the main stop is where Calle Santander meets Calle Real. **Rebuli** to **Guatemala City**, 3½ hrs, US$3.30, crowded, hourly between 0500 and 1500. To **Guatemala City** via **Escuintla** south coast, 8 a day plus 3 **Pullman** a day. Direct bus to **Quetzaltenango**, 7 a day between 0530 and 1415, US$2.70, 2½ hrs. There are direct buses to **Los Encuentros** on the Pan-American Hwy (US$0.75). To **Chichicastenango** direct, Thu and Sun, 0645, 0700, 0730 and then hourly to 1530. Other days between 0700-1500, US$2, 1½ hrs. There are 4 daily direct buses to **Cuatro Caminos**, US$1.60 from 0530, for connections to Totonicapán, Quetzaltenango, Huehuetenango, etc. To **Antigua** take a bus up to Los Encuentros through Sololá. Change for a bus to **Chimaltenango** US$3.10, and change there for Antigua. There is also a direct bus (**Rebuli**) to **Antigua** leaving 1030-1100, daily, US$4.40. To **Sololá**, US$0.40, 20 mins, every 30 mins. You can wait for through buses by the market on Calle Real. The fastest way to southern **Mexico** is probably by bus south to Cocales, 2½ hrs, 5 buses between 0600 and 1400, then many buses along the Pacific Hwy to **Tapachula** on the border. For **La Mesilla**, take a bus up to Los Encuentros, change west for Cuatro Caminos. Here catch a bus north to La Mesilla. Some travel agencies go direct to **San Cristóbal de las Casas** via La Mesilla, daily at 0600. See Tour operators, above.

Shuttles Services are run jointly by travel agencies, to **Guatemala City**, **Antigua**, **Quetzaltenango**, **Chichi** and more. Around 4 a day. **Antigua**, US$14, **Chichicastenango**, on market days, US$15, **Quetzaltenango** US$20 and the Mexican border US$40. Atitrans, Calle Santander, next to Hotel Regis, T7762-0146, is recommended.

Bicycle
Several rental agencies on Calle Santander, eg **Maco Cycle Rental** and **Tono Cycle Rental**. Also **Alquiler de Bicicletas Emanuel**, on Calle 14 de Febrero. Prices start at US$2 per hr or about US$10 for a day.

Motorcycle
Motorcycle hire About US$6 per hr, plus fuel and US$100 deposit. Try **Maco Cycle** near the junction of Calle Santander and 14 de Febrero, T7762-0883.
Motorcycle parts David's Store, opposite **Hotel Maya Kanek**, has good prices and also does repairs.

Santa Catarina Palopó *p59*
There are frequent pickups from Panajachel and boat services.

San Antonio Palopó *p59*
Frequent pickups from Panajachel. Enquire about boats.

San Lucas Tolimán *p59*
Boat Enquire about boats. Private *lancha*, US$35.
Bus To **Santiago Atitlán**, hourly and to **Guatemala City** via **Panajachel**.

Santiago Atitlán *p60*
Bus To **Guatemala City**, US$2.60 (5 a day, first at 0300). 2 **Pullmans** a day, US$3.40. To **Panajachel**, 0600, 2 hrs, or take any bus and change on main road south of San Lucas.

Boat 4 sailings daily to Pana with *Naviera*, 1¼ hrs, US$1.80, or by *lancha* when full, 20-35 mins, US$1.30-2. To **San Pedro** by *lancha* several a day, enquire at the dock for times, 45 mins, US$1.80.

San Pedro La Laguna *p61, map p61*
Boat

Up to 10 *lanchas* to **Panajachel**. To **Santiago**, leave when full (45 mins, US$2.50). To **San Marcos**, every 2 hrs. Private *lanchas* (10 people at US$2 each).

Bus

There are daily buses to **Guatemala City**, several leave in the early morning and early afternoon, 4 hrs, US$4.50, to **Antigua** and to **Quetzaltenango**, in the morning, 3½ hrs, US$3.

San Marcos La Laguna *p63*
Boat Service roughly every ½ hr to **Panajachel** and to **San Pedro**. Wait on any dock. Fare US$1.80 to either. **Bus** San Pedro to Pan-American Hwy can be boarded at San Pablo. **Pickup** Frequent pickups from the village centre and anywhere along the main road. To **San Pedro**, US$0.50, less to villages en route.

Chichicastenango *p64, map p65*
Bus

Buses passing through Chichi all stop at 5 Av/5 Calle by the **Hotel Chugüilá**, where there are always police and bus personnel to give information. To **Guatemala City**, every 15 mins 0200-1730, 3 hrs, US$3.70. To **Santa Cruz del Quiché**, every ½ hr 0600-2000, US$0.70, 30 mins or 20 mins, if the bus driver is aiming for honours in the graduation from the School of Kamikaze Bus Tactics. To **Panajachel**, ½ hr, US$2, several until early afternoon or take any bus heading south and change at Los Encuentros. Same goes for **Antigua**, where you need to change at Chimaltenango. To **Quetzaltenango**, 5 between 0430-0830, 2½ hrs, US$3.80. To **Mexico**, and all points west, take any bus to Los Encuentros and change. To **Escuintla** via Santa Lucía Cotzumalguapa, between 0300 and 1700, 3 hrs, US$2.80. There are additional buses to local villages especially on market days.

Shuttles operate to the capital, **Xela**, **Panajachel**, **Huehuetenango** and Mexican border. **Maya Chichi Van**, see Tour operators, above.

Santa Cruz del Quiché and around *p66*
Bus

Terminal at 10 Calle y 1 Av, Zona 5. To **Guatemala City**, passing through Chichicastenango, at 0300 until 1700, 3 hrs, US$4.50. To **Nebaj** and **Cotzal**, 8 a day, US$3.20, 2 hrs. Buses leave, passing through Sacapulas (1 hr, US$2.50), roughly every hour from 0800-2100. To **Uspantán**, via **Sacapulas**, for **Cobán** and **San Pedro Carchá** every hour, 2 hrs, US$3.90. To **Joyabaj**, several daily, via Chiché and Zacualpa, US$1.80, 1½ hrs. First at 0800 with buses going on to the capital. Last bus back to Quiché at 1600. It is possible to get to **Huehuetenango** in a day via Sacapulas, then pickup from bridge to **Aguacatán** and bus from there to Huehuetenango. Last bus to Huehue from Aguacatán, 1600. Daily buses also to **Quetzaltenango**, **San Marcos**, and to **Panajachel**. To **Joyabaj**, Joyita bus from **Guatemala City**, 10 a day between 0200 and 1600, 5 hrs, US$1.80. There are buses from **Quiché** to **San Andrés Sajcabaja**.

The road east to Cobán *p66*
Bus and truck

Several trucks to Cobán, daily in the morning from **Sacapulas**; 7 hrs if you're lucky, usually much longer. Start very early if you wish to make it to Cobán the same day. **Transportes Mejía** from Aguacatán to **Cobán** stops in Sacapulas on Tue and Sat mornings. Also possible to take Quiché–Uspantán buses (0930, 1300, 1500), passing Sacapulas at about 1030, 1400, 1600. Then take the early morning buses at 0300 and 0500 from Uspantán to Cobán or the **Transportes Mejía** buses. After that, pickups leave when full. Hitchhiking to Cobán is also possible. Buses to **Quiché** 0300, 2200, other early-morning departures.

Nebaj and around p67
Bus
The bus ride to Quiché is full of fabulous views and hair-raising bends but the road is now fully paved. Buses to **Quiché** (US$3.20, 2½ hrs) passing through **Sacapulas** (1¾ hrs from Nebaj, US$1.30) leave hourly from 0500-1530. Bus to **Cobán** leaves Gazolinera Quetzal at 0500, 4-5 hrs, US$6.50. Cobán to Nebaj at 1300. Alternatively get to Sacapulas on the main road, and wait for a bus.

Chajul and Cotzal p68
Bus
Buses to Chajul and Cotzal do not run on a set schedule. It is best to ask the day before you want to travel, at the bus station. There are buses and numerous pickups on Sun when villagers come to Nebaj for its market, which would be a good day to visit the villages. Alternatively, bargain with a local pickup driver to take you on a trip.

ⓘ Directory

Panajachel p56, map p57
Banks Banco Industrial, Calle Santander (TCs and Visa ATM), Calle Real, US$, TCs and cash, Visa ATM opposite. There is a *cambio* on the street near **Mayan Palace** for US$ cash and TCs. **Internet** Many in centre, shop around for best prices; standard is US$1 per hr. Cheaper in the old town. **Medical services** Centro de Salud Calle Real, just downhill from the road to San Antonio Palopó. **Farmacia Santander**, top end of Calle Santander, very good and helpful. **Post** Calle Santander. Difficult but not impossible to send parcels of up to 1 kg abroad as long as packing requirements are met. **Get Guated Out**, Centro Comercial, Av Los Arboles, T/F7762-0595, good but more expensive service, they use the postal system but pack and deal with formalities for you. **DHL**, Edif Rincón Sai, Calle Santander. **Telephone** Telgua, Calle Santander and internet cafés. **Language schools** Jardín de América, Calle 14 de Febrero, T7762-2637, www.jardindeamerica.com. US$80 for 20 hrs per week tuition, lodging with family costs an additional US$60 per week. **Jabel Tinamit**, behind Edif Rincón Sai, T7762-0238, www.jabeltinamit.com. Similar tariff.

San Lucas Tolimán p59
Banks Banrural and Corpobanco.
Internet Available in the plaza.

Santiago Atitlán p60
Banks G&T Continental, opposite the church. **Internet** Next to Chim-ni-ya.

San Pedro La Laguna p61, map p61
Banks Banrural changes cash and TCs; Visa ATM. **Internet** There are several internet and phone offices. **Language schools** This is a popular place for learning Spanish. Students may make their own accommodation arrangements but homestays are possible. **Casa Rosario**, www.casarosario.com, offers classes from US$70 a week for 20 hrs a week. **Corazón Maya**, T7721-8160, www.corazonmaya.com, from US$49 a week. Tz'utujil classes also. Run by the welcoming Marta Navichoc. **San Pedro**, T5715-4604, www.sanpedrospanish school.org, from US$75 per week. School has a great location with gardens close to the lakeshore. **Medical services** Centro Médico opposite Educación Básica school has a good doctor who does not speak English.

San Juan La Laguna p62
Banks Banrural, diagonally opposite Nick's Place. Changes cash and TCs.
Internet There are a couple of places in town.

San Marcos La Laguna p63
Language schools Casa Rosario, T5613-6401. **San Marcos Spanish School**, T5852-0403, www.sanmarcos spanishschool.com. From US$76 per week.

Chichicastenango *p64, map p65*
Banks There are a number of banks in town taking Visa and MasterCard. **Mayan Inn** will exchange cash. **Internet** Aces, inside **Hotel Girón**, 6 Calle, 4-52. **Post** 7 Av, 8-47. **Cropa Panalpina**, 7 Av, 8-60, opposite post office, T7756-1028, www.cropa.com.gt. Will pack and ship your purchases back home by air cargo. **Telephone** Telgua, 6 Calle between 5 y 6.

Santa Cruz del Quiché and around *p66*
Banks Banco Industrial, 3 Calle y 2 Av, top corner of Parque Central, cash on Visa cards and TCs; **G&T Continental**, 6 Calle y 3 Av, Visa and MasterCard TCs. **Post** 3 Calle between 1 Av and 0 Av, Zona 5. **Telephone** Telgua, 1 Av/2 Calle, Zona 5.

Nebaj and around *p67*
Banks Banrural, TCs and Visa ATM. There are now a couple of ATMS. **Internet** There are a couple of internet services in town. **Language schools** The Nebaj Language School, www.nebajlanguageschool.com, US$145 a week including accommodation. **Post** Behind the bank.

Western highlands

Just before the volcanic highlands reach their highest peaks, this part of the western highlands takes the form of scores of small market towns and villages, each with its own character – the loud animal market at San Francisco El Alto, the extra-planetary landscape at Momostenango, and its Maya cosmovision centre, and the dancing extravaganzas at Totonicapán. The modern ladino town of Huehuetenango sits at the gateway to the Sierra de los Cuchumatanes, within which hides, in a cold gash in a sky-hugging valley, the indigenous town and weaving centre of Todos Santos Cuchumatán.

Ins and outs

This area is well connected by buses from the Cuatro Caminos junction, Quetzaltenango or Huehuetenango. The road from Cobán is another access option, although a much slower one. ▶▶ *See Transport, page 92.*

Nahualá and Cuatro Caminos

Before the major four-way junction of Cuatro Caminos, the Pan-American Highway runs past Nahualá, a Maya village at 2470 m. The traditional *traje* is distinctive and best seen on market days on Thursday and Sunday, when finely embroidered cuffs and collars are sold, as well as very popular *huípiles*. The **Fiesta de Santa Catalina** is on 23-26 November (25th is the main day). There is an unpaved all-weather road a little to the north and 16 km longer, from Los Encuentros (on the Pan-American Highway) through Totonicapán (40 km) to San Cristóbal Totonicapán. The route from Chichicastenango to Quiché, Xecajá and Totonicapán takes a day by car or motorcycle, but is well worth taking and recommended by cyclists. There are no buses. There is also a scenic road from Totonicapán to Santa Cruz del Quiché via San Antonio Ilotenango. It takes one hour by car or motorcycle and two hours by pickup truck. There are no buses on this route either.

Cuatro Caminos is a busy junction with roads, east to Totonicapán, west to Los Encuentros, north to Huehuetenango and south to Quetzaltenango. Buses stop here every few seconds so you will never have to wait long for a connection. There is a petrol station and lots of vendors to keep you fed and watered. Just north of Cuatro Caminos is **San Cristóbal Totonicapán**, noted for its *huípiles*.

Totonicapán → *Altitude: 2500 m.*

The route to San Miguel Totonicapán, the capital of its department, passes through pine-forested hillsides, pretty red-tiled roofs and *milpas* of maize on the road side. The 18th-century beige church stands on one of the main squares, unfortunately now a parking lot, at 6 y 7 Avenida between 3 and 4 Calle. The market is considered by Guatemalans to be one of the cheapest, and it is certainly very colourful. Saturday is the main market noted for ceramics and cloth, with a small gathering on Tuesdays. There is a traditional dance fiesta on 12-13 August, music concerts and a chance to see *cofradía* rituals. The annual **feria** is on 24-30 September in celebration of the Archangel San Miguel, with the main fiesta on 29 September. The **Casa de Cultura** ① *8 Av, 2-17, T5630-0554, www.larutamayaonline.com/aventura.html*, run by Carlos Humberto Molina, displays an excellent collection of fiesta masks, made on site at the mask factory, and for sale. It has a cultural programme with a number of tour options, cultural activities and bicycle adventures. You need to reserve in advance.

San Francisco El Alto

San Francisco stands high on a great big mound in the cold mountains at 2640 m above the great valley in which lie Totonicapán, San Cristóbal and Quetzaltenango. It is famous for its market, which is stuffed to capacity, and for the animal market held above town, where creatures from piglets to kittens to budgies are for sale. The town's fiesta is on 1-6 October, in honour of St Francis of Assisi.

The market is packed to bursting point on Fridays with locals buying all sorts, including woollen blankets for resale throughout the country. It's an excellent place for buying woven and embroidered textiles of good quality, but beware of pickpockets. Go early to see as much action as possible. Climb up through the town for 10 minutes to see the animal market (ask for directions all the time as it's hard to see 5 m ahead, the place is so packed).

The **church** on the main square is magnificent; notice the double-headed Hapsburg eagle. It is often full on market days with locals lighting candles, and their live purchases ignoring the 'Silencio' posters. The white west front of the church complements the bright colours of the rest of the plaza, especially the vivid green and pink of the Municipalidad.

Momostenango

Momostenango is set in a valley with ribbons of houses climbing higgledy-piggledy out of the valley floor. Momostenango, at 2220 m, represents *Shol Mumus* in K'iche', meaning 'among the hills', and on its outlying hills are numerous altars and a hilltop image of a Maya god. Some 300 medicine men are said to practise in the town. Their insignia of office is a little bag containing beans and quartz crystals. Momostenango is the chief blanket-weaving centre in the country, and locals can be seen beating the blankets (*chamarras*) on stones, to shrink them. There are also weird stone peaks known as the *riscos* – eroded fluted columns and draperies formed of volcanic ash – on the outskirts of town.

The town is quiet except on Wednesday and Sunday market days, the latter being larger and good for weaving, especially the blankets. On non-market days try **Tienda Manuel de Jesús Agancel** ① *1 Av, 1-50, Zona 4, near bank*, for good bargains, especially blankets and carpets. There is also **Artesanía Paclom** ① *corner of 1 Calle and 3 Av, Zona 2*, just five minutes along the road to Xela. This family have the weaving looms in their back yard and will show you how it's all done if you ask.

The **Feast of Wajshakib Batz' Oj** (pronounced 'washakip'), is celebrated by hundreds of *Aj Kij* (Maya priests) who come for ceremonies. New priests are initiated on this first day of the ritual new year; the initiation lasting the year. The town's very popular fiesta is between 21 July and 4 August, with the town's patron saint of Santiago Apóstol celebrated on 25 July. The **Baile de Convites** is held in December with other dances on 8, 12 and 31 December and 1 January. At **Takilibén Maya Misión** ① *3 Av 'A', 6-85, Zona 3, T7736-5537, wajshakibbatz13@yahoo.es*, just after the Texaco garage on the right on the way in from Xela, Chuch Kajaw (day keeper/senior priest) Rigoberto Itzep welcomes all interested in learning more about Maya culture and cosmology. He offers courses in culture and does Maya horoscope readings. He also has a **Maya sauna** (*Tuj*).

Just outside town are three sets of *riscos* (eroded columns of sandstone with embedded quartz particles), creating a strange eerie landscape of pinnacles that look like rocket lollipop ice creams. To get there, take the 2 Calle, Zona 2, which is the one to the right of the church, for five minutes until you see a sign on a building pointing to the left. Follow the signs until you reach the earth structures (five to 10 minutes).

Huehuetenango and around → *For listings, see pages 90-93. Altitude: 1905 m.*

Huehuetenango – colloquially known as Huehue – is a pleasant, large town with little to detain the visitor. However, it is a busy transport hub serving the Cuchumatanes Mountains and the Mexican border. Its bus terminal, 2 km from town, is one of the busiest in the country. There are Maya ruins near the town, which were badly restored by the infamous **United Fruit**

Huehuetenango

Sleeping 🛏	Todos Santos Inn 7	La Fonda de
Casa Blanca 1		Don Juan 4
Cascata 2	**Eating 🍴**	Mi Tierra Café 5
Gobernador 3	Café Bugambilias 1	Perkys Pizza 7
La Sexta 4	El Jardín 2	
Mary 5	La Cabaña del Café 3	

Company, and new adventure tourism opportunities opening up nearby. Trips, including horse rides, to more remote spots in the Huehuetenango region to see forests, haciendas and lakes are organized by **Unicornio Azul**. A useful website is www.interhuehue.com.

The neoclassical **cathedral** was built between 1867 and 1874, destroyed by earthquake in 1902, and took 10 years to repair. In 1956, the image of the patron saint, the Virgen de la Concepción was burnt in a fire. Then, during the 1976 earthquake, 80% of it was damaged, save the bells, façade and cupola. The skyline to the north of the city is dominated by the Sierrra de los Cuchumatanes, the largest area over 3000 m in Central America.

The ruins of **Zaculeu** ① *0800-1800, US$6.40*, the old capital of the Mam Maya, are 5 km west of Huehuetenango on top of a rise with steep drops on three sides – a site chosen because of these natural defence measures. Its original name in Mam was *Xinabajul*, meaning 'between ravines'. In K'iche' it means 'white earth'. It was first settled in the Early Classic period (AD 250-600), but it flourished during the late post-Classic (AD 1200-1530). In July 1525, Gonzalo de Alvarado, the brother of Guatemala's conqueror, Pedro de Alvarado, set out for Zaculeu with 80 Spaniards, 40 horses and 2000 indigenous fighters, passing Mazatenango and Totonicapán on the way. The battle lasted four months, during which time the soldiers and residents of Zaculeu were dying of hunger, and eating their dead neighbours. The weakened Kaibil Balam, the Zaculeu *cacique* (chief), called for a meeting with Gonzalo. Gonzalo told the Mam chief that peace was not on the cards. Negotiations followed with the outcome being that Kaibil Balam be instructed in Christianity, obey the Spanish king and leave the city, whereupon Gonzalo de Alvarado would take possession of the Mam kingdom settlement in the name of the Spanish crown.

Aguacatán → *Altitude: 1670 m.*
The women of Aguacatán wear the most stunning headdresses in the country. On sale in *tiendas* in town, they are a long, slim belt of woven threads using many colours. The women also wear beautiful clothes – the *cortes* are dark with horizontal stripes of yellow, pink, blue and green. The town fiesta is 40 days after Holy Week, Virgen de la Encarnación.

Towards Todos Santos Cuchumatán
To get to Todos Santos, you have to climb the front range of the Cuchumatanes Mountains above Chiantla by a steep road from Huehuetenango. **Chiantla** has the **Luna Café** with art gallery and the nearby paleontological site of **El Mamutz**. Looking down on a clear day the cathedral at Huehuetenango resembles a blob of orange blancmange on the plain. At the summit, at about 3300 m, there is **El Mirador**. The paved road continues over bleak moorland to Paquix where the road divides. The unpaved road to the north continues to Soloma. The other to the west goes through Aldea Chiabel, noted for its outhouses, more obvious than the small dwellings they serve. Here, giant agave plants appear to have large pom-poms attached – reminiscent of the baubles on Gaudí's Sagrada Familia in Barcelona. On this journey you often pass through cloud layer, eventually surfacing above it. On cloudier days you will be completely submerged until descending again to Huehuetenango. The road crosses a pass at 3394 m before a difficult long descent to Todos Santos, about 50 km from Huehuetenango. The walk northwest from Chiantla to Todos Santos Cuchumatanes can be done in around 12-14 hours, or better, two days, staying overnight at **El Potrillo** in the barn owned by Rigoberto Alva. This route crosses one of the highest parts of the sierra at over 3500 m. Alternatively, cycle the 40-km part-gravel road, which is steep in places, but very rewarding.

Todos Santos Cuchumatán → *For listings, see pages 90-93. Altitude: 2470 m.*

High in the Cuchumatanes, the Mam-speaking Todos Santeros maintain a traditional way of life with their striking, bright, traditional dress and their adherence to the 260-day Tzolkin calendar. The town is hemmed in by 3800-m-high mountains either side that squeeze it into one long, 2-km street down the valley. The town is famous for its weaving, and even more famous for the horse race, see box, page 89.

Some of Guatemala's best weaving is done in Todo Santos. Fine *huípiles* may be bought in the cooperative on the main street and direct from the makers. The men wear the famous red-and-white striped trousers. Some wear a black wool over-trouser piece. Their jackets are white, pink, purple and red-striped with beautifully coloured, and intricately embroidered, collars and cuffs. Their straw hat is wrapped with a blue band. You can buy the embroidered cuffs and collars for men's shirts, the red trousers, and gorgeous colourful crocheted bags made by the men. The women wear navy blue *cortes* with thin, light blue, vertical stripes.

There is a colourful Saturday market and a smaller one on Wednesday. The **church** near the park was built in 1580.

Around Todos Santos

The closest walk is to **Las Letras**, where the words 'Todos Santos' are spelt out in white stone on a hillside above the town. The walk takes an hour. To get there take the path down the side of **Restaurant Cuchumatlán**. The highest point of the Cuchumatanes, and the highest non-volcanic peak in the country, **La Torre** at 3837 m, is to the northeast of Todos Santos and can be reached from the village of **Tzichem** on the road to Concepción Huista. When clear, it's possible to see the top of Volcán Santa María, one of the highest volcanoes in Guatemala. The hike takes about five hours. The best way to do it is to start in the afternoon and spend the night near the top. It is convenient for camping, with wood but no water. A compass is essential in case of mist. From Todos Santos, you can also hike south to **San Juan Atitán**, four to five hours, where the locals wear an interesting *traje típico*. Market days are on Mondays and Thursdays. From there you can hike to the Pan-American Highway – it's a one day walk. The local fiesta is 22-26 June.

Jacaltenango to the Mexican border

The road from Todos Santos continues northwest through **Concepción Huista**. Here the women wear towels as shawls and Jacalteco is spoken. The fiesta, 29 January-3 February, has fireworks and dancing. The hatmaker in Canton Pilar supplies the hats for Todos Santos, he welcomes viewers and will make a hat to your specifications (but if you want a typical Todos Santos leather *cincho*, buy it there).

Beyond Jacaltenango is **Nentón**, and **Gracias a Dios** at the Mexican border. When the road north out of Huehue splits at Paquix, the right fork goes to **San Mateo Ixtatán**, with ruins nearby. The road from Paquix crosses the roof of the Cuchumatanes, before descending to **San Juan Ixcoy**, **Soloma** and **Santa Eulalia**, where the people speak O'anjob'al as they do in Soloma. East along a scenic route is **Barillas**. There are several *pensiones* in these places and regular buses from Huehue.

Todos Santos festival

The horse racing festival of Todos Santos is one of the most celebrated and spectacular in Central America – it is also a frenzied day that usually degenerates into a drunken mess. Quite simply riders race between two points, having a drink at each turn until they fall off.

According to Professor Margarito Calmo Cruz, the origins of the fiesta lie in the 15th or 16th century with the arrival of the *conquistadores* to Todos Santos. They arrived on horses wearing large, colourful clothes with bright scarves flowing down their backs and feathers in their hats. The locals experimented, imitating them, enjoyed it and the tradition was born. When the day begins, the men are pretty tipsy, but sprightly and clean. The race is frantic and colourful with scarves flying out from the backs of the men. As the day wears on, they get completely smashed, riding with arms outstretched – whip in one hand and beer bottle in the other. They are mudspattered, dishevelled and are moaning and groaning from the enjoyment and the alcohol which must easily have reached near comatose level.

At times the riders fall, and look pretty lifeless. They are dragged by the scruff of the neck, regardless of serious injury or death, to the edge of the fence as quickly as possible, to avoid trampling.

The men guzzle gallons of beer and the aim is to continue racing all day. A fall means instant dismissal from the race. There are wardens on the side lines with batons, whose primary job is the welfare of the horses, changing them when they see necessary. But they also deal with protesting fallen riders, who try and clamber back onto their horses. By the end of the day the spectacle is pretty grotesque. The horses are drenched with sweat and wild-eyed with fear. The men look hideous and are paralytic from booze. The edge of the course and the town is littered with bodies.

The race takes place on the road that winds its way out of town, not the incoming road from Huehue. It starts at 0800. There are about 15 riders on the course at any one time. It continues until noon, stops for cerveza guzzling and begins again at 1400, ending at 1700.

◉ Western highlands listings

For Sleeping and Eating price codes and other relevant information, see pages 12-13.

▣ Sleeping

Totonicapán *p84*
$ Hospedaje San Miguel, 3 Calle, 7-49, Zona 1, T7766-1452. Rooms with or without bath, hot water, communal TV.
$ Pensión Blanquita, 13 Av and 4 Calle. 20 rooms, hot showers, good. Opposite this *pensión* is a Shell station.

San Francisco El Alto *p85*
$ Hotel Vásquez, 4 Av, 11-53, T7738-4003. Rooms all with private bathroom. Parking.
$ Vista Hermosa, 2 Calle, 2-23, T7738-4010. 36 rooms, cheaper without bathroom, hot water, TV.

Momostenango *p85*
$ Estiver Ixcel, 1 Calle, 4-15, Zona 4, downhill away from plaza, T7736-5036. 12 rooms, hot water, cheaper without bath, clean.
$ Hospedaje y Comedor Paclom, close to central plaza, at 1 Calle, 1-71, Zona 4. Pretty inner courtyard with caged birds and plants, hot water in shared bathrooms.
$ La Villa, 1 Av, 1-13, Zona 1, below bank, T7736-5108. 6 rooms, warm water only, clean and nicely presented.

Huehuetenango and around *p86, map p86*
$$ Casa Blanca, 7 Av, 3-41, T7769-0777. Comfortable, good restaurant in a pleasant garden, buffet breakfast, set lunch, very popular and good value, parking.
$$ Cascata, Lote 4, 42, Zona 5, Col Alvarado, Calzada Kaibil Balam, close to the bus station, T7769-0795, www.hotelcascata.ya.st. Newish hotel with 16 rooms with Wi-Fi and private bathrooms. It is owned by Dutch, French and English folk and the service is excellent.

$ Hotel Gobernador, 4 Av 1-45, T7764-1197. Garden, parking, with bath cheaper without, clean, good value.
$ La Sexta, 6 Av, 4-29, T7764-6612. With bath, cheaper without, cable TV, restaurant, good for breakfast, clean, good value, phone call facility, stores backpacks without charge.
$ Mary, 2 Calle, 3-52, T7764-1618. With bath, cheaper without, good beds, hot water, cable TV, parking, clean, quiet, safe, well-maintained, good value. Recommended.
$ Todos Santos Inn, 2 Calle, 6-74, T7764-1241. Shared bath and private bath available, hot water, TV, helpful, clean, laundry, some rooms a bit damp, luggage stored. Recommended.

Todos Santos Cuchumatán *p88*
Reservations are necessary in the week before the Nov horse race, but even if you turn up and the town is full, locals offer their homes.
$ Casa Familiar, up the hill, close to central park, T7783-0656. Run by the friendly family of Santiaga Mendoza Pablo. Hot shower, sauna, breakfast, dinner, delicious banana bread, spectacular view, popular. The Mendoza family make and sell *típicas* and give weaving lessons.
$ Hospedaje El Viajero, around the corner and then right from **Hotelito Todos Santos**, 5 rooms, 2 shared baths with hot water.
$ Hotel La Paz. Friendly, great view of the main street from balconies, excellent spot for the 1 Nov fiesta, shared showers have seen better days, enclosed parking.
$ Hotel Mam, above the central park, next to **Hotelito Todos Santos**. Friendly, clean, hot water, but needs 1 hr to warm up, not too cold in the rooms as an open fire warms the building, good value.
$ Hotelito Todos Santos, above the central park. Hot water, clean, small café, but beware of boys taking you to the hotel quoting one price, and then on arrival, finding the price has mysteriously gone up.

Around Todos Santos *p88*
$ Hospedaje San Diego, San Juan Atitán. Only 3 beds, basic, friendly, clean, food available.

Totonicapán *p84*
$ Comedor Brenda 2, 9 Av, 3-31. Good, serving local food.
$ Comedor Letty, 3 Calle, 8-18. Typical Guatemalan fare.

Momostenango *p85*
$ Comedor Santa Isabel, next door to Hospedaje y Comedor Paclom. Friendly, cheap and good breakfasts.
$ Flipper, 1 Calle y 2 Av A. Good *licuados* and a range of fruit juices.
$ Hospedaje y Comedor Paclom, close to the central plaza and where buses arrive from Xela, 1 Calle, 1-71, Zona 4. Cheap meals, including snacks in a pretty inner courtyard.

Huehuetenango and around
p86, map p86
$$-$ Casa Blanca, see Sleeping. Open 0600-2200. Try the breakfast pancake with strawberries and cream. The plate of the house is a meat extravaganza, fish and good salads served, set lunch good value.
$$-$ La Cabaña del Café, 2 Calle, 6-50. Log cabin café with to-die-for cappuccino, snack food and good *chapín* breakfasts, good atmosphere. Recommended.
$ Café Bugambilias, 5 Av 3-59, on the plaza. large, unusual 4-storey building, most of which is a popular, cheap, restaurant, very good breakfasts, *almuerzos*, sandwiches. Recommended.
$ El Jardín, 6 Av 2-99, Zona 1. Meat dishes, breakfasts, good pancakes and local dishes. It's worth eating here just to check out the toilets, which are right out of the 3rd-and-a-half floor of the office in the movie *Being John Malkovich*!

$ La Fonda de Don Juan, 2 Calle, 5-35. Italian restaurant and bar (try the *cavatini*), sandwiches, big choice of desserts, *licuados*, coffees, good pizzas, also *comida típica*, with reasonable prices all served in a bright environment with red and white checked tablecloths.
$ Mi Tierra Café, 4 Calle, 6-46, T7764-1473. Good drinks and light meals, Mexican offerings – try the *fajitas*, nice setting, popular with locals and travellers. Recommended.
$ Perkys Pizza, 3 Av esq, 4 Calle. Wide variety of pizzas, eat in or takeaway, modern, clean, good value.

Todos Santos Cuchumatán *p88*
There are *comedores* on the 2nd floor of the market selling very cheap meals.
$ Comedor Katy. Will prepare vegetarian meals on request, good-value *menú del día*.
$ Cuchumatlán. Has sandwiches, pizza and pancakes, and is popular at night.

Todos Santos Cuchumatán *p88*
1 Nov Horse race. The festival begins on 21 Oct. See box, page 89.
2 Nov Day of the Dead, when locals visit the cemetery and leave flowers and food.

Todos Santos Cuchumatán *p88*
The following shops all sell bags, trousers, shirts, *huipiles*, jackets and clothes. Prices have more or less stabilized at the expensive end, but the best bargains can be had at the **Tienda Maribel**, further up the hill from Casa Familiar and the **Cooperativa Estrella de Occidente**, on the main street. **Casa Mendoza**, just beyond Tienda Maribel, is where Telésforo Mendoza makes clothes to measure. **Domingo Calmo** also makes clothes to measure. His large, brown house with tin roof is on the main road to the Ruinas (5 mins) – follow the road up from Casa Familiar. Ask for the **Casa de Domingo**.

▲ Activities and tours

Huehuetenango and around *p86, map p86*

Unicornio Azul, based in Chancol, T5205-9328, www.unicornioazul.com. Horse-riding trips, trekking, mountain biking and birdwatching in the Cuchumatanes.

◉ Transport

Totonicapán *p84*

Bus Every 15 mins to **Quetzaltenango**, US$0.40, 45 mins. To **Los Encuentros**, US$2.20. To **Cuatro Caminos**, 30 mins, US$0.30.

San Francisco El Alto *p85*

Bus 2 km along the Pan-American Hwy heading north from Cuatro Caminos is a paved road, which runs to San Francisco El Alto (3 km) and then to Momostenango (19 km). Bus from **Quetzaltenango**, 50 mins on Fri, US$0.75. The last bus back is at 1800.

Momostenango *p85*

Bus From **Cuatro Caminos** (US$0.50) and **Quetzaltenango**, 1-1½ hrs. Buses to **Xela** every 30 mins from 0430-1600.

Huehuetenango and around *p86, map p86*

Bus and taxi

Local From the terminal to town, take 'Centro' minibus, which pulls up at cathedral, 5 mins. Taxis from behind the covered market. Walking takes 20-25 mins. Bus leaves Salvador Osorio School, final Calle 2, every 30 mins, 15 mins, to **Zaculeu**, last return 1830. Taxi, US$8, including waiting time. To walk takes about 1 hr – either take 6 Av north, cross the river and follow the road to the left, through Zaculeu modern village to the ruins, or go past the school and turn right beyond the river. The signs are barely visible.

Long distance To **Guatemala City**, 5 hrs, US$11, **Los Halcones**, 7 Av, 3-62,

Zona 1 (they do not leave from the terminal) at 0430, 0700, 1400, reliable. From the bus terminal there are numerous services daily to the capital from 0215-1600 via **Chimaltenango**, 5 hrs, US$4. Via **Mazatenango** there are 5 daily.

North To **Todos Santos Cuchumatán**, 10 daily until 1630, 2-3 hrs, US$3.60. To **Barillas**, via **San Juan Ixcoy** (2½ hrs), **Soloma** (3 hrs), and **San Mateo Ixtatan** (7 hrs), 10 daily from 0200-2330, US$7. There are also buses to **San Rafael la Independencia** passing through Soloma and **Sta Eulalia**.

Northwest To **La Mesilla** for Mexico, frequent buses between 0530-1800, US$3.50, 2½ hrs, last bus returning to Huehue, 1800. To **Nentón**, via La Mesilla twice a day. To **Gracias a Dios**, several times a day.

South To **Quetzaltenango**, 13 a day from 0600-1600, US$3, 2-2¼ hrs. To **Cuatro Caminos**, US$2, 2 hrs. To **Los Encuentros**, for Lake Atitlán and Chichicastenango, 3 hrs.

East To **Aguacatán**, 12 daily, 0600-1900, 1 hr 10 mins, US$1.20. To **Nebaj** you have to get to Sacapulas via Aguacatán. To **Sacapulas**, 1130, 1245. To **Cobán**, take the earliest bus/pickup to Aguacatán and then Sacapulas and continue to Uspantán to change for Cobán.

Aguacatán *p87*

Bus From **Huehue**, 1 hr 10 mins. It is 26 km east of Huehuetenango on a semi-paved route (good views). Returning between 0445 and 1600. Buses and pickups for **Sacapulas** and for onward connections to Nebaj and Cobán leave from the main street going out of town. Wait anywhere along there to catch your ride. It is 1½ hrs from Aguacatán to Sacapulas. To **Guatemala City** at 0300, 1100.

Todos Santos Cuchumatán *p88*

Bus To **Huehuetenango**, 2-3 hrs, crowded Mon and Fri, 0400, 0500, 0600, 0615-0630,

1145, 1230, 1300. Possible changes on Sat so ask beforehand. For petrol, ask at **El Molino**.

Jacaltenango to the Mexican border *p88*
Bus From **Huehuetenango** at 0330, 0500, returning at 1130 and 1400; also pickups.

ℹ Directory

San Francisco El Alto *p85*
Banks G&T Continental, 2 Av, 1-95, takes MasterCard and changes TCs; **Banco Industrial**, 2 Calle, 2-64, cashes TCs, takes Visa.

Momostenango *p85*
Banks Banrural, on plaza, TCs only.
Language schools Patzite, 1 Calle, 4-33, Zona 2, T7736-5159, www.patzite.20m.com.

Huehuetenango and around *p86, map p86*
Banks Some banks open Sat morning. The bigger banks change TCs. Mexican pesos available from **Camicard**, 5 Av, 6-00.
Internet Several places around town.
Language schools Some operate in summer months only (see box, page 51). Huehuetenango is a good spot to learn Spanish, as there are fewer chances of meeting gringos and conversing in your own tongue. **Señora de Mendoza**, 1 Calle, 1-64, Zona 3, T7764-1987. **Rodrigo Morales** (at Sastrería La Elegancia), 9 Av, 6-55, Zona 1. Recommended. **Spanish Academy Xinabajul**, 4 Av, 14-14, Zona 5, T7764-6631, www.world wide.edu/guatemala/xinabaj/index.html. **Abesaida Guevara de López**, 10 Calle 'A', 10-20, Zona 1, T7764-2917. Recommended. Information on schools and other tourist info is posted in **Mi Tierra Café**. **Post** 2 Calle, 3-54. **Telephone** **Telgua**, Edif El Triángulo, 9 Av, 6-142, on main road out of town.

Todos Santos Cuchumatán *p88*
Bank Banrural TCs and dollars cash only.
Language schools All local coordinators are on friendly terms but are competing for your business. Take your time and visit all 3 schools. **Hispano Maya**, opposite Hotelito Todos Santos, www.hispanomaya.org. **Nuevo Amanecer**, escuela_linguistica@yahoo.com. Working There is also a volunteer project to teach English in a nearby village where food and board is provided. Weaving can be taught. **Post** Parque Central.

Quetzaltenango and around

Quetzaltenango (commonly known as Xela – pronounced 'shayla') is the most important city in western Guatemala. The country's second city is set among a group of high mountains and volcanoes, one of which, Santa María, caused much death and destruction after an eruption in 1902. The bulk of the city is modern, but its 19th-century downtown revamp and its narrow streets give the centre more of a historic feel. There are breathtaking views and a pleasant park with its beautifully restored façade of the colonial church. It is an excellent base from which to visit nearby hot springs, religious idols, volcanoes and market towns.

Ins and outs → *Altitude: 2335 m.*

Getting there Most visitors arrive by bus, a 30-minute (14.5 km) journey southwest of Cuatro Caminos. Buses pull into the Zona 3 Minerva Terminal. To get a bus into the city centre, take a path through the market at its far left or its far right, which brings you out in front of the Minerva Temple. Watch out for very clever pickpockets walking through this market. Buses for the town centre face away (left) from the temple. All Santa Fe services go to Parque Centro América, US$0.15. Alternatively take a taxi. ▶ *See Transport, page 104.*

Getting around The town centre is compact and all sites and most services are within walking distance. The Santa Fe city bus goes between the terminal, the *rotonda* and the town centre. Out of town destination buses stop at the *rotonda* and it is quicker to get here from the town centre than to the Minerva Terminal. City buses for the terminal leave from 4 Calle and 13 Avenida, Zona 1, and those straight for the *rotonda* leave from 11 Avenida and 10 Calle, Zona 1, US$0.15. A taxi within Zona 1, or from Zona 1 to a closer part of Zona 3, is about US$3.20.

Tourist information INGUAT ① *7 Calle, 11-35, on the park, T7761-4931, Mon-Fri 0900-1600, Sat 0900-1300.* Not recommended. Try the recommended tour operators (page 103) for information instead. General information can be found at www.xelapages.com and www.xelawho.com, which has good listings.

Background

The most important battle of the Spanish conquest took place near Quetzaltenango when the great K'iche' warrior Tecún Umán was slain. In October 1902 the Volcán Santa María erupted, showering the city with half a metre of dust. An ash cloud soared 8.6 km into the air and some 1500 people were killed by volcanic fallout and gas. A further 3000 people died a short while later from malaria due to plagues of mosquitoes which had not been wiped out by the blast. Some 20 years on, a new volcano, born after the 1902 eruption, began to erupt. This smaller volcano, Santiaguito, spews clouds of dust and ash on a daily basis and is considered one of the most dangerous volcanoes in the world. The city's prosperity, as seen by the grand neoclassical architecture in the centre, was built on the back of the success of the coffee *fincas* on the nearby coastal plain. This led to the country's first bank being established here. The town's fiestas are 9-17 September, Holy Week and the October fiesta of La Virgen del Rosario.

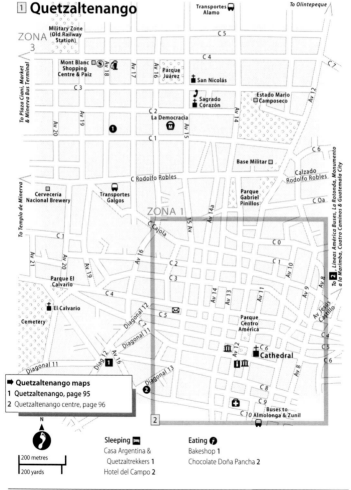

Quetzaltenango

➡ Quetzaltenango maps
1 Quetzaltenango, page 95
2 Quetzaltenango centre, page 96

N

200 metres
200 yards

Sleeping 🛏
Casa Argentina &
    Quetzaltrekkers 1
Hotel del Campo 2

Eating 🍴
Bakeshop 1
Chocolate Doña Pancha 2

Sights

The central park, **Parque Centro América**, is the focus of the city. It is surrounded by the cathedral, with its beautifully restored original colonial façade, and a number of elegant neoclassical buildings, constructed during the late 19th and early 20th century. The

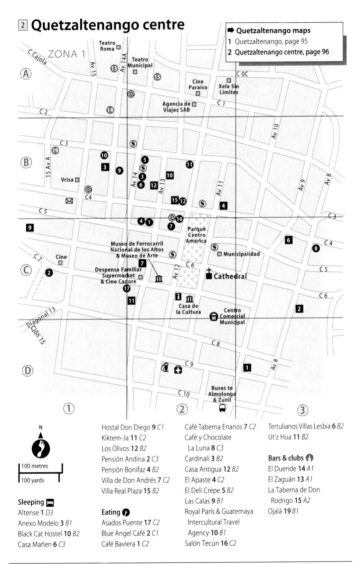

② Quetzaltenango centre

➡ **Quetzaltenango maps**
1 Quetzaltenango, page 95
2 Quetzaltenango centre, page 96

N

100 metres

100 yards

Sleeping 🛏
Altense **1** *D3*
Anexo Modelo **3** *B1*
Black Cat Hostel **10** *B2*
Casa Mañen **6** *C3*
Hostal Don Diego **9** *C1*
Kiktem-Ja **11** *C2*
Los Olivos **12** *B2*
Pensión Andina **2** *C3*
Pensión Bonifaz **4** *B2*
Villa de Don Andrés **7** *C2*
Villa Real Plaza **15** *B2*

Eating 🍴
Asados Puente **17** *C2*
Blue Angel Café **2** *C1*
Café Baviera **1** *C2*
Café Taberna Enanos **7** *C2*
Café y Chocolate
  La Luna **8** *C3*
Cardinali **3** *B2*
Casa Antigua **12** *B2*
El Apaste **4** *C2*
El Deli Crepe **5** *B2*
Las Calas **9** *B1*
Royal París & Guatemaya
  Intercultural Travel
  Agency **10** *B1*
Salón Tecún **16** *C2*
Tertulianos Villas Lesbia **6** *B2*
Ut'z Hua **11** *B2*

Bars & clubs 🍸
El Duende **14** *A1*
El Zaguán **13** *A1*
La Taberna de Don
  Rodrigo **15** *A2*
Ojalá **19** *B1*

modern cathedral, **Catedral de la Diócesis de los Altos**, was constructed in 1899 and is set back behind the original. The surviving façade of the 1535 **Catedral del Espíritu Santo** is beautiful, intricately carved and with restored portions of murals on its right side. On the south side of the park is the **Casa de la Cultura**. Inside are the **Museo de la Marimba** with exhibits and documents relating to the 1871 Liberal Revolution. On the right-hand side of the building is the totally curious **Museo de Historia Natural** ① *Mon-Fri 0800-1200, 1400-1800, US$0.90*. Deformed stuffed animals are cheek by jowl with pre-Columbian pottery, sports memorabilia, fizzy drink bottles, a lightning-damaged mirror and dinosaur remains. It satisfies the most morbid of curiosities with displays of a two-headed calf, Siamese twin pigs, an eight-legged goat, and a strange sea creature that looks like an alien, known as *Diabillo del Mar* (little sea devil). On the park's southwest side is the **Museo de Arte**, with a collection of contemporary Guatemalan art, and the **Museo del Ferrocarril Nacional de los Altos** ① *7 Calle and 12 Av, Mon-Fri 0800-1200, 1400-1800, US$0.90*, recounting the story of an electric railway between Xela and the Pacific slope. The **Banco de Occidente**, founded in 1881, and the first bank to opened in Guatemala, dominates the northern edge of the park. The overly wired-up **Municipalidad** straddles the eastern edge of the park with its neoclassical columns. Its first building blocks were laid in 1881, but it wasn't completed until 1897. The stately **Teatro Municipal** (1892-1896) is on 14 Avenida y 1 Calle and can be visited outside of performance hours. Restored at a cost of four million quetzales, it has an imposing presence. To its left, on Avenida 14 "A", is the Teatro Roma. Building began in 1898, but was not completed until 1931, when it became the first cinema to open in Guatemala. It was restored in 2000 as a theatre with a capacity for 1400 and is open for performances.

There is a sickly green modern church, the **Sagrado Corazón**, on the Parque Benito Juárez near the market. Inside is a gigantic, free-standing, Chagall-influenced painting with swooping angels, and Christ in a glass box, built into the picture. The church of **La Transfiguración** ① *near the corner of 11 Calle and 5 Av, Zona 1*, houses the largest crucified Christ figure (San Salvador del Mundo) to be found in Central America – it is almost 3 m in height and now housed behind glass. At 20 Avenida and 4 Calle is the city's **Cementerio** ① *0700-1900*. Inside are the remains of the Quetzalteco President, Estrada Cabrera (1898-1920) in a small cream neoclassical temple. Behind his tomb are the unmarked graves of a large number of cholera victims wiped out in a 19th-century epidemic. Manuel Lisandra Barillas (Guatemalan President 1885-1892) is also entombed here. There is a small patio area known as Colonia Alemana lined with graves of German residents; a large area where those that died as martyrs in the civil war lie; and a memorial to those that perished in the September Revolution of 1897.

North of Quetzaltenango → *For listings, see pages 101-107.*

Heading south to Quetzaltenango from Cuatro Caminos you pass the small *ladino* town of **Salcajá**, where *jaspé* skirt material has been woven since 1861. If you fancy a taste or a whiff of some potent liquor before bracing yourself for an entry into Quetzaltenango, then this is the place to halt. It is worth a visit not only for the booze but its famous church – the oldest in Central America – and for its textiles, often seen being produced in the streets. In 1524 the first church in Central America was founded by the conquering Spaniards. **San Jacinto** is a small church on 6 Avenida y 2 Calle; it may not always be open.

Caldo de frutas, a highly alcoholic drink with quite a kick, is not openly sold but is made in the town and drunk on festive occasions. It is illegal to drink it in public places. It is a concoction of nances, cherries, peaches, apples and quinces and is left to ferment in rum. There is also *rompope*, a drink made with eggs. Salcajá is a town that also revolves around textiles, with shops on every street. Yarn is tied and dyed, untied, and wraps are then stretched around telephone poles along the road or on the riverside. One of these can be seen outside San Jacinto church. Market day is Tuesday.

San Andrés Xecul is a small village in stunning surroundings with an extraordinarily lurid coloured church, 8 km north of Xela. Painted a deep-mustard yellow in 1900, its figurines, including angels, have been given blue wings and pastel-pink skirts. Climb the hill a bit above the town and catch a glimpse of the fantastic dome – mulitcoloured like a beach ball. With your back to the church climb the cobbled street leading up the right-hand side of the plaza to a yellow and maroon chapel peering out across the valley. The view from here is spectacular. Market day is Thursday, opposite the church. The town's fiestas are on 21 November, 30 November and 1 December.

South of Quetzaltenango → *For listings, see pages 101-107.*

Souteast of Xela is **Cantel** which has the largest and oldest textile factory in the country. Sunday is market day and the town's fiesta is 12-18 August (main day 15 August). At Easter a passion play is performed. A little further on, on the outskirts of town, on the right-hand side (one minute on the bus), is the white **Copavic glass factory** ① *T7763-8038, www.copavic.com, Mon-Fri 0500-1300, Sat 0500-1200*, where you can watch and photograph the workers blow the recycled glass.

Zunil
Pinned in by a very steep-sided valley is the town of Zunil, 9 km from Quetzaltenango. It is visited for the nearby hot thermal baths that many come to wallow in, and for its worship of its well-dressed idol San Simón (Maximón). The market is held on Mondays. The town's fiesta is 22-26 November (main day 25) and there is a very colourful Holy Week. The church is striking both inside and out. It has a large decorated altarpiece and a small shrine to murdered Bishop Gerardi at the altar. The façade is white with serpentine columns wrapped in carved ivy.

San Simón (Maximón) is worshipped in the town and is often dressed in different clothes at different times. A small charge is made for the upkeep and to take photos; ask anyone in the town to escort you to his house. To the left of the church is the **Santa Ana Cooperative**, which sells beautiful *huípiles*, shirt and skirt materials, as well as bags and bookmarks.

The nearby extinct **Volcán Pico Zunil**, rises to 3542 m to the southeast of the town. On its slopes are the **thermal baths of Fuentes Georginas** ① *0700-1900, US$2.70*, which you'll know you're approaching by the wafts of sulphurous fumes that come your way. There are several different-sized pools set into the mountainside surrounded by thick, luscious vegetation and enveloped in the steam that continuously rises up in wafts from the hot pools. There are spectacular views on the way to the baths.

The thermal baths of **Aguas Amargas** ① *0800-1700, US$2, children, US$1.30*, are on Zunil Mountain below Fuentes Georginas. They are reached by following the road south and heading east (left) by Estancia de La Cruz. This road passes fields of flowers and would make a great trip on a bike.

El Viejo Palmar

This is Guatemala's Pompeii. The river that cuts through here flows directly down from the active Santiaguito volcanic cone following a series of serious lahars (mudflows of water and volcanic material) that took place in the 1990s. The small town of 10,000 was evacuated, leaving an extraordinary legacy. In August 1998, the whole south end of the ghost town was destroyed by a massive lahar that crushed the church. This also shifted the course of the Río Nimá I, which began to flow directly through the centre of the church remains. Very heavy erosion since has left the west front and the altar separated by a 30-m-deep ravine – an unbelievable sight.

Volcán Santa María and Santiaguito

Santiaguito's mother, Santa María (3772 m), is a rough 5½-hour climb (1500 m). You can see Santiaguito (2488 m) below, erupting mostly with ash blasts and sometimes lava flows from a mirador. It is possible to camp at the summit of Santa María, or on the saddle west of the summit, but it is cold and windy, but worth it because dawn provides views of the entire country's volcanic chain and an almighty shadow is cast across the area by Santa Maria's form. Santiaguito is a fairly new volcano that formed after the eruption of Santa María out of its crater. Do not attempt to climb Santiaguito: it erupts continuously on a daily basis throwing up ash and is considered one of the most dangerous volcanoes in the world. To see it erupting you need to climb Santa María, where you can look down on this smaller volcano. ▸▸ *See Tour operators, page 103.*

Laguna Chicabal

San Martín rangers' station ⓘ *0700-1800, US$2,* is where the two-hour climb to Laguna Chicabal starts. This is a lime-green lake, at 2712 m, in the crater of the extinct volcano (2900 m) of the same name, with wild white lilies, known as *cartucho,* growing at the edges. The Maya believe the waters are sacred and it is thought that if you swim in the lake you will become ill. The highlight of a trip here is the sight of the clouds tumbling down over the circle of trees that surround the lake, and then appearing to bounce on the surface before dispersing. Ceremonies of Maya initiation are held at the lake in early May, known as *Jueves de la Ascensión*. The walk from San Martín takes about two hours.

West of Quetzaltenango → *For listings, see pages 101-107.*

To Mexico from Quetzaltenango

It takes half an hour to reach **San Juan Ostuncalco**, 15 km away. It's a pleasant, prosperous town with a big white church noted for its good weekly market on Sunday and beautiful sashes worn by men. Its fiesta, Virgen de la Candelaria, is held on 29 January to 2 February. The road, which is paved, switchbacks 37 km down valleys and over pine-clad mountains to a plateau looking over the valley in which are San Pedro and San Marcos. **San Marcos** has a few places to stay and eat. It is a transport hub with little to see. **San Pedro Sacatepéquez** has a huge market on Thursday. The Maya women wear golden and purple skirts.

The extinct **Volcán Tajumulco**, at 4220 m, is the highest in Central America. Start very early in the day if you plan to return to San Marcos by nightfall. It's about a five-hour climb and a three-hour descent. Once you have reached the ridge on Tajumulco, turn right along the top of it; there are two peaks, the higher is on the right. The peak on the left (4100 m) is used for shamanistic rituals.

Dormant **Volcán Tacaná** (4093 m) on the Mexican border may be climbed from the village of Sibinal. Its last eruption was 1949, but there was activity in 2001, so check before climbing. It is the second highest volcano in Guatemala with a 400-m-wide crater and fumaroles on its flanks. Take a bus to Sibinal from San Marcos. It is a six-hour difficult climb to the summit and it's recommended that you ask for a guide in the village. About 15 km west of San Marcos the road begins its descent from 2500 m to the lowlands. In 53 km to **Malacatán** it drops to 366 m. It is a winding ride with continuous bends, but the scenery is attractive. There is accommodation.

The road to the coastal plain from San Juan Ostuncalco is the most attractive of all the routes down from the highlands, bypassing most of the small towns through quickly changing scenery as you lose height. After San Juan, go south for 1.5 km to **Concepción Chiquirichapa**, with a bright blue and yellow church, which is one of the wealthiest villages in the country. It has a small market early every Thursday morning and a fiesta on 5-9 December. About 6 km beyond is **San Martín Sacatepéquez**, which used to be known as San Martín Chile Verde, and is famous for its hot chillies. This village appears in Miguel Angel Asturias' *Mulata de Tal*. It stands in a windy, cold gash in the mountains. The slopes are superbly steep and farmed, giving fantastic vistas on the climb up and down from Laguna Chicabal (see above). The men wear very striking long red and white striped tunics, beautifully embroidered around the hem. Market day is Sunday. The fiesta runs from 7-12 November (main day 11 November).

Quetzaltenango and around listings

For Sleeping and Eating price codes and other relevant information, see pages 12-13.

● Sleeping

Quetzaltenango *p94, maps p95 and p96*
At Easter, 12-18 Sep and Christmas, rooms need to be booked well in advance.
$$ Casa Mañen, 9a Av, 4-11, Zona 1, T7765-0786. Reports are consistently good, serves great breakfasts and friendly staff offer a very warm welcome. Room 2 is a great option with a bed on a mezzanine. Some rooms have microwave, fridge and TV. All are comfortable, and furnished with attractive wooden accessories. There is a small, pretty courtyard area and secure parking.
$$ Hotel del Campo, Km 224, Carretera a la Costa Sur, T7931-9393, www.hoteldel campo.com.gt. Large red-brick hotel 4 km from town, popular with family weekenders, with indoor heated swimming pool, playground and meeting rooms. 92 spacious bedrooms with private bath, cable TV, and Wi-Fi, breakfast included. Recommended.
$$ Hotel Villa de Don Andrés, 13 Av 6-16, Zona 1, T7761-2014. www.hotelvilladedon andres.com. Boutique B&B hotel in old city centre one block from Parque Central, 5 prettily decorated rooms with private bath, minibar, cable TV and Wi-Fi, breakfast extra. Laundry service and parking space. Recommended.
$$ Los Olivos, 13 Av, 3-22, T7761-0215, Zona 1. 26 pleasant rooms above parking area with private bathroom, TV and a restaurant with cheap breakfasts and meals.
$$ Pensión Bonifaz, 4 Calle, 10-50, Zona 1, T7765-1111. 75 clean, comfortable rooms with TV. Pool, which is occasionally heated. Good restaurant and bar. Parking.
$$ Villa Real Plaza, 4 Calle, 12-22, Zona 1, T7761-4045. Dignified colonial building, 58 rooms with TV. Restaurant has good vegetarian food, and is good value. Parking.

$ Altense, 9 Calle, 8-48, Zona 1, T7765-4648. 16 rooms with bath, hot water, parking, secure and friendly. However, if your room is on the 9 Av side, you'll be woken by rush-hour traffic. This is a good town centre deal for single travellers. Recommended.
$ Black Cat Hostel, 13 Av, 3-33, Zona 1, T7761-2091, www.blackcathostels.net. A hostel in the old Casa Kaehler. Dorms and private rooms all with shared bathrooms. Breakfast included.
$ Casa Argentina, Diagonal 12, 8-37, Zona 1, T7761-2470. 25 clean rooms, hot water, 10 shared bathrooms, cheaper in 18-bed dorm, rooms with private bath, cooking facilities with purified water, friendly, laundry service. Ask about cheap monthly room rates.
$ Hostal Don Diego, 6 Calle, 15-12, Zona 1, www.hostaldondiegoxela.com. Sweet hostel, set about an interior courtyard with rooms with shared bathroom. Hot water and breakfast included. Bright and clean. Weekly and monthly rents available; tours office (branch of **Adrenalina Tours**).
$ Kiktem-Ja, 13 Av, 7-18, Zona 1, T7761-4304. A central location with 16 colonial-style rooms, nicely furnished, locally made blankets on the beds, wooden floors, all with bath, hot water, open fires, car parking inside gates.
$ Pensión Andina, 8 Av, 6-07, Zona 1, T7761-4012. Private bathrooms, hot water, friendly, clean, sunny patio, restaurant, good value, parking.

Zunil *p98*
$$$-$$ Las Cumbres Eco-Saunas y Gastronomía, T5399-0029, www.las cumbres.com.gt. Daily 0700-1800. Beyond Zunil on the left-hand side of the road heading to the coast (Km 210). This is the place for some R&R with saunas emitting natural steam from the geothermal activity

nearby. There are 12 rooms with sauna, cheaper without, and separate saunas and jacuzzis for day visitors (US$2.50 per hr) and a restaurant serving good regional food and natural juices. Highly recommended. See Transport, page 105, for transfers.

$ Turicentro Fuentes Georginas. 6 cold bungalows with 2 double beds and 2 bungalows with 3 single beds. They have cold showers, fireplaces with wood, electricity 1700-2200 and barbecue grills for guests' use near the baths. Guests can use the baths after public closing times. Reasonably priced restaurant with breakfasts, snacks and drinks, 0800-1800 (destroyed by Tropical Storm Agatha in 2010, but being rebuilt early 2011).

🍴 Eating

Quetzaltenango *p94, maps p95 and p96*
$$$-$$ Cardinali, 14 Av, 3-25, Zona 1. Owned by Benito, a NY Italian, great Italian food, including large pizzas with 31 varieties: 2 for 1 on Tue and Thu; tasty pastas of 20 varieties, extensive wine list. Recommended. Also does home delivery in 30 mins (T7761-0924).
$$$-$ Las Calas, 14 Av "A", 3-21, Zona 1. Mon-Sat. Breakfasts, salads, soups, paella and pastas served around a courtyard with changing art hanging from walls. The food is tasty with delicious bread to accompany, but small portions are served. The breakfast service is far too slow. Adjoining bar.
$$$-$ Restaurante Royal París, 14 Av "A", 3-06, Zona 1. Delicious food (try the fish in a creamy mushroom sauce), excellent choices, including vegetarian. Also cheap options. Run by Stéphane and Emmanuelle. Recommended. Live music from 2000 on Fri.
$$$-$ Restaurante Tertulianos Villa Lesbia, 14 Av, 5-26, Zona 3, T7767-4666. Gourmet quality, specializing in meat, cheese and chocolate fondues, and scrumptious desserts. Recommended.
$$ El Apaste, 5 Calle, 14-48, Zona 3, T7776-6249. Local Xela cuisine, rich stews and

meats, traditionally served in the eponymous *apaste* (terracotta dish).
$$ Ut'z Hua, Av 12, 3-02, Zona 1. This prettily decorated restaurant with purple tablecloths does typical food, which is always very good and filling. Don't miss the *pollo con mole* or fish. Recommended.
$$-$ Asados Puente, 7 Calle, 13-29. Lots of veggie dishes with tofu and tempeh. Also ceviche. Popular with expats. Run by Ken Cielatka and Eva Melgar. Some profits go towards helping ill children.
$$-$ Salón Tecún, Pasaje Enríquez, off the park at 12 Av y 4 Calle, Zona 1. Bar, local food, breakfasts also, TV. Always popular with gringos and locals.
$ Café Taberna Enanos, 5 Calle near Av 12 and Parque Central, Zona 1. Mon-Sat 0715-2000. Good cheap breakfast, also has *menú del día*.
$ El Deli Crepe, 14 Av, 3-15, Zona 1. Good tacos, *almuerzo* with soup, great milkshakes, savoury and sweet crêpes, juicy *fajitas* that arrive steaming.

Cafés and bakeries
Bakeshop at 18 Av, 1-40, Zona 3. Mennonite bakery that is Xela's answer to *dulce* heaven. They bake a whole range of cookies, muffins, breads and cakes and sells fresh yoghurt and cheeses. Tue and Fri 0900-1800 so get there early as the goodies go really fast.
Blue Angel Café, 7 Calle, 15-79, Zona 1. Great salads, light meals, service a little slow though, movies shown on a monthly rotation, useful noticeboard.
Café Baviera, 5 Calle, 13-14, Zona 1. Open 0700-2000. Good cheap meals and excellent pies, huge cake portions (try the carrot cake) and coffee in large premises, with walls lined from ceiling to floor with old photos and posters. Good for breakfasts, but a little on the expensive side. Popular, but lacks warmth.
Chocolate Doña Pancha, 10a Calle 16-67 Zona 1, T7761-9700. High-quality chocolate

factory, with great range of drinks, cakes and pastries, also chocolate products to take away.
Café y Chocolate La Luna, 8 Av, 4-11, Zona 1. Delicious hot chocolate with or without added luxuries, good cheap snacks, also top chocolates and *pasteles* (the strawberry and cream pie is recommended), pleasant atmosphere in a colonial house decorated with moon symbols, fairy lights, and old photos; a good meeting place.

Entertainment

Quetzaltenango *p94, maps p95 and p96*
Bars and clubs
El Duende, 14 Av "A", 1-42, Zona 1. Popular café-bar, 1800-2330. A favourite among Guatemalans and gringos.
El Zaguán, 14 Av "A", A-70, Zona 1. A disco-bar Wed, Thu 1900-2430, Fri, Sat 2100-2430, US$3.25, drink included; plays salsa music.
La Taberna de Don Rodrigo, 14 Av, Calle C-47, Zona 1. Cosy bar, reasonable food served in dark wood atmosphere, draught beer.
Ojalá, 15 Av "A", 3-33, an entertainment venue, popular with locals and gringos, which also shows films.

Cinemas
Cine Sofía, 7 Calle 15-18. Mon-Fri 1800. See Blue Angel and Ojala, above.
La Pradera, 5 screens in shopping mall in Zona 3, next to bus terminal. Latest releases.

Dance
Trópica Latina, 5 Calle 12-24, Zona 1, T5892-8861, tropicalatina@xelawho.com. Classes Mon-Sat.

Theatre
Teatro Municipal, 14 Av and 1 Calle, main season May-Nov, theatre, opera, etc.

Shopping

Quetzaltenango *p94, maps p95 and p96*
Bookshops
Vrisa, 15 Av, 3-64, T7761-3237, a good range of English-language second-hand books.

Markets
The **main market** is at Templo de Minerva on the western edge of town (take the local bus, US$0.10); at the southeast corner of Parque Centro América is the **Centro Comercial Municipal**, a shopping centre with craft and textile shops on the upper levels, food, clothes, etc below. There is another **market** at 2 Calle y 16 Av, Zona 3, south of Parque Benito Juárez, known as La Democracia. Every first Sun of the month there also is an art and handicrafts market, around Parque Centro América.

Supermarkets
Centro Comercial Mont Blanc, Paiz, 4 Calle between 18-19 Av, Zona 3.
Despensa Familiar, 13 Av, 6-94.
La Pradera, near the Minerva Terminal.

North of Quetzaltenango *p97*
The smallest bottle of bright yellow *rompope* is sold in various shops around Salcajá, including the **Fábrica de Pénjamo**, 2 Av, 4-03, Zona 1, US$1.55, and it slips down the throat very nicely!

Activities and tours

Quetzaltenango *p94, maps p95 and p96*
When climbing the volcanoes make sure your guides stay with you all the time; it can get dangerous when the cloud rolls down.
Adrenalina Tours, inside Pasaje Enríquez, T7761-4509, www.adrenalinatours.com. Numerous tours are on offer including bike, fishing, rafting, horse riding, rock climbing and volcano tours as well as packages to Belize, Honduras and the Petén and trips to Huehue and Todos Santos. Specializes

in hikes and treks all over Guatemala. Highly recommended.

Agencia de Viajes SAB, 1 Calle, 12-35, T7761-6402. Good for cheap flights.

Guatemaya Intercultural Travel Agency, 14 Av "A", 3-06, T7765-0040. Very helpful.

Mayaexplor, T7761-5057, www.maya explor.com. Run by Thierry Roquet, who arranges a variety of trips around Xela and around the country. He can also arrange excursions into Mexico, Belize and Honduras and treks, eg Nebaj–Todos Santos. French-speaking. His website offers useful info for travellers. A proportion of funds goes towards local development projects. Recommended.

Quetzaltrekkers, based inside **Casa Argentina** at Diagonal 12, 8-37, T7765-5895, www.quetzaltrekkers.com. This recommended, established, non-profit agency is known for its 3-day hike (Sat am-Mon pm) from Xela across to Lake Atitlán. Proceeds go to the **Escuela de la Calle School** for kids at risk, and a dorm for homeless children. Also offers trek from Nebaj–Todos Santos, 6 days, full-moon hike up Santa María and others. Hiking volunteers are also needed for a 3-month minimum period: hiking experience and reasonable Spanish required.

Tranvia de los Altos, www.tranviadelos altos.com, provides daytime and nighttime walking tours in Xela as well as excursions. Guided city tour is only US$4. Recommended.

Zunil *p98*
See **Las Cumbres Eco-Saunas y Gastronomía**, T5399-0029, under Sleeping, above.

⊖ **Transport**

Quetzaltenango *p94, maps p95 and p96*
Bus
Local City buses run between 0600 and 1900. Between the town centre and Minerva Terminal, bus No 6, Santa Fe, US$0.20, 15-30 mins, depending on traffic. Catch the bus at the corner of 4 Calle and 13 Av

by Pasaje Enríquez. Buses to the Rotonda leave from the corner of 11 Av and 10 Calle, US$0.20, or catch bus No 6, 10 or 13, from Av 12 y 3 Calle as they come down to the park, 15 mins. To catch buses to **San Francisco El Alto**, **Momostenango**, the **south coast** and **Zunil**, get off the local bus at the Rotonda, then walk a couple of steps away from the road to step into a feeder road where they all line up.

Long distance To **Guatemala City**, **Galgos**, Calle Rodolfo Robles, 17-43, Zona 1, T7761-2248, 1st-class buses, at 0400, 1230, 1500, US$5, 4 hrs, will carry bicycles; **Marquensita** several a day (office in the capital 21 Calle, 1-56, Zona 1), leaves from the Minerva Terminal, US$4.60, comfortable, 4 hrs. **Líneas América**, from 7 Av, 3-33, Zona 2, T7761-2063, US$5, 4 hrs, between 0515-2000, 6 daily. **Línea Dorada**, 12 Av and 5 C, Zona 3, T7767-5198, 0400 and 1530, US$9. **Transportes Alamo** from 14 Av, 5-15, Zona 3, T7763-5044, between 0430 and 1430, 7 a day, US$5, 4 hrs.

The following destinations are served by buses leaving from the Minerva Terminal, Zona 3 and the Rotonda. For **Antigua**, change at Chimaltenangoby either taking a chicken bus or Pullman. To **Almolonga**, via **Cantel**, every 30 mins, US$0.50, 10 mins. (Buses to Almolonga and Zunil not via Cantel, leave from the corner of 10 Av and 10 Calle, Zona 1.) To **Chichicastenango** with **Transportes Veloz Quichelense de Hilda Esperanza**, several from 0500 to 1530, US$3.80, 2½ hrs. To **Cuatro Caminos** US$0.50, 30 mins. To **Huehuetenango** with **Transportes Velásquez**, every 30 mins 0500-1730, US$2.50, 2½ hrs. To **La Mesilla** at 0500, 0600, 0700, 0800, 1300, 1400 with **Transportes Unión Fronteriza**, US$3.60, 4 hrs. To **Los Encuentros**, US$2.20. To **Malacatán**, US$3.60, 5 hrs. To **Momostenango**, US$1.20, 1½ hrs. To **Panajachel**, with **Transportes Morales**, at 0500, 0600, 1000, 1200, 1500, US$3.20, 2½-3 hrs. To **Retalhuleu**, US$1.20, 1½ hrs. To **Salcajá**, every 30 mins, US$0.40, 15 mins. To **San Andrés Xecul** every 2 hrs, US$0.60, 30 mins. To **San Cristóbal Totonicapán**, every 30 mins, US$0.40, 20 mins. To **San Francisco El Alto**, US$0.70. **San Marcos**, every 30 mins, US$1, 1 hr. **San Martín Sacatepéquez/San Martín Chile Verde**, US$0.70, 1 hr. **Santiago Atitlán**, with Ninfa de Atitlán at 0800, 1100, 1230, 1630, 4½ hrs. To **Ciudad Tecún Umán** every 30 mins, 0500-1400, US$3.60, 4 hrs. To **Totonicapán**, every 20 mins, US$1.20, 1 hr. To **Zunil**, every 30 mins, US$0.70, 20-30 mins.

Shuttle Adrenalina Tours, see Tour operators, above, runs shuttles. To **Cobán**, US$45, Panajachel, US$20 and Antigua, US$25. Adrenalina also runs a shuttle to and from **San Cristóbal de las Casas**, Mexico, US$35.

Car
Car hire Tabarini Renta Autos, 9 Calle, 9-21, Zona 1, T7763-0418. **Mechanic** José Ramiro Muñoz R, 1 Calle, 19-11, Zona 1, T7761-8204. Also **Goodyear Taller** at the Rotonda and for motorbikes **Moto Servicio Rudy**, 2 Av, 3-48, Zona 1, T7765-5433.

Taxi
Found all over town, notably lined up along Parque Centro América.
Taxis Xelaju, T7761-4456.

North of Quetzaltenango *p97*
Bus All buses heading to Quetzaltenango from Cuatro Caminos pass through **Salcajá**, 10 mins. From Xela to **San Andrés Xecul**, US$0.60, 30 mins. Or take any bus heading to Cuatro Caminos and getting off at the Esso station on the left-hand side, and then almost doubling back on yourself to take the San Andrés road. There are pickups from here.

South of Quetzaltenango *p98*
Bus Cantel is 10-15 mins by bus (11 km), and US$0.24 from Xela on the way to Zunil, but you need to take the bus marked for Cantel Fábrica and Zunil, not Almolonga and Zunil. From **Zunil** to Xela via Almolonga leaves from the bridge. Walk down the left-hand side of the church to the bottom of the hill, take a left and you'll see the buses the other side of the bridge, US$0.60. **Fuentes Georginas** is reached either by walking the 8 km uphill just to the south of Zunil, 2 hrs (300-m ascent; take the right fork after 4 km, but be careful as robbery has occurred here), by pickup truck in 15 mins (US$10 return with a 1-hr wait), or hitch. If you come by bus to Zunil and are walking to the Fuentes, don't go down into town with the bus, but get off on the main road at the Pepsi stand and walk to the entrance road, which is visible 100 m away on the left. See also Shuttles, above, for transfer to the thermal pools.

El Viejo Palmar *p99*
Bus Just before San Felipe, and just before the Puente Samalá III, if you're heading south, is the turn to the right for El Viejo Palmar. Take any bus heading to the south coast, and asked to be dropped off at the entrance and walk. Or, take a pickup from San Felipe park. Ask for Beto or Brígido.
Taxi From Xela round trip is US$25, or take a tour from town.

Volcán Santa María and Santiaguito *p99*
Bus To reach the volcano take the bus to **Llano del Pinal**, 7 km away, from the Minerva Terminal (every 30 mins, last bus back 1800). Get off at the crossroads and follow the dirt road towards the right side of the volcano until it sweeps up the right (about 40 mins), take the footpath to the left (where it is marked for some distance); bear right at the saddle where another path comes in from the left, but look carefully as it is easily missed.

Laguna Chicabal *p99*

Bus/car The last bus to **Quetzaltenango** leaves at 1900, 1 hr. Parking at the entrance, US$2. It is a 40-min walk from the car park (and you'll need a sturdy vehicle if you attempt the steep first ascent in a car).

To Mexico from Quetzaltenango *p99*

Bus Volcán Tajumulco can be reached by getting to the village of **San Sebastián** from San Marcos, which takes about 2 hrs.

Directory

Quetzaltenango *p94, maps p95 and p96*
Banks Many banks on Parque Centro América. Non-Amex TCs are difficult to change here. Maestro can't be used in ATMs. There is a **Bancard**, 24 hr Visa ATM on the park next to **Banrural** which has a MasterCard ATM **Banco Industrial**, corner of 5 Calle y 11 Av, 24 hr Visa ATM, Visa accepted. **G&T Continental**, 14 Av, 3-17. Advances on MasterCard. **Embassies and consulates** Mexican Consulate, 21 Av, 8-64, Zona 3, T7767-5542, Mon-Fri 0800-1100, take photocopies of your passport. **Emergencies** Police: T7761-5805; Fire: T7761-2002; Red Cross: T7761-2746. **Internet** Lots of places around town. **Language schools** See also box, page 51. Many of Xela's schools can be found at www.xelapages.com/schools.htm. There are many schools offering individual tuition, accommodation with families, extra-curricular activities and excursions. Some also offer Mayan languages. Several schools fund community-development projects, and students are invited to participate with voluntary work. Some schools are non-profit making; enquire carefully. Extra-curricular activities are generally better organized at the larger schools. Prices start from US$130 per week including accommodation, but rise in Jun-Aug to US$150 and up. The following have been recommended: **Centro de Estudios de Español Pop Wuj**, 1 Calle, 17-72, T7761-8286, www.pop-wuj.org.

Guatemalensis, 19 Av, 2-14, Zona 1, T7765-1384, www.geocities.com/spanland/. **Sol Latino**, Diagonal 12, 6-58, Zona 1, T5613-7222, www.spanishschoollatino.com. **Instituto Central América (ICA),** 19 Av, 1-47 Calle, Zona 1, T/F7763-1871. **INEPAS** (Instituto de Estudios Español y Participación en Ayuda Social), 15 Av, 4-59, T7765-1308, www.inepas. org. Keen on social projects and has already founded a primary school in a Maya village, extremely welcoming. **Juan Sisay Spanish School**, 15 Av, 8-38, Zona 1, T7761-1586, www.juansisay.com. **Kie-Balam**, Diagonal 12, 4-46, Zona 1, T7761-1636, kie_balam@ hotmail.com. Offers conversation classes in the afternoon in addition to regular hours. **La Paz**, Diagonal 11, 7-36, T7761-2159, xela.escuela lapaz@gmail.com. **Minerva Spanish School**, 24 Av, 4-39, Zona 3, T7767-4427, www.minervaspanishschool.com. **Proyecto Lingüístico Quetzalteco de Español**, 5 Calle, 2-40, Zona 1, T7765-2140, hermandad@plqe.org. Recommended. **Proyecto Lingüístico 'Santa María'**, 14 Av "A", 1-26, T/F7765-1262. Volunteer opportunities and free internet access. **Sakribal**, 6 C, 7-42, Zona 1, T7763-0717, www.sakribal.com. Community projects are available. **Ulew Tinimit**, 4 C, 15-23, Zona 1, T7761-6242, www.spanish guatemala.org. **Utatlán**, 12 Av, 14-32, Pasaje Enríquez, Zona 1, T7763-0446, utatlan_ xela@hotmail.com. Voluntary work opportunities, one of the cheaper schools. **Laundry** Minimax, 14 Av, C-47. **Lavandería Pronto**, 7 Calle, 13-25, good service. **Lavandería El Centro**, 15 Av, 3-51, Zona 1, very good service. **Medical services** San Rafael Hospital, 9 Calle, 10-41, T7761-2956. **Hospital Rodolfo Robles**, a private hospital on Diagonal 11, Zona 1, T7761-4229. **Hospital Privado Quetzaltenango**, Calle Rodolfo Robles, 23-51, Zona 1, T7761-4381. Medical tourism, www.turismoysaludquetzaltenango.com, T5308-5106, a new service supported by many doctors, and Adrenalina Tours (see above). **Post** 15 Av y 4 Calle. **Telephone** Telgua, 15 Av "A" y 4 Calle. **Kall Shop**, 8 Av, 4-24, Zona 1. **Voluntary work** Asociación Hogar Nuevos Horizontes, www.ahnh.org, T7761-6140.

EntreMundos, El Espacio, 6 Calle, 7-31, Zona 1, T7761-2179, www.entremundos.org, puts people in touch with opportunities. **Hogar de Niños**, Llanos de Urbina, Cantel, T7761-1526, hogardeninos@hotmail.com.

Southern Guatemala

The southern coastal plain of Guatemala supports many plantations of coffee, sugar and tropical fruit trees and its climate is unbearably hot and humid. Amid the fincas some of the most curious archaeological finds have been unearthed, a mixture of monument styles such as Maya and Olmec, including Abaj Takalik, the cane field stones at Santa Lucía Cotzumalguapa and the big 'Buddhas' of Monte Alto.

On the coast are the black-sand beaches and nature reserves of the popular and laid-back Monterrico and Sipacate resorts, where nesting turtles burrow in the sand and masses of birds take to the skies around. Casting a shadow over the coast, the Central Highland volcanoes of Lake Atitlán, and the Antigua trio of Fuego, Acatenango and Agua, look spectacular, looming on the horizon above the lowlands.

Ins and outs
Numerous buses travel from Guatemala City and along the CA2 Highway that runs through the transport hub of Escuintla and through towns either side to the Mexican and El Salvadorean borders. ▸▸ *See Transport, page 114.*

Guatemala City to the Pacific coast
The main road from the capital heads to Escuintla, which connects Guatemala City with all the Pacific ports. There is also a direct route to Escuintla from Antigua. South of Guatemala City is **Amatitlán** on the banks of the lake of the same name. The lake is seriously polluted. The main reason for coming here would be for the **Day of the Cross** on 3 May, when the Christ figure is removed from the church and floated out of a boat amid candles and decorations. A *teleférico* has opened on the lake. **Palín** has a Sunday market in a plaza under an enormous ceiba tree. The textiles are exceptional, but are increasingly difficult to find. There are great views of Pacaya to the east as you head down to the coast, Volcán Agua to the northwest, and the Pacific lowlands to the west. An unpaved road runs northwest from here to Antigua via **Santa María de Jesús**. The town's fiesta is on 24-30 July. **Escuintla** is a large, unattractive provincial centre in a rich tropical valley. It is essentially a transport hub for travellers in the area.

Puerto San José, Chulamar and Iztapa
South of Escuintla the fast tarmacked highway heads to Puerto San José. Puerto San José used to be the country's second largest port and first opened for business (especially the coffee trade) in 1853. The climate is hot, the streets and most of the beaches dirty, and at weekends the town fills up with people from the capital. There are swimming beaches near by, but beware of the strong undercurrent. Some 5 km to the west of Puerto San José is Chulamar, a popular beach at weekends with good bathing. **Iztapa** is world renowned

for deep-sea fishing. Sail fish, bill fish, marlin, tuna, dorado, roosterfish, yellowfin and snapper are to be found in large numbers. The **Chiquimulilla Canal** runs either side of Puerto San José parallel to the coast, for close to 100 km. From here a trip can be taken through the canal by *lancha* to the old Spanish port of Iztapa, now a bathing resort, a short distance to the east.

Monterrico → *For listings, see pages 113-116.*

Monterrico is a small, black-sand resort where the sunsets are a rich orange and the waves crash spectacularly on to the shore. If you are in the area between September and January, you can sponsor a baby turtle's waddle to freedom.

Ins and outs
The landing stage is 10 minutes' walk from the ocean front, where you'll find the main restaurants and places to stay. When you step off the dock take the first left, and keep left, which heads directly to the main cluster of beach hotels. This road is known as Calle del Proyecto or Calle del Muelle. Walking straight on from the dock takes you to the main drag in town. When you get to the main drag and want to walk to the main group of hotels, take a left along the beach or take the sandy path to the left one block back from the beach where the sand is a tiny bit easier to walk on.

Sights
Monterrico's popularity is growing fast but mainly as a weekend and holiday resort with views that are undisturbed by high-rise blocks. All the hotels, mostly rustic and laid-back, are lined up along the beach, and there are a few shops and *comedores* not linked to hotels, in this village of just 1500 people. The village is surrounded by canals carpeted in aquatic plants and mangrove swamps with bird and turtle reserves in their midst. These areas make up the **Monterrico Nature Reserve**. Anteater, armadillo, racoon and weasel live in the area. It is worth taking a boat trip at sunrise or sunset, to see migratory North and South American birds, including flamingo. However, the real stars in this patch are the olive ridleys – *Parlama blanca* and *Parlama negra* turtles, which lay eggs between July and October, and the Baule turtle, which lays between between October and February. There is a **turtle hatchery** ① *daily 0800-1200, 1400-1700, US$1.* Just behind the hatchery there are 300 breeding crocodiles, 150 turtles and iguanas. The turtle liberation event takes place every Saturday night between October and February.

Santa Lucía Cotzumalguapa → *For listings, see pages 113-116.*

Amid the sugar-cane fields and *fincas* of this Pacific town lie an extraordinary range of carved stones and images with influences from pre-Maya civilizations, believed mostly to be ancient Mexican cultures, including the Izapa civilization from the Pacific coast area of Mexico near the Guatemalan border. The town is just north of the Pacific Highway, where some of the hotels and banks are.

Ins and outs

You can visit all the sites on foot. However, you are advised not to go wandering in and out of the cane fields at the Bilbao site as there have been numerous assaults in the past. You can walk along the tarmacked road north to the El Baúl sites (6 km and 8 km respectively from town), but there is no shade, so take lots of water. Ask for directions. There is an occasional 'Río Santiago' bus, which goes as far as Colonia Maya, close to the El Baúl hilltop. Only workers' buses go to **Finca El Baúl** in the morning, returning at night. To get to the museum, walk east along the Pacific Highway and take a left turn into the *finca* site. Alternatively, take a taxi from town (next to the plaza) and negotiate a trip to all four areas. They will charge around US$20. **Note** Do not believe any taxi driver who tells you that Las Piedras (the stones) have been moved from the cane fields to the museum because of the increasing assaults.

Sights

There is considerable confusion about who carved the range of monuments and stelae scattered around the town. It is safe to say that the style of the monuments found in the last 150 years is a blend of a number of pre-Columbian styles. Some believe the prominent influence is Toltec, the ancestors of the Maya K'iche', Kaqchikel, Tz'utujil and Pipiles. It is thought the Tolteca-Pipil had been influenced in turn by the Classic culture from Teotihuacán, a massive urban state northeast of the present Mexico City, which had its zenith in the seventh century AD. However, some experts say that there is no concrete evidence to suggest that the Pipiles migrated as early as AD 400 or that they were influenced by Teotihuacán. All in all, the cultural make-up of this corner of Guatemala may never be known.

Four main points of interest entice visitors to the area. Bilbao, El Baúl, Finca El Baúl and the Museo de Cultura Cotzumalguapa. The remnants at **Bilbao**, first re-discovered in 1860, are mainly buried beneath the sugar cane but monuments found above ground show pre-Maya influences. It is thought that the city was inhabited 1200 BC-AD 800. There are four large boulders – known as *Las Piedras* – in sugar-cane fields, which can be reached on foot from the tracks leading from the end of 4 Avenida in town. **El Baúl** is a Late Classic ceremonial centre, 6 km north of Santa Lucía, with two carved stone pieces to see; most of its monuments were built between AD 600 and 900. **Finca El Baúl** has a collection of sculptures and stelae gathered from the large area of the *finca* grounds. The **Museo de Cultura Cotzumalguapa** ① *Finca Las Ilusiones, Mon-Fri 0800-1600, Sat 0800-1200, US$1.30, less than 1 km east of town, ask the person in charge for the key,* displays numerous artefacts collected from the *finca* and a copy of the famous Bilbao Monument 21 from the cane fields.

Santa Lucía Cotzumalguapa to the Mexican border

Beyond Santa Lucía Cotzumalguapa is **Cocales**, where a good road north leads to Patulul and after 30 km, to Lake Atitlán at San Lucas Tolimán. The Pacific Highway continues through San Antonio Suchitepéquez to **Mazatenango** (where just beyond are the crossroads for Retalhuleu and Champerico) and on to Coatepeque and Ciudad Tecún Umán for the Mexican border. Mazatenango is the chief town of the Costa Grande zone. While not especially attractive, the Parque Central is very pleasant with many fine trees providing shade. There is a huge fiesta in the last week of February, when hotels are full and double their prices. At that time, beware of children carrying (and throwing) flour.

Retalhuleu and around

Retalhuleu, normally referred to as 'Reu' (pronounced 'Ray-oo') is the capital of the department. The entrance to the town is grand with a string of royal palms lining the route, known as Calzada Las Palmas. It serves a large number of coffee and sugar estates and much of its population is wealthy. The original colonial church of **San Antonio de Padua** is in the central plaza. Bordering the plaza to the east is the neoclassical **Palacio del Gobierno**, with a giant quetzal sculpture on top. The **Museo de Arqueología y Etnología** ① *Tue-Sat 0830-1300, 1400-1800, Sun 0900-1230, US$1.30, next to the palacio*, is small. Downstairs are exhibits of Maya ceramics.

If you fancy cooling off, near Reu are the **Parque Acuático Xocomil** ① *Km 180.5 on the road from Xela to Champerio, T7722-9400, www.irtra.org.gt, Thu-Sun 0900-1700, US$9.60.* Nearby is the enormous theme park with giant pyramids of **Xetulul** ① *T7722-9450, www.irtra.org.gt, Thu-Sun 100-1800, US$26.*

Abaj Takalik

① *Daily 0700-1700, US$3.25, guides are volunteers so tips are welcomed.*

One of the best ancient sites to visit outside El Petén is Abaj Takalik, a ruined city that lies, sweltering, on the southern plain. Its name means 'standing stone' in K'iche'. The site was discovered in 1888 by botanist Doctor Gustav Brühl. It is believed to have flourished in the late pre-Classic period of 300 BC to AD 250 strategically placed to control commerce between the highlands and the Pacific coast. There are some 239 monuments, which include 68 stelae, 32 altars and some 71 buildings, all set in peaceful surroundings. The environment is loved by birds and butterflies, including blue morphos, and by orchids, which flower magnificently between January and March. The main temple buildings are mostly up to 12 m high, suggesting an early date before techniques were available to build Tikal-sized structures.

Towards the Mexican border

The main road runs 21 km east off the Pacific Highway to **Coatepeque**, one of the richest coffee zones in the country. There is a bright, modern church in the leafy Plaza Central. The local fiesta takes place from 11-19 March. There are several hotels, *hospedajes* and restaurants. **Colomba**, an attractive typical village east of Coatepeque in the lowlands, has a basic *hospedaje*.

Routes to El Salvador

Three routes pass through Southern Guatemala to El Salvador. The main towns are busy but scruffy with little to attract the visitor. If travelling by international bus to El Salvador, see page 32.

Route 1 The Pan-American Highway: The first route heads directly south along the paved Pan-American Highway from Guatemala City (CA1) to the border at San Cristóbal Frontera. **Cuilapa**, the capital of Santa Rosa Department, is 65 km along the Highway. About 9 km beyond Los Esclavos is the El Molino junction. Beyond, just off the Pan-American Highway, is the village of **El Progreso**, dominated by the imposing Volcán Suchitán, at 2042 m, now part of the Parque Regional Volcán Suchitán run by La Fundación de la Naturaleza. There is accommodation. The town fiesta with horse racing is from 10-16 November. From El

Progreso, a good paved road goes north 43 km to Jalapa through open, mostly dry country, with volcanoes always in view. There are several crater lakes including **Laguna del Hoyo** near Monjas that are worth visiting. The higher ground is forested. Beyond Jutiapa and El Progreso the Pan-American Highway heads east and then south to Asunción Mita. Here there is a turning left to Lago de Güija. Before reaching the border at **San Cristóbal Frontera**, the Pan-American Highway dips and skirts the shores (right) of **Lago Atescatempa**, with several islands set in heavy forest.

Route 2 Via Jalpatagua: The second, quicker way of getting to San Salvador is to take a highway that cuts off right from the first route at El Molino junction, about 7 km beyond the Esclavos bridge. This cut-off goes through El Oratorio and Jalpatagua to the border at **Valle Nuevo**, continuing then to Ahuachapán and San Salvador.

Route 3 El Salvador (La) via the border at Ciudad Pedro de Alvarado: This coastal route goes from Escuintla to the border bridge over the Río Paz at La Hachadura (El Salvador). It takes two hours from Escuintla to the border. You pass **Auto Safari Chapín** ⓘ *Km 87.5, T2363-1105, Tue-Sun 0900-1700, US$5*, east of Escuintla, an improbable wildlife park, but busy at weekends and holidays. **Taxisco** is 18 km beyond and just off the road. It's a busy place, which has a white church with a curious hearts and holly design on the façade. To the east is Guazacapán, which merges into **Chiquimulilla**, 3 km to the north, the most important town of the area, with good-quality leather goods available. There is accommodation on offer. A side excursion can be made from Chiquimulilla up the winding CA 16 through coffee *fincas* and farmland. About 20 km along there is a turning to the left down a 2- to 3-km steep, narrow, dirt road that goes to **Laguna de Ixpaco**, an impressive, greenish-yellow lake that is 350 m in diameter. It is boiling in some places, emitting sulphurous fumes and set in dense forest. This trip can also be made by heading south off the Pan-American Highway after Cuilapa (just before Los Esclavos) towards Chiquimulilla on the CA 16, with old trees on either side, some with orchids in them, where you will reach the sign to Ixpaco, after 20 km. Thirty kilometres beyond on the Pacific Highway is **Ciudad Pedro de Alvarado** on the border.

Southern Guatemala listings

For Sleeping and Eating price codes and other relevant information, see pages 12-13.

🛏 Sleeping

Puerto San José, Chulamar and Iztapa *p108*

There are a number of *comedores* in town.

$$$$ Soleil Pacífico, Chulamar, T7879-3131, www.gruposoleil.com. Usual luxuries with day passes available.

$$$ Hotel y Turicentro Eden Pacific, Barrio El Laberinto, Puerto San José, T7881-1605. 17 a/c rooms with TV, private beach and pools.

$$-$ Hotel Club Sol y Playa Tropical, 1 Calle, 5-48, on the canal, Iztapa, T7881-4365. With pool, friendly staff and standard rooms with fans. Good food at restaurant.

Monterrico *p109*

Most hotels are fully booked by Sat midday and prices rise at weekends – book beforehand if arriving at the weekend.

$$ Hotel Pez de Oro, at the end of main strip to the east, T2368-3684, www.pezdeoro.com. 18 spacious bungalows attractively set around a swimming pool. All rooms have private bathroom, mosquito lamps, pretty bedside lights and fan. Some with a/c. Recommended.

$$ Hotel Restaurante Dulce y Salado, some way away from the main cluster of hotels and a 500-m hard walk east through sand if you are on foot, T5817-9046. The sea view and the uninterrupted view of the highland volcanoes behind is fantastic. Run by a friendly Italian couple, Fulvio and Graziella. Clean, nice rooms, with bath, fans and mosquito nets, set around a pool. Breakfast included, good Italian food.

$$ San Gregorio, Calle del Proyecto, behind El Kaimán, T2238-4690. 29 modern rooms with bath, fan and mosquito nets. There is a large part-shaded pool, a restaurant set around the pool. Non-guests can pay to use the pool.

$$-$ Café del Sol, 250 m west of the main drag next to **Eco Beach Place**, T5810-0821, www.cafe-del-sol.com. 13 rooms pleasant rooms. Rooms across the road in an annexe are much more spartan. There is a pleasant bar area and a restaurant.

$$-$ El Mangle, main strip, T5514-6517. Rooms with fans, bathrooms, and mosquito nets (some are a little dark), centred around a nice, clean pool, set a little back from the beach front. It's quieter than some of the others. Recommended.

$$-$ Johnny's Place, main strip. Equipped bungalows, rooms with bath, cheaper without, and a dorm (**$** per person). All windows have mosquito netting. Internet, table tennis, swimming pools, fishing and a restaurant with free coffee fill-ups. Recommended.

$ El Delfín, T5904-9167, eldelfin99@ yahoo.com. Bungalows, with mosquito nets, fans and private bathroom and rooms. Restaurant with vegetarian food. Organizes shuttles at any hour. Recommended.

$ Hotel y Restaurant Kaiman, on the beach side, T5617-9880, big bar ('1000 'til you're done' at the weekends) and restaurant. The rooms are very clean, with bath, fan, and mosquito nets. There are 2 pools for adults and children, but they're not in top shape. Discounts for longer stays.

Santa Lucía Cotzumalguapa *p109*

$$ Santiaguito, Pacific Hwy at Km 90.4, T7882-5435. A/c, TV and hot and cold water, pool and restaurant. Non-guests can use the pool for US$2.60.

$ Hospedaje La Reforma, a stone's throw from the park on 4 Av, 4-71. Lots of dark box rooms and dark shared showers. Clean.

$ Hotel El Camino, diagonally opposite Santiaguito across the highway at Km 90.5, T7882-5316. Rooms with bath, tepid water, fan, some rooms with a/c (more expensive). All have TV. Good restaurant.

Retalhuleu and around *p111*
$$ Astor, 5 Calle, 4-60, T7771-2559, hotelastor@intelnett.com. A colonial-style place with with 27 rooms, a/c, hot water, TV, set around a pretty courtyard where there's a pool and jacuzzi. Parking and restaurant. **Bar La Carreta** is inside the hotel. Non-guests can use the pool and jacuzzi here (nicer than the one at **Posada de Don José**) for a fee.

$$ La Colonia, 1.5 km to the north at Km 180.5, T7772-2048. Rooms with a/c and TV, pool, and good food.

$$ Posada de Don José, 5 Calle, 3-67, T7771-0180, posadadonjose@hotmail.com. Rooms with a/c and fan, TV. Also a very good restaurant serving such mouth-watering temptations as lobster sautéed in cognac. Restaurant and café are set beside the pool. Non-guests can use the pool for a small fee.

$$ Siboney, 5 km northwest of Reu in San Sebastián, Km 179, T7772-2174, www.hotelsiboney.com. Rooms are with bath, a/c and TV, set around pool. Try the *caldo de mariscos* or *paella* in the excellent restaurant. Non-guests can pay to use the pool.

🍴 Eating

Monterrico *p109*
Be careful especially with *ceviche*. There are lots of local *comedores* along Calle Principal, which leads to the beach.

$$ Restaurant Italiano, at the end of the main strip to the east, at **Hotel Pez de Oro**. Popular and consistently good. Recommended.

Santa Lucía Cotzumalguapa *p109*
$ Pastelería Italiana, Calzada 15 de Septiembre, 4-58. Open early for bakery.

Retalhuleu and around *p111*
$$ Restaurante La Luna, 5 Calle, 4-97, on the corner of the plaza. Good *típico* meals served.

$ El Patio, corner of 5 Calle, 4 Av. *Menú del día* and cheap breakfasts. Limited.

🎭 Entertainment

Monterrico *p109*
El Animal Desconocido, on beach close to **Johnny's Place**. Open from 2000 in the week.

⛰ Activities and tours

Monterrico *p109*
Tour operators
Those preferring to stay on land can rent horses for a jaunt on the beach. *Lancha* and turtle-searching tours are operated by a couple of agencies in town.

⊖ Transport

Guatemala City to the Pacific coast
p108
Bus To and from Guatemala City to **Amatitlán** (every 30 mins, US$0.50) from 0700-2045 from 14 Av, between 3 y 4 Calle, Zona 1, Guatemala City. From **Escuintla** (1½ hrs) to the capital from 8 Calle and 2 Av, Zona 1, near the corner of the plaza in Escuintla. Buses that have come along the Pacific Hwy and are going on to the capital pull up at the main bus terminal on 4 Av. From the terminal there are buses direct to **Antigua** every 30 mins, 1-1½ hrs, US$1.20. To **Taxisco** from Escuintla, every 30 mins, 0700-1700, 40 mins, for connections onwards (hourly) to La Avellana, for boats to Monterrico. Frequent buses to **Iztapa** with the last bus departing at 2030.

If you are changing in Escuintla for **Santa Lucía Cotzumalguapa** to the west, you need to take a left out of the bus terminal along the 4 Av up a slight incline towards the police fortress and take a left here on its corner, 9 Calle, through the market. Head for 3 blocks straight, passing the **Cinammon Pastelería y Panadería** on the right at 9 Calle and 2 Av. At the end here are buses heading to Santa Lucía and further west along the Pacific Hwy. It is a 5- to 10-min walk. Buses leave here every 5 mins. To **Santa Lucía Cotzumalguapa** (the bus *ayudantes* shout 'Santa'), 35 mins, US$1.20. On the return, buses pull up at the corner of the 8 Calle and 2 Av, where Guatemala City buses also pass.

Puerto San José, Chulamar and Iztapa *p108*
Bus Regular buses from the capital passing through **Escuintla**, 2-3 hrs. If you are heading further east by road from Iztapa along the coast to **Monterrico** (past loofah plantations), see below.

Monterrico *p109*
Bus and boat
There are 3 ways of getting to Monterrico: 2 by public transport, the 3rd by shuttle. The **first route** to Monterrico involves heading direct to the Pacific coast by taking a bus from the capital to **Puerto San José**, 1 hr, and changing for a bus to **Iztapa**. Or take a direct bus from Escuintla to Iztapa. Then cross river by the toll bridge to **Pueblo Viejo** for US$1.60 per vehicle (buses excluded), or US$0.80 per foot passenger, 5 mins. The buses now continue to Monterrico, about 25 km east, 1 hr. Buses run to and from Iztapa between 0600-1500, from the corner of main street and the road to Pueblo Viejo to the left, 3 blocks north of the beach, just past the Catholic church on the right.

The **second route** involves getting to Taxisco first and then La Avellana. There are also direct buses to La Avellana from Guatemala City, see page 30. If you are coming from Antigua, take a bus to **Escuintla** 1-1½ hrs. From there, there are regular departures to **Taxisco**, 40 mins. From Taxisco to La Avellana, buses leave hourly until 1800, US$1, 20 mins. If you take an international bus from Escuintla (45 mins), it will drop you off just past the

Taxisco town turn-off, just before a bridge with a slip road. Walk up the road (5 mins) and veer to the right where you'll see the bus stop for **La Avellana**. At La Avellana take the **motor boats** through mangrove swamps, 20-30 mins, US$0.60 for foot passengers, from 0630 and then hourly until 1800. The journey via this route from Antigua to Monterrico takes about 3¼ hrs if your connections are good. Return boats to La Avellana leave at 0330, 0530, 0700, 0800, 0900, 1030, 1200, 1300, 1430, 1600. Buses leave La Avellana for Taxisco hourly until 1800. Buses pull up near the **Banco Nor-Oriente** where numerous buses heading to Guatemala and Escuintla pass.

Shuttles Alternatively, numerous travel agencies in Antigua run shuttles, US$10-12 1 way. You can book a return shuttle journey in Monterrico by going to the language school on the road that leads to the dock. There are also mini buses operating from Monterrico to **Iztapa** and vice-versa.

Santa Lucía Cotzumalguapa *p109*
Bus Regular departures to the capital. Buses plying the Pacific Hwy also pass through, so if you are coming from Reu in the west or Escuintla in the east you can get off here.

Car If you are driving, there are a glut of 24-hr **Esso** and **Texaco** gas stations here. See under Guatemala City to the Pacific coast for catching transport from **Escuintla**.

Santa Lucía Cotzumalguapa to the Mexican border *p110*
Bus 5 a day **Cocales-Panajachel**, between 0600 and 1400, 2½ hrs. Frequent buses to **Mazatenango** from Guatemala City, US$5. To the border at **Ciudad Tecún Umán**, US$2.10, an irregular service with Fortaleza del Sur.

Retalhuleu and around *p111*
Bus Services along the Pacific Hwy to Mexico leave from the main bus terminal,

which is beyond the city limits at 5 Av 'A'. To **Coatepeque** (0600-1800), **Malacatán**, **Mazatenango** and **Champerico** (0500-1800). Buses also leave from here to **El Asintal**, for Abaj Takalik, 30 mins, every 30 mins from 0600-1830, last bus back to Reu 1800. Or catch them before that from the corner of 5 Av 'A' and the Esso gas station as they turn to head for the village. Leaving from a smaller terminal at 7 Av/10 Calle, there are regular buses to **Ciudad Tecún Umán**, **Talismán** and **Guatemala City** via the Pacific route, and to **Xela** (1¾ hrs, every hour 0500-1800).

Abaj Takalik *p111*
Bus Take a bus to El from **Retalhuleu** and walk the hot 4 km to the site entrance. Or, take any bus heading along the Pacific Hwy and get off at the **El Asintal** crossroads. Take a pickup from here to El Asintal; then a pickup from the town square to Abaj Takalik. As there are only *fincas* along this road, you will probably be on your own, in which case it is US$5 to the site or US$10 round trip, including waiting time. Bargain hard.

Taxi and tour A taxi from central plaza in Reu to the site and back including waiting time is US$13. Alternatively, take a tour from Xela.

Towards the Mexican border *p111*
Bus From Quetzaltenango to **Coatepeque**, catch any bus heading to Ciudad Tecún Umán from Reu.

Directory

Monterrico *p109*
Language school Proyecto Lingüístico Monterrico, http://monterrico-guatemala. com/spanish-school.htm. **Medical services** There is a clinic behind El Delfín open at weekends. **Post** Near Hotel Las Margaritas on the Calle Principal.

Santa Lucía Cotzumalguapa *p109*
Banks Banco G&T Continental, on the highway, accepts MasterCard. **Banco Industrial**, accepts Visa, 3 Av between 2 and 3 Calle. There's a **Bancared** Visa ATM on the plaza. **Telephone** Telgua, Cda 15 de Septiembre near the highway.

Retalhuleu and around *p111*
Banks There are plenty of banks in town taking Visa and MC. ATMs also. **Embassies and consulates** Mexico, inside the Posada de Don José. Mon-Fri 0700-1230, 1400-1800. **Medical services** Hospital Nacional de Retalhuleu, Blvd Centenario, 3 Av, Zona 2, 10 mins along the road to El Asintal, T7771-0116. **Post** On the plaza. **Telephone** 5 Calle, 4-18.

Guatemala City to the Caribbean

From the capital to the Caribbean, the main road passes through the Río Motagua Valley, punctuated by cacti and bordered by the Sierra de Las Minas mountains rising abruptly in the west. Dinosaur remains, the black Christ and the Maya ruins of Quiriguá can be found on or close to the highway. The banana port of Puerto Barrios is a large transport and commercial hub and jumping-off point for the Garífuna town of Lívingston. Trips down the lush gorge of the Río Dulce are a highlight; nearby are some great places to see and stay on its banks, as well as accommodation around Lago de Izabal.

Ins and outs
Getting there The Carretera al Atlántico, or Atlantic Highway, stretches from Guatemala City all the way to Puerto Barrios on the Caribbean coast in the department of Izabal. Most of the worthwhile places to visit are off this fast main road, along the Río Motagua valley, where cactus, bramble, willow and acacia grow. There are numerous buses plying the route. ▶▶ *See Transport, page 128.*

Along the Atlantic Highway
Before Teculután is **El Rancho** at Km 85, the jumping-off point for a trip north to Cobán (see page 134). There are a few places to stay here. Geologists will be interested in the **Motagua fault** near Santa Cruz, between Teculután and Río Hondo. Just before Río Hondo (Km 138), a paved road runs south towards Estanzuela. Shortly before this town you pass a monument on the right commemorating the 1976 earthquake, which activated a fault line that cut across the road. It can still be seen in the fields on either side of the road. The epicentre of this massive earthquake, which measured 7.5 on the Richter scale, and killed 23,000 people, was at **Los Amates**, 65 km further down the valley towards Puerto Barrios.

Estanzuela
Estanzuela is a small town fronting the highway. Its **Museo de Palaeontología, Arqueología y Geología** ① *daily 0800-1700, free*, displays the incredible reconstructed skeletal remains of a 4-m prehistoric giant sloth found in Zone 6, Guatemala City and a giant armadillo, among others. Take a minibus south from Río Hondo and ask to be dropped at the first entrance to the town on the right. Then walk right, into the town, and continue for 600 m to the museum, 10 minutes. When you reach the school, walk to the right and you will see the museum.

Chiquimula, Volcán de Ipala and the Honduran border
Chiquimula is a stop-off point for travellers who stay here on their way to or from Copán Ruinas, Honduras, if they can't make the connection in one day. The fiesta, which

includes bullfighting, is from 11-18 August. An alternative route to Chiquimula and Esquipulas is from the southeast corner of Guatemala City (Zona 10), where the Pan-American Highway heads towards the Salvadorean border. After a few kilometres there is a turning to **San José Pinula** (fiesta: 16-20 March). After San José, an unpaved branch road continues for 203 km through fine scenery to **Mataquescuintla**, **Jalapa** (several *hospedajes*, good bus connections; fiesta: 2-5 May), **San Pedro Pinula**, **San Luis Jilotepeque** and **Ipala** to Chiquimula. Southwest of Chiquimula, the extinct Volcán de Ipala (1650 m) can be visited. The crater lake is cool and good for swimming.

At **Vado Hondo**, 10 km south of Chiquimula on the road to Esquipulas, a smooth dirt road branches east to the Honduran border (48 km) and a further 11 km to the great Maya ruins of Copán. The border is 1 km after the village.

Esquipulas

Esquipulas is dominated by a large, white basilica, which attracts millions of pilgrims from across Central America to view the image of a Black Christ. The town has pulled out the stops for visitors, who, as well as a religious fill, will lack nothing in the way of food, drink and some of the best kitsch souvenirs on the market. If it's possible, stop at the mirador, 1 km from the town, for a spectacular view on the way in of the basilica, which sits at the end of a 1.5-km main avenue. The history of the famous *Cristo Negro* records that in 1735 Father Pedro Pardo de Figueroa, suffering from an incurable chronic illness, stood in front of the image to pray, and was cured. A few years later, after becoming Archbishop of Guatemala he ordered a new church to be built to house the sculpture. The **basilica** ⓘ *open until 2000*, was completed in 1758 and the *Cristo Negro* was transferred from the parish church shortly after that. Inside the basilica, the Black Christ is on a gold cross, elaborately engraved with vines and grapes. It was carved by Quirio Cataño in dark balsam wood in 1595. The image attracts over 1,000,000 visitors per year, some crawling on their hands and knees to pay homage. The main pilgrimage periods are 1-15 January (with 15 January being the busiest day), during Lent, Holy Week and 21-27 July.

Quiriguá

ⓘ *Daily 0730-1630, US$4. Take insect repellent. There are toilets, a restaurant, a museum and a jade store and you can store your luggage with the guards. There is no accommodation at the site (yet), but you can camp (see Sleeping). The site is reached by a paved road from the Atlantic Highway. The village of Quiriguá is about halfway between Zacapa and Puerto Barrios on the highway, and about 3 km from the entrance road to the ruins.*

The remarkable Late Classic ruins of Quiriguá include the tallest stelae found in the Maya world. The UNESCO World Heritage Site is small, with an excavated acropolis to see, but the highlight of a visit is the sight of the ornately carved tall stelae and the zoomorphic altars. The Maya here were very industrious, producing monuments every five years between AD 751 and 806, coinciding with the height of their prosperity and confident rule. The earliest recorded monument dates from AD 480.

It is believed that Quiriguá was an important trading post between Tikal and Copán, inhabited since the second century, but principally it was a ceremonial centre. The Kings of Quiriguá were involved in the rivalries, wars and changing alliances between Tikal, Copán and Calakmul. It rose to prominence in the middle of the eighth century, around the time of Cauac Sky who ascended to the throne in AD 724. Cauac Sky was appointed to the position by 18 Rabbit, powerful ruler of Copán (now in Honduras), and its surrounding settlements. It seems that he was fed up with being a subordinate under the domination of Copán, and during his reign, Quiriguá attacked Copán and captured 18 Rabbit. One of the stelae tells of the beheading of the Copán King in the plaza at Quiriguá as a sacrifice after the AD 738 battle. After this event 18 Rabbit disappears from the official chronicle and a 20-year hiatus follows in the historical record of Copán. Following this victory, Quiriguá became an independent kingdom and gained control of the Motagua Valley, enriching itself in the process. And, from AD 751, a monument was carved and erected every five years for the next 55 years. The tallest stelae at Quiriguá is **Stelae E**, which is 10.66 m high with another 2.5 m or so buried beneath. It is 1.52 m wide and weighs 65 tonnes. One of its dates corresponds with the enthronement of Cauac Sky, in AD 724, but it's thought to date from AD 771. All of the stelae, in parkland surrounded by ceiba trees and palms, have shelters, which makes photography difficult. Some monuments have been carved in the shape of animals, some mythical, all of symbolic importance to the Maya.

Thirteen kilometres from Quiriguá is the turn-off for **Mariscos** and Lago de Izabal (see page 123). A further 28 km on are the very hot twin towns of Bananera/Morales. From Bananera there are buses to Río Dulce, Puerto Barrios and the Petén.

Puerto Barrios

Puerto Barrios, on the Caribbean coast, is a hot and dusty port town, still a central banana point, but now largely superseded as a port by Santo Tomás. The launch to the Garífuna town of Lívingston leaves from the municipal dock here. While not an unpleasant town, it is not a destination in itself, but rather a launch pad to more beautiful and happening spots in Guatemala. It's also the departure point for the Honduran Caribbean. On the way into town, note the cemetery on the right-hand side, where you will pass a small Indian mausoleum with elephant carvings. During the 19th century, *culi* (coolies) of Hindu origin migrated from Jamaica to Guatemala to work on the plantations. The fiesta is 16-22 July.

Lívingston and around → *For listings, see pages 123-131.*

Lívingston, or La Buga, is populated mostly by Garífuna, who bring a colourful flavour to this corner of Guatemala. With its tropical sounds and smells, it is a good place to hang out for a few days, sitting on the dock of the bay, or larging it up with the locals, *punta*-style. *Coco pan* and *cocado* (a coconut, sugar and ginger *dulce*) and locally made jewellery are sold in the streets. The town is the centre of fishing and shrimping in the Bay of Amatique and only accessible by boat. It is nearly 23 km by sea from Puerto Barrios and there are regular daily boat runs that take 35 minutes in a fast *lancha*. The bulk of the town is up a small steep slope leading straight from the dock, which is at the mouth of the Río Dulce estuary. The other part of town is a linear spread along the river estuary, just north of the dock and then first left. The town is small and everything is within walking distance. The Caribbean beach is pretty dirty nearer the river estuary end, but a little further up the coast, it is cleaner, with palm trees and accommodation. Closer to the town are a couple of bars and weekend beach discos. The town's **Centro Cultural Garífuna-Q'eqchi'** is perched on a hillock, and has the best views in the whole of Lívingston. The town's fiestas are 24-31 December, in honour of the Virgen del Rosario, with dancing including the *punta*, and Garífuna Day, 26 November. The small but helpful **tourist office** ① *on the east side of the Parque Municipal, www.livingston.com.gt, daily 0600-1800*, with a café and exhibition space behind.

Around Lívingston

Northwest along the coastline towards the Río Sarstún, on the border with Belize (where manatee can be seen), is the **Río Blanco beach** (45 minutes by *lancha* from Lívingston), followed by **Playa Quehueche** (also spelt Keueche). Beyond Quehueche, about 6 km (1½ hours) from Lívingston, are **Los Siete Altares**, a set of small waterfalls and pools hidden in the greenery. They are at their best during the rainy season when the water cascades down to the sea. In the drier seasons much of the water is channelled down small, eroded grooves on large slabs of grey rock, where you can stretch out and enjoy the

Lívingston

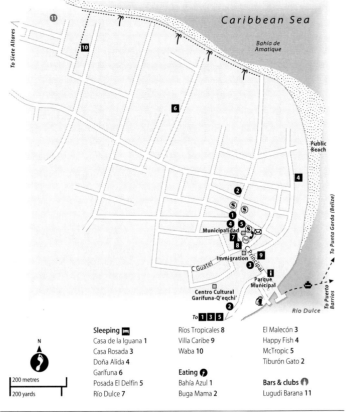

Sleeping 🛏
Casa de la Iguana **1**
Casa Rosada **3**
Doña Alida **4**
Garífuna **6**
Posada El Delfín **5**
Río Dulce **7**

Ríos Tropicales **8**
Villa Caribe **9**
Waba **10**

Eating 🍴
Bahía Azul **1**
Buga Mama **2**

El Malecón **3**
Happy Fish **4**
McTropic **5**
Tiburón Gato **2**

Bars & clubs 🍸
Lugudi Barana **11**

sun. Early *Tarzan* movies were filmed here. Don't stroll on the beach after dark and be careful of your belongings at the Siete Altares end. Police occasionally accompany tourists to the falls; check on arrival what the security situation is. Boats can be hired in Lívingston to visit beaches along the coast towards San Juan and the Río Sarstún.

For one of the best trips in Guatemala take a boat up the **Río Dulce** through the sheer-sided canyon towards El Golfete, where the river broadens. Trees and vegetation cling to the canyon walls, their roots plunging into the waters for a long drink below. The scenery here is gorgeous, especially in the mornings, when the waters are unshaken. Tours can be arranged from Lívingston for US$12. You can also paddle up the Río Dulce gorge on *cayucos*, which can be hired from some of the hotels in Lívingston.

The **Biotopo Chocón Machacas** ① *0700-1600, US$2.50 (private hire at US$125 is the only transport option)*, is one place where the elusive manatee (sea cow) hangs out, but you are unlikely to see him munching his way across the lake bottom, as he is very shy and retreats at the sound of a boat motor. (The manatee is an aquatic herbivore, which can be up to 4 m long when adult, and weigh more than 450 kg. It eats for six to eight hours daily and can consume more than 10% of its body weight in a 24-hour period.) Administered by CECON, the reserve is a mangrove zone, halfway between Río Dulce town and Lívingston, on the northern shore of **El Golfete** – an area where the Río Dulce broadens into a lake 5 km across. Four Q'eqchi' communities of 400 people live on land within the 6245-ha reserve. Within the reserve are carpets of water lilies, dragonflies, blue morpho butterflies, pelicans and cormorants. On land, spot army ants, crabs, mahogany trees and the *labios rojos* ('hot lips') flower.

Proyecto Ak' Tenamit ① *www.aktenamit.org*, meaning 'new village' in Q'eqchi', is 15 minutes upriver from Lívingston. It was set up to help 7000 Q'eqchi' Maya displaced by the civil war. Volunteers are needed for a minimum of a month's work (board and transport, and weekends off). A working knowledge of Spanish is required. There's also a shop and restaurant, with excursions, run by locally trained volunteer guides, and accommodation is available (see Sleeping). Near here is the **Río Tatín tributary** the wonderfully sited **Finca Tatín** and **Hotelito Perdido**, see Sleeping. **Reserva Ecológica Cerro San Gil**, with its natural pools, karstic caves and biostation, can be visited from here, or from Río Dulce. Contact FUNDAECO ① *www.fundaeco.org.gt*.

Punta de Manabique

Punta de Manabique is a fine, finger-shaped peninsula northeast of Puerto Barrios and just visible across the bay from Lívingston, coated in a beach of white sand on its eastern side, and by mangrove on the other. Travelling north to the point of the peninsula, you pass the Bahía de Graciosa, where dolphins frolic and manatees silently graze under the surface. In its virgin tropical forest live howler monkeys, parrots, snakes, pizote, tapirs and peccary and, on its beaches, turtles. There is a visitor centre, scientific station and a hotel. For more information contact the **Fundación Mario Dary** ① *www.guate.net/fundary manabique/fundacion.htm*, which operates conservation, health, education and ecotourism projects.

Lago de Izabal → *For listings, see pages 123-131.*

The vast Lago de Izabal narrows to form a neck at the town of Fronteras. Better known as Río Dulce, it is famed for its riverside setting and there are some beautiful places around the lake and river in which to stay. Just south of Río Dulce on the lake is the Castillo de San Felipe. On the northern shore of the lake is the town of El Estor, and on its southern shore the smaller town of **Mariscos**. Further east, beyond Río Dulce, the river broadens out to El Golfete, where there is the Biotopo Chacón Machacas, see above. It then narrows into one of the finest gorges in the world, and opens out at its estuary, with Lívingston at its head. This area can be wet in the rainy season, but it experiences a lull in July, known as the *canícula*.

Fronteras/Río Dulce and around

Río Dulce is a good place to stop and kick back for a couple of days. Allow yourself to be tempted to laze on a boat for the afternoon, walk in the nearby jungle, or eat and drink at one of several dockside restaurants. Río Dulce, www.mayaparadise.com, is 23 km upstream from Lívingston at the entrance to Lago de Izabal, is easily accessible from Puerto Barrios by road, and is the last major stop before the Petén. It's also a good place to collect information about the area stretching from El Estor to Lívingston.

On the shore of Lago de Izabal is **Casa Guatemala** ① *14 Calle, 10-63, Zona 1, Guatemala City, T2231-9408, www.casa-guatemala.org,* (also known as **Hotel Backpacker's**) an orphanage where you can work in exchange for basic accommodation and food. At the entrance to Lago de Izabal, 2 km upstream, is the old Spanish fort of **Castillo de San Felipe** ① *0800-1700, US$3.30.* The fortification was first built in 1643 to defend the coast against attacks from pirates; it has been well preserved and in lovely grounds; great views from the battlements. Between Río Dulce and El Estor is **Finca El Paraíso**, a hot waterfall with waters that plunge into a cool-water pool below.

El Estor and around

El Estor enjoys one of the most beautiful vistas in Guatemala. It is strung along the northwest shore of Lago de Izabal, backed by the Santa Cruz mountain range and facing the Sierra de las Minas. The lake is the largest in Guatemala at 717 sq km. It's a great place to relax, swim (down a nearby canyon), go fishing and spot manatee. Some businesses are expecting the new road to bring a surge of tourists visitors. For the next few years, you'll still have the place mostly to yourself. The town dates back to the days when the Europeans living in the Atlantic area got their provisions from a store situated at this spot, now the **Hotel Vista al Lago**. Briton Skinner and Dutchman Klee supplied the region from *el store* 1815-1850. Nickel-mining began just outside town in 1978, but was suspended at the **Exmibal plant** after the oil crisis of 1982, because the process depended on cheap supplies of energy.

You can hire a boat from Río Dulce to El Estor, passing near the hot waterfall, inland at Finca El Paraíso, which can be reached by a good trail in about 40 minutes. The Río Sauce cuts through the impressive **Cañón El Boquerón**, where you can swim with the current all the way down the canyon, which is brilliant fun. It's a deep canyon with lots of old man's beard hanging down, strange rock formations and otters and troops of howler monkeys whooping about. One of the locals will paddle you upstream for about 800 m (US$1).

Exploring the Río Zarco, closer to town, also makes for a good trip, with cold swimming. The **Refugio de Vida Silvestre Bocas del Polochic** (Bocas del Polochic Wildlife Reserve) is a 23,000-ha protected area on the western shores of the lake. Howler monkeys are commonly seen. In addition to over 350 bird species, there are iguanas, turtles and the chance of sighting crocodiles and manatees. The NGO **Defensores de la Naturaleza** ① *2 Calle and 5 Av, El Estor, T2440-8138 in the capital, www.defensores.org.gt*, has a research station at Selempim with bunk beds (**$** per person), food, showers and kitchen. Its a two- or three-hour boat ride from El Estor to Ensenada Los Lagartos. Tours available from town for US$30 for two people. Contact the office in El Estor or ask at a hotel about boat services.

Mariscos is on the southern shore of Lago de Izabal. The best reason to come here is the nearby Denny's Beach.

Guatemala to the Caribbean listings

For Sleeping and Eating price codes and other relevant information, see pages 12-13.

😊 Sleeping

Chiquimula *p117*

$$ Posada Perla del Oriente, 2 Calle between 11 and 12 Av, T7942-0014. All rooms with TV, some with a/c, parking, pool, quiet. Restaurant. Recommended.

$ Hernández, 3 Calle, 7-41, T7942-0708. Cheaper without bathroom, fans. TVs in rooms and a pool add to its attractions. Family-run, quiet and friendly.

$ Hotel Posada Don Adán, 8 Av, 4-30, T7942-0549. All rooms with private bathroom, a/c, TV. Run by a friendly, older couple.

$ Victoria, 2 Calle, 9-99, next to the bus station (so ask for rooms away from street), T7942-2732. All rooms have bath, cold water, fan, cable TV, towels, soap, shampoo, some rooms have a/c, drinking water provided, good restaurant, good value, will store luggage. Recommended.

Esquipulas *p118*

There are plenty of hotels, *hospedajes* and *comedores* all over town, especially in and around 11 Calle, also known as Doble Vía Quirio Cataño. Prices tend to double before the Jan feast day. They also rise at Easter and at weekends. When quiet, midweek, bargain for lower room prices.

$$$ Payaquí, 2 Av, 11-26, T7943-1143, www.hotelpayaqui.com. The 40 rooms are lovely, with *frigobars,* full of beers for the pilgrims to guzzle, hot-water showers and free drinking water, swimming pool, parking, restaurant, bar; credit cards, Honduran lempiras and US dollars accepted.

$$ Hotel Chortí, on the outskirts of town at Km 222, T7943-1148. All 20 rooms have a/c, TV, phone and *frigobar*. There are 2 pools, a restaurant and bar.

$$ Hotel El Peregrino, 2 Av, 11-94, T7943-1054. Clean rooms in the newer part.

$$ Hotel Villa Zonia, 10 Calle, 1-84, T7943-1133. Looks a little Alpine and very nice.

$$ Legendario, 3 Av and 9 Calle, T7943-1824, www.portahotels.com. Built around a garden with 2 pools, restaurant, parking.

$$ Los Angeles, 2 Av, 11-94, T7943-1254. Spotless rooms with bath, TV and fans, parking, friendly service. Recommended.

$ Hotel Calle Real, 3 Av, 10-00, T7943-2405. Rooms all with private bathroom, with TV, hot water, clean.

$ Pensión Casa Norman, 3 Av, 9-20, T7943-1503. Rooms with bath and hot water.

$ San Carlos 2, used to be known as **París**, 2 Av, 10-48, T7943-1276. 28 very clean rooms. Cheaper without bath, hot water showers.

Quiriguá p118

$$ Hotel Restaurante Santa Mónica, in Los Amates, 2 km south of Quiriguá village on the highway, T7947-3838. 17 rooms all with private bath, TV and fan, pool, restaurant. It is opposite a 24-hr Texaco gas station. Convenient if you don't want to walk the 10-15 mins into Quiriguá village for the 2 hotels there. There are a couple of shops, banks, and *comedores* here.

$ Hotel y Cafetería Edén, T7947-3281. Helpful, cheaper with shared bath, basement rooms are very dark, clean. The bus comes as far as here, which is where the back route walk to the ruins starts.

$ Hotel y Restaurante Royal, T7947-3639. With bath, cheaper without, clean, mosquito netting on all windows, good place to meet other travellers, restaurant.

Camping

You can camp in the car park of the ruins for free, but facilities are limited to toilets and very little running water. There is a restaurant and a project in the pipeline to open a hotel and waterpark opposite the entrance.

Puerto Barrios p119

$$ El Reformador, 16 Calle and 7 Av 159, T7948-5489. 51 rooms with bathroom, a/c and TV, some with a/c, restaurant, laundry service, clean, quiet, accepts credit cards. Recommended. The same management run the **Oguatour** travel agency across the road.

$$ Hotel Valle Tropical, 12 Calle between 5 and 6 Av, T7948-7084, vtropical@guate.net. 59 rooms with a/c and private bathroom, inviting pool and restaurant, parking. Non-guests can use pool (US$7).

$$-$ Hotel del Norte, at the end of 7 Calle, T7948-2116. A rickety, old wooden structure with sloping landings on the seafront side. All rooms have bath, some with a/c. There's a pool and expensive restaurant, but worth it for the English colonial tearoom atmosphere, no credit cards, but will change dollars.

$ Hotel Europa, 8 Av, between 8 and 9 Calle, T7948-1292. 23 clean rooms, with bath, fan, 2 more expensive rooms with a/c, good restaurant, parking, friendly Cuban management.

$ Hotel Lee, 5 Av, between 9 and 10 Calle, T7948-0830. Convenient for the bus station and dock, 24 rooms with fan and TV, with private bath, cheaper without. Noisy restaurant opposite. Friendly service.

$ Hotel Xelajú, 9 Calle, between 6 and 7 Av, T7948-0482. Rooms, with bath, cheaper without, fans, quiet, and ultra-clean shared bathrooms.

Lívingston p119, map p120

$$$ Hotel Villa Caribe, up Calle Principal from the dock on the right, T7947-0072, www.villasdeguatemala.com. All rooms have sea view and baths. There is a swimming pool (available to non-guests when the hotel is not busy for US$6.50), bar and a large restaurant overlooking the sea.

$$ Hotel Doña Alida, in a quiet location, T7947-0027, hotelalida@yahoo.es. Direct access to the beach, some rooms with great sea views and balconies, with restaurant.

$$ Posada El Delfín, T7947-0694, www.posadaeldelfin.com. Good-quality hotel, with over 20 attractive rooms with a/c and hot water.

$ Casa de la Iguana, T7947-0064. Very cool hostel with jungle hut style accommodation and hot showers. 3 private rooms, each with bath as well as dorms and space for tents and hammocks.

$ Casa Rosada, 600 m from the dock, T7947-0303, www.hotelcasarosada.com. A pastel-pink house set on the waterfront, 10 bungalows furnished with attractive hand-painted furniture. The room upstairs overlooks the bay. Meals are set for the day, ranging from pasta to delicious shrimps bathed in garlic. Reservations advisable.

$ Garífuna (see map), T7947-0183. 8 comfortable, ultra-clean rooms with private bath, laundry and internet. Recommended.

$ Hotel Río Dulce, main street, T7947-0764, An early 19th-century wooden building, with a seriously sloping landing on the 1st floor, a good place from which to watch life pass by. Try and get a room upstairs rather than behind the old building. Rooms with or without bathrooms. There is a restaurant on the ground floor with some tables directly on the street.

$ Hotel Ríos Tropicales, T7947-0158, www.mctropic.com. This place has some nice touches to distinguish it from the majority of other places in town, like terracotta-tiled floors. 11 rooms, with fans, 5 with private bath, book exchange and the **McTropic** restaurant up the road with internet and a tour operator.

$ Waba, Barrio Pueblo Nuevo, T7947-0193. Run by a friendly family offering upstairs rooms with a balcony and sea views. All rooms have private bath and are clean and cool, with fan. *Comida típica* is served at a little wooden restaurant (0700-2130) on site. Good value and recommended.

Around Lívingston *p120*
$ Centro Turístico Quehueche, 15 mins upriver from Lívingston, T254 1560, www.aktenamit.org; run by Ak'Tenamit Foundation, community-led project. Ecolodge wooden cabins with private bath, lovely jungle setting. Highly recommended.

$ Finca Tatín, Río Tatín tributary, with great dock space to hang out on, T5902-0831, www.fincatatin.centro america.com. It's B&B, whether you opt for a room with private bath, or a dorm bed. Tours available. Take a *lancha* from Lívingston (US$4) to get there.

$ Hotel Ecológico Salvador Gaviota, along the coast, towards Siete Altares, beyond **Hotel Ecológico Siete Altares**, T7947-0874, www.hotelecologicosalvador gaviota.com. Rooms are with shared bath, but the bungalows for 2 or 4 people have private bath. Rooms available for monthly rent. All set in lush surroundings. There is a bar and restaurant (0730-2200), and free

lancha service – ring beforehand. Tours available. The beach here is lovely, hummingbirds flit about and the owner Lisette is friendly. Highly recommended.

$ Hotelito Perdido, hideaway on the River Lampara, can be dropped off on the Lívingston–Río Dulce boat service, T5725-1576, www.hotelitoperdido.com. Quiet hideaway, with rustic, basic and clean accommodation. Food extra at around US$15 a day (no local alternatives available).

Camping
Biotopo Chocón Machacas, 400 m from the entrance, next to a pond, with grills for cooking on, and toilets, but no food or drink for sale.

Punta de Manabique *p121*
$ Eco-Hotel El Saraguate, www.guate.net/ fundarymanabique/saraguate.htm. Rooms and a restaurant run by Fundación Mario Dary.

Fronteras/Río Dulce and around *p122*
$$$ Catamaran Island Hotel, T7930-5494, www.catamaranisland.com. Finely decorated *cabañas*, 40 rooms set around the lake edge, an inviting pool, large restaurant with good food, *lancha* from Río Dulce, 10 mins downstream, or call for a pickup. Recommended.

$$$ Hotel La Ensenada, Km 275, in town 500 m to the right at the Shell station on road to Petén, T7930-5340. Riverside location, breakfast included, restaurant, pool, nice gardens, camping and campervan facilities.

$$ Hacienda Tijax, T7930-5505, www.tijax.com. 2 mins by *lancha* from the dock, jungle lodges and cabins (a/c costs extra); yacht moorings available. There is a beautiful jungle trail with canopy walkway, a rubber plantation, bird sanctuary, pool with whirlpool and jacuzzi, natural pools to swim in, horse riding, kayaking, sailing and rowboat hire and a medicine trail. Excellent food in the riverside bar and restaurant, tranquil and beautiful. Highly recommended.

$$-$ Bruno's, in town on the lake, a stone's throw from the where the buses stop, T7930-5721, www.mayaparadise.com/brunoe.htm. Best rooms overlook the lake, also dorms, camping, campervan parking, pool, restaurant. Non-guests can pay to use pool. The marina has 28 berths. Restaurant service is consistently not up to scratch.

$$-$ Tortugal Marina, T5306-6432, www.tortugal.com. 3 beautifully presented bungalows with gorgeous soft rugs on the floor and other types of accommodation. Plentiful hot water. There is a riverside restaurant and bar, pool table in a cool upstairs attic room with books, satellite TV, internet, phone and fax service. Very highly recommended.

$ Café Sol, in town 500 m north of the bridge on the road to Tikal, T7930-5143. Friendly, clean, fans, good-value rooms, cheaper without bath, TV costs a bit extra. Useful if you have to catch an early bus.

$ Hotel Backpacker's, in town by the bridge on the south bank of the river, T7930-5169, www.hotelbackpackers.com. Restaurant and bar, dorms with lockers, and private rooms with bathroom, internet and telephone service, profits go to **Casa Guatemala** (see page 122). Recommended.

$ La Cabaña del Viajero, 500 m from the castle, T7930-5062. Small place with pool, traditional *cabañas* as well as larger family-style *cabañas* with private bathroom and some cute little attic rooms as well.

El Estor and around *p122*

$$ Marisabela, 8 Av and 1 Calle on the waterfront, T7949-7215. Large rooms with tiled private bathrooms, some with TV, internet service.

$ Denny's Beach, T5398-0908, www.dennysbeach.com. With its gorgeous lakeside location, accessible by *lancha* from Río Dulce (minimum fee US$41), or free from Mariscos if you call ahead. Tours, wake boarding and horse riding arranged. Internet service. A remote and complete get away.

$ Hotel Vista al Lago, 6 Av, 1-13, T7949-7205. 21 clean rooms with private bath and fan. Ask for the lakeview rooms, where there is a pleasant wooden balcony on which to sit. Friendly owner Oscar Paz will take you fishing, and runs ecological and cultural tours.

$ Villela, 6 Av, 2-06, T7949-7214. 9 big rooms with bath, clean, some quite dark though. Flower-filled garden with chairs to sit out in. Recommended.

🍴 Eating

Chiquimula *p117*

$ Magic, corner of 8 Av and 3 Calle. A good place from which to watch the world go by, and most of what's on offer is seriously cheap. Sandwiches, *licuados* and burgers.

$ Pastelería Las Violetas, 7 Av, 4-80, and another near **Hotel Victoria**. An excellent cake shop with a fine spread, good-value sandwiches too, plus great cappuccino, and a/c. Next door is its bakery.

Esquipulas *p118*

There are plenty of restaurants, but prices are high for Guatemala.

$$$ La Hacienda, 2 Av, 10-20. Delicious barbecued chicken and steaks. Kids' menu available, breakfasts available. One of the smartest restaurants in town.

$$ Restaurante Payaquí, 2 Av, 11-26, inside the hotel of the same name. Specialities include turkey in *pipián*, also lunches and breakfasts. A poolside restaurant makes a pleasant change.

$ Café Pistachos, close to **Hotel Calle Real**. Clean, cheap snack bar with burgers, hotdogs, etc.

Puerto Barrios *p119*

$$$-$$ Restaurante Safari, at the north end of 5 Av and 1 Calle, overlooking the bay with views all around. Basically serving up oceans of fish, including whole fish, *ceviche* and fishburgers.

$$ La Fonda de Quique, an orange and white wooden building at 5 Av and corner of 12 Calle. Nicely a/c with handmade wooden furniture, serving lobster, fish and meats, plus snacks.

Lívingston p119, map p120

Fresh fish is available everywhere; ask for *tapado* in restaurants – a rich soup with various types of seafood, banana and coconut. Women sell *pan de coco* on the streets.

$$ Bahía Azul, Calle Principal. Excellent breakfasts, but dreadful coffee. Tables on the street as well as a dining-room. Specializes in salsas, *camarones* and *langosta*. There is a tourist service and the **Exotic Travel Agency**.

$$ Buga Mama, an excellent example of an innovative development project. Local Mayan young people staff this large restaurant located next to the water as part of their training with the Ak'Tenamit project (www.aktenamit.org). The food is OK, the service excellent, and a great spot too – well worth checking out.

$$ El Malecón, 50 m from the dock on the left. Serves *chapín* and Western-style breakfasts, seafood and chicken *fajitas*, all in a large, airy wooden dining area.

$$ Happy Fish, just along from the **Hotel Río Dulce**. A popular restaurant with internet café. Serves a truckload of fish (not quite so happy now) with good coffee. Occasional live music at weekends.

$$ Hotel Río Dulce, see Sleeping. The restaurant serves delicious Italian food prepared with panache. Recommended.

$ McTropic, opposite the **Hotel Río Dulce**. Street tables, great breakfasts, and cocktails. Good service and popular.

$ Rasta Mesa Restaurant, in Barrio Nevago, just past the cemetery, www.site.rasta mesa.com. Garífuna cultural centre and restaurant. Music, history, classes in cooking and drumming. Great place to hang out.

$ Tiburón Gato, far end of Calle Principal. A simple open-fronted place, serving a good range of fish, seafood and pasta; open for breakfasts too.

Fronteras/Río Dulce and around p122

There are restaurants in the hotels – **Bruno's** is a relaxing location – and a couple along the main road.

$$-$ Ranchón Mary, El Relleno, T7930-5103. Thatch-roofed waterfront deck with tables, serving delicious fish and seafood and ice-cold beer.

$$-$ Rosita's Restaurant, San Felipe de Lara, T5054-3541. Lovely waterfront location with open deck, overlooking the bridge, 5 mins by *lancha* from Río Dulce. Great seafood, nachos and home-made banana pie.

El Estor and around p122

$ Dorita. A *comedor* serving seafood, very good meals, excellent value and popular with the locals.

$ Marisabela, 8 Av and 1 Calle. Good and cheap spaghetti, as well as fish and chicken, with lake views.

$ Restaurant del Lago, west side of main square. Restaurant overlooking the main square. Popular with local dishes.

$ Restaurant Elsita, 2 blocks north of the market on 8 Av. This is a great people-watching place. There's a large menu and the food's good.

🎭 Entertainment

Puerto Barrios p119

The Container, just past the **Hotel del Norte** overlooking the sea. Open 0700-2300. An unusual bar constructed from the front half of an old ship equipped with portholes, and a number of banana containers from the massive banana businesses just up the road.

Mariscos de Izabal, one of the most popular spots in Puerto Barrios. A thatched bar that is mostly a drinking den but with tacos, tortillas and burgers served amid beating Latin rhythms. You can hang out until here 0100.

Lívingston *p119, map p120*
Lugudi Barana. Sun only, 1500-0100.
A disco that's also on the beach and
popular with visitors and locals.

⚙ Festivals and events

Lívingston *p119, map p120*
26 Nov Garífuna Day.
24-31 Dec In honour of the **Virgen
del Rosario**, with traditional dancing.

⛰ Activities and tours

Lívingston *p119, map p120*
Captain Eric, located at the Pitchi Mango
snack bar on the main street, T4265-5278.
Will arrange 1- to 2-day boat tours for groups
of up to 5 people to the surrounding region.
Exotic Travel Agency, in the **Bahía
Azul** restaurant, T7947-0133, www.blue
caribbeanbay.com.
Happy Fish, on the main road, T7947-0661,
www.happyfishresort.com.
    You can also contract any of the *lancheros*
at the dock to take you to Río Dulce, Playa
Blanca and Siete Altares.

Fronteras/Río Dulce *p122*
Sailing
Captain John Clark's sailing trips on his 46-ft
Polynesian catamaran, *Las Sirenas*, are highly
recommended. Food, taxes, snorkelling and
fishing gear, and windsurf boards included.
Contact **Aventuras Vacacionales SA**,
Antigua, www.sailing-diving-guatemala.com,
see page 48.
    Coastguard For emergencies, call Guarda
Costa on VHF channel 16, T4040-4971.

Tour operators
Atitrans Tours, on the little road heading to
the dockside. To **Finca Paraíso** for US$20.
Otiturs, opposite Tijax Express, T5219-4520.
Run by the friendly and helpful Otto Archila.
Offers a minibus service as well as tours to
local sites, internal flights and boat trips.

Tijax Express, opposite Atitrans, T7930-
5505, info@tijax.com. Agent for Hacienda
Tijax (over the river).
    Lancheros offer trips on the river and
on Lago de Izabal. They can be contacted
at the muelle principal, under the bridge.
Ask for Cesár Mendez, T5819-7436, or ask
at **Atitrans** for collection.

⊖ Transport

Estanzuela *p117*
Bus From **Guatemala City** to Zacapa, with
Rutas Orientales, 0430-1800, every 30 mins,
2¾-3 hrs. To **Esquipulas** with same service
that continues from Zacapa, US$6, 1½ hrs.

Chiquimula, Volcán de Ipala and
the Honduran border *p117*
Bus Take an early bus to **Ipala** from
Chiquimula; stay on the bus and ask the
driver to let you off at Aldea El Chaparroncito
(10 mins after Ipala). From here it's a 1½-hr
ascent, following red arrows every now and
then. Another ascent goes via Municipio
Agua Blanca. Take a minibus to **Agua Blanca**
from Ipala and get out at the small village of
El Sauce, where the trail starts. The last
bus from Ipala to Chiquimula is 1700.

Chiquimula
Bus There are 3 terminals in Chiquimula,
all within 50 m of each other. To **Guatemala
City**, Transportes Guerra and Rutas
Orientales, hourly, US$4, 3¼-3½ hrs, leave
from 11 Av between 1 and 2 Calle, as do
buses for **Puerto Barrios**, several companies,
every 30 mins, between 0300-1500, 4 hrs,
US$6.50. To **Quiriguá**, US$3.20, 1 hr 50 mins.
Take any Puerto Barrios-bound bus. On to
Río Dulce take the Barrios bus and get off
at La Ruidosa junction and change, or
change at Bananera/Morales. To **Flores** with
Transportes María Elena, 8 hrs, 0400, 0800,
1300. Buses to **Ipala** and **Jalapa** also leave
from here; 4 buses daily to Jalapa between
0500-1230, 4½ hrs, US$5.80; to Ipala, US$2.20.

Supplemented by minibuses 0600-1715 to Ipala. To **Zacapa**, 25 mins, from the terminal inside the market at 10 Av between 1 and 2 Calle. Same for those to **Esquipulas**, every 10 mins, US$2.70, until 1900. To and from **Cobán** via El Rancho (where a change must be made). Buses to **El Florido** (Honduras border) leave with **Transportes Vilma** from inside the market at 1 Calle, between 10 and 11 Av, T7942-2253, between 0530-1630, US$2.70, 1½ hrs. Buses return from the border at 0530, 0630 and then hourly 0700-1700.

Esquipulas *p118*

Bus Rutas Orientales. Leaving Esquipulas, 1 Av "A" and 11 Calle, T7943-1366, for **Guatemala City** every 30 mins from 0200-1700, 4½ hrs, US$8.50. To **Chiquimula** by minibus, every 30 mins, 0430-1830, US$1.40.

Quiriguá *p118*

Bus Emphasize to the bus driver if you want Quiriguá *pueblo* and not the *ruinas*. Countless travellers have found themselves left at the ruins and having to make a return journey to the village for accommodation.

To get to the **ruins** directly, take any bus heading along the highway towards Puerto Barrios and ask to be let off at the *ruinas*. At this ruins crossroads, take a pickup (very regular), 10 mins, US$0.50, or bus (much slower and less regular) to the ruins 4 km away. Last bus back to highway, 1700. You can walk, but take lots of water, as it's hot and dusty with little shade.

To get to the **village** of Quiriguá, 3 km south from the ruins entrance road, it is only a 10-min walk to the **Hotel Royal**. Keep to the paved road, round a left-hand bend, and it's 100 m up on the left. Or take a local bus heading from the highway into the village. The **Hotel Edén** is a further 5 mins on down the hill. There is a frequent daily bus service that runs a circular route between Los Amates, Quiriguá village and then on to the entrance road to the ruins. You can also walk through the banana plantations from Quiriguá village to the ruins as well. From **Hotel Royal** walk past the church towards the old train station and the **Hotel Edén**, and follow the tracks branching to the right, through the plantation to the ruins.

Puerto Barrios *p119*
Boat

It's a 10-min walk to the municipal dock at the end of Calle 12, from the **Litegua** bus station. Ferries *(barca)* leave for Lívingston at 1030 and 0500 (1½ hrs, US$2.50). *Lanchas* also leave when a minimum of 12 people are ready to go, 30 mins, US$3.80. The only scheduled *lanchas* leave at 0630, 0730, 0900 and 1100, and the last will leave, if there are enough people, at 1800. **Transportes El Chato**, 1 Av, between 10 and 11 Calle, T7948-5525, pichilingo2000@yahoo.com, also does trips from here to Punta de Manabique, and other places near and far.

To Belize *Lanchas* leave for **Punta Gorda** at 1000 with **Transportes El Chato**, address above, returning at 1400, 1 hr 20 mins, US$22. Also services with Requena to Punta Gorda at 1400, returning at 0900.

Bus

To **Guatemala City**, with **Litegua**, 6 Av between 9 and 10 Calle, T7948-1002, www.litegua.com. 18 a day, 5 hrs, US$11-7.50. Bus to **El Rancho** (turn-off for Biotopo del Quetzal and Cobán), 4 hrs, take any bus to Guatemala City. To **Quiriguá**, 2 hrs, take any capital-bound bus. To **Chiquimula**, operated by **Carmencita**, 4 hrs. Alternatively, catch a bus to Guatemala City, getting off at Río Hondo, and catch a *colectivo* or any bus heading to Chiquimula. For **Río Dulce**, take any bus heading for Guatemala City and change at **La Ruidosa** (15 mins). For minibuses to **Entre Ríos**, for the El Cinchado border crossing to **Honduras** (**Corinto**), with connections to **Omoa**, **Puerto Cortés** and **La Ceiba**.

Lívingston *p119, map p120*
Boat

Ferry to **Puerto Barrios** to (22.5 km), 1½ hrs, US$1.60 at 0500 and 1400 Mon-Sat. Private *lanchas* taking 16-25 people also sail this route, 30 mins, US$4. They leave at 0630 and 0730 each day and at 0900 and 1100 Mon-Sat to Puerto Barrios and then when full. Lívingston to **Río Dulce**, with short stops at **Aguas Calientes** and the **Biotopo Chacón Machacas**, US$15.50 1 way. *Lanchas* definitely leave at 0900 and 1430 for **Río Dulce**, but these make no stops. To **Honduras** (Omoa, Puerto Cortés, La Ceiba), *lanchas* can be organized at the dock or through tour operators, see above. To **Belize** (Punta Gorda, Placencia, Cayos Zapotillos), check with tour operators, see above, about boats to Belize. Anyone who takes you must have a manifest with passengers' names, stamped and signed at the immigration office. On Tue and Fri fast *lanchas* make the trip to Punta Gorda (US$22). Enquire at the dock and negotiate a fare with the *lanchero* association. Boats to Placencia and the Zapotilla cayes can also be arranged.

Fronteras/Río Dulce and around *p122*
Boat

Lanchas colectivas leave for **Lívingston** at 0900 and 1300, US$15.50. Private *lanchas* can be arranged at the dock to any of the river or lakeside hotels.

Bus

Local To get to **Castillo de San Felipe**, take a boat from Río Dulce, or *camioneta* from the corner of the main road to Tikal, and the first turning left after the bridge by **Pollandia**, 5 mins, or a 5-km walk. From Río Dulce to **Finca El Paraíso**, take the same road, 45 mins, US$1.70. Buses to Río Dulce pass the *finca* between 40 and 50 mins past the hour. To **El Estor**, from the same Pollandia turn-off, US$2.50, 1½ hrs on a paved road, 0500-1600, hourly, returning 0500-1600. To **Puerto**

Barrios, take any bus to **La Ruidosa** and change, 35 mins to junction then a further 35 mins to Puerto Barrios.

Long-distance To **Guatemala City** and **Flores**: through buses stop at Río Dulce. To **Guatemala City** with Litegua, T7930-5251, www.litegua.com, 7 a day between 0300 and 1515, US$7.54, 6 hrs. **Fuente del Norte**, T5692-1988, 23 services daily, US$6.30. Luxury service 1300, 1700 and 2400, US$13. **Línea Dorada**, at 1300, luxury service, 5 hrs, US$13. To **Flores** from 0630-0300, 25 buses daily, 4½ hrs with **Fuente del Norte**, US$8. Luxury service, 1430, US$13. This bus also stops at **Finca Ixobel** and **Poptún**, US$3.90. **Línea Dorada**, to Flores, 1500, 3 hrs, luxury service with a/c, TV and snacks, US$13, and on to **Melchor de Mencos** for Belize. **Fuente del Norte**, also to **Melchor de Mencos**, at 1300, 2130 and 2330, 6 hrs, US$12.50. Also to, **Sayaxché** at 2200 and one to **Naranjo** at 2100.

Shuttles Atitrans, T7930-5111, www.atitrans.com, runs shuttles to **Antigua**, **Flores**, **Copán Ruinas** and **Guatemala City**.

El Estor and around *p122*
Bus The ferry from Mariscos no longer runs, but a private *lancha* can be contracted.

To **Río Dulce**, 0500-1600, hourly, 1 hr, US$2.20. Direct bus to **Cobán**, at 1300, 7 hrs, US$5.60. Also via either Panzós and Tactic, or Cahabón and Lanquín, see page 141. For the **Cañón El Boquerón**, take the Río Dulce bus and ask to be dropped at the entrance. Or hire a bike from town (8 km) or a taxi, US$6.50, including waiting time.

To **Cobán**, with Transportes Valenciana, 1200, 0200, 0400 and 0800, 8 long and dusty hrs, with no proper stop. To **Guatemala City**, 0100 direct, via Río Dulce, 7 hrs, US$6.30, or go to Río Dulce and catch one. At 2400 and 0300 via Río Polochic Valley. For **Santa Elena, Petén** take a bus to Río Dulce and pick on up from there.

Chiquimula *p117*

Banks There are several banks accepting MasterCard and Visa, and ATMs. **Post** Close to the bus terminal inside the market. **Telephone** Office on the plaza.

Esquipulas *p118*

Banks There are a number of banks and ATMs in town close to the park, Visa and MasterCard accepted. There are money changers in the centre if you need *lempiras*. Better rates than at the borders. **Post** End of 6 Av, 2-43.

Puerto Barrios *p119*

Banks Banco G&T Continental, 7 Calle and 6 Av, with ATMs. TCs. **Banco Industrial**, 7 Av, 7-30, 24-hr Visa ATM and cash on Visa cards. **Immigration** Corner of 12 Calle and 3 Av, open 24 hrs. **Internet** A couple of places in town. **Post** Corner of 6 Calle and 6 Av. **Telephone** Telgua, corner of 10 Calle and 8 Av.

Lívingston *p119, map p120*

Banks Banco Reformador, cash advance on Visa and MasterCard, TCs and cash changed. Has a 24-hr Visa-only ATM. There is also a **Banrural**. Some hotels will change cash, including **Casa Rosada**.

Immigration Calle Principal, opposite Hotel Villa Caribe, T7947-0240. Just knock if the door is shut. **Internet** There are a couple of places in town, including Café Buga Net, opposite Buga Mama, daily 0730-2100, US$0.80 per hr. **Gaby's** in Barrio Marcos Sánchez Díaz is open 0900-2100 daily and charges US$1.25 an hour. **Laundry** Lavandería Doña Chila, opposite Casa Rosada. **Language schools** Livingston Spanish School, T5715-4604, www.livingstonspanish school.org. 1-2-1 classes, 20 hrs a week, US$95 a week including food and lodging. **Post** Next to Telgua, behind the Municipalidad, take the small road to the right. **Telephone** Telgua, behind the Municipalidad, 0800-1800.

Fronteras/Río Dulce and around *p122*

Banks There are 2 banks: Visa, TCs and cash only. ATMS available. **Internet** Captain Nemo's Communications behind Bruno's, and phone call service and **Tijax Express**. **Post** Near the banks.

El Estor *p122*

Banks Banco Industrial and Banrural have ATMs. **Internet** Xbox 360 open 0800-2100, Mon-Sat. Good machines with a/c keeping machines and people cool. **Post** In the park.

The Verapaces

Propped up on a massive limestone table eroded over thousands of years, the plateau of the Verapaz region is riddled with caves, underground tunnels, stalagtites and stalagmites. Cavernous labyrinths used by the Maya for worship, in their belief that caves are the entrances to the underworld, are also now visited by travellers who marvel at the natural interior design of these subterranean spaces. Nature has performed its work above ground too. At Semuc Champey, pools of tranquil, turquoise-green water span a monumental limestone bridge; beneath the bridge a river thunders violently through. The quetzal reserve also provides the opportunity to witness a feather flash of red or green of the elusive bird, and dead insects provide curious interest in Rabinal, where their body parts end up on ornamental gourds. The centre of this region – the imperial city of Cobán – provides respite for the traveller with a clutch of museums honouring the Maya, coffee and orchid, and a fantastic entertainment spectacle at the end of July with a whirlwind of traditional dances and a Maya beauty contest.

Ins and outs

The principal road entrance to the Verapaces leaves the Atlantic Highway at El Rancho heading up to Cobán. This junction is one hour from Guatemala City. ▸▸ *See Transport, page 140.*

Background

Before the Spanish conquest of the region, Las Verapaces had a notorious reputation – it was known as Tezulutlán (land of war) for its aggressive warlike residents, who fought repeated battles with their neighbours and rivals, the K'iche' Maya. These warring locals were not going to be a pushover for the Spanish conquerors and they strongly resisted when their land was invaded. The Spanish eventually retreated and the weapon replaced with the cross. Thus, Carlos V of Spain gave the area the title of Verdadera Paz (true peace) in 1548. The region's modern history saw it converted into a massive coffee- and cardamom-growing region. German coffee *fincas* were established from the 1830s until the Second World War, when the Germans were invited over to plough the earth by the Guatemalan government. Many of the *fincas* were expropriated during the war, but some were saved from this fate by naming a Guatemalan as the owner of the property. The area still produces some of Guatemala's finest coffee – served up with some of the finest cakes! The Germans also introduced cardamom to the Verapaces, when a *finquero* requested some seeds for use in biscuits. Guatemala is now the world's largest producer of cardamom.

Baja Verapaz → *For listings, see pages 138-142.*

The small region of Baja Verapaz is made up of a couple of Achi'-Maya speaking towns, namely Salamá, Rabinal, San Jerónimo and Cubulco. The department is known for the quetzal reserve, the large Dominican *finca* and aqueduct, and the weird decorative technique of the crafts in Rabinal.

Sierra de las Minas Biosphere Reserve
ⓘ *To visit, get a permit in San Augustín from the office of La Fundación de Defensores de la Naturaleza, Barrio San Sebastián, 1 block before the Municipalidad, T7936-0681, ctot@ defensores.org.gt, www.defensores.org.gt. The contact is César Tot. Alternatively, contact the Fundación offices in Santa Elena, Petén, at 5 Calle, 3 Av "A", Zona 2, T7926-3095, lacandon@ defensores.org.gt, or in the capital at 7 Av, 7-09, Zona 13, T2440-8138.*

Just north of El Rancho, in the Department of El Progreso, is **San Agustín Acasaguastlán**, an entrance for the Sierra de las Minas Biosphere Reserve, one of Guatemala's largest conservation areas with peaks topping 3000 m and home to the quetzal, harpy eagle and peregrine falcon, puma, jaguar, spider monkey, howler monkey, tapir and pizote.

Biotopo del Quetzal
ⓘ *Daily 0700-1600, US$2.60, parking, disabled entrance. Run by Centro de Estudios Conservacionistas (CECON), Av Reforma, 0-63, Zona 10, Guatemala City, T2331-0904, cecon@usac.edu.gt.*

The Biotopo del Quetzal, or **Biosphere Mario Dary Rivera**, is between Cobán and Guatemala City at Km 160.5, 4 km south of Purulhá and 53 km from Cobán. There are two trails. Increasing numbers of quetzals have been reported in the Biotopo, but they are still very elusive. Ask for advice from the rangers. The area around the Biotopo has been protected as a Corredor Biológico Bosque Nuboso, with numerous privately run reserves and restaurants by the roadside offering birdwatching trails, waterfalls, natural swimming holes and caves. For more information, see www.bosquenuboso.com.gt.

Salamá, Rabinal and Cubulco
Just before Salamá is **San Jerónimo**, where there is a Dominican church and convent, from where friars tended vineyards, exported wine and cultivated sugar. There is an old sugar mill (*trapiche*) on display at the *finca* and a huge aqueduct of 124 arches to transport water to the sugar cane fields and the town. Salamá sits in a valley with a colonial cathedral, containing carved gilt altarpieces as its centrepiece. The town also has one of a few remaining *Templos de Minerva* in the country, built in 1916. Behind the Calvario church is the hill Cerro de la Santa Cruz, from where a view of the valley can be seen. Market day is Monday and is worth a visit. The village of **Rabinal** was founded in 1537 by Fray Bartolomé de las Casas. It has a 16th-century church, and a busy Sunday market, where lacquered gourds, beautiful *huípiles* and embroidered napkins are sold. The glossy lacquer of the gourd is made from the body oil of a farmed scaly insect called the *niij*. The male *niij* is boiled in water to release its oil, which is then mixed with soot powder to create the lacquer. The **Museo Rabinal Achí** ⓘ *2 Calle y 4 Av, Zona 3, T5311-1536, museoachi@hotmail.com*, displays historical exhibits and has produced bilingual books about the Achí culture. West of Rabinal, set amid maize fields and peach trees, Cubulco is

known for its tradition of performing the pole dance, *Palo Volador*, which takes place every 20-25 July. Men, attached by rope, have to leap from the top of the pole and spiral down, accompanied by marimba music. There are three basic *hospedajes* in town.

Alta Verapaz → *For listings, see pages 138-142.*

The region of Alta Verapaz is based on a gigantic mountain, Sierra de Chamá. Dinosaurs roamed the area more than 65 million years ago before it was engulfed by sea. It later emerged, covered with limestone rock, which over millions of years has left the area riddled with caves, and dotted with small hills. In the far northwest of the department are the mystical, emerald-green waters of **Laguna Lachuá**.

Santa Cruz Verapaz and around

Santa Cruz Verapaz has a fine white 16th-century church with a fiesta between 1-4 May when you can see the wonderful Danza de los Guacamayos (scarlet macaws). This **Poqomchi' Maya** village is 15 km northwest of Tactic, at the junction with the road to Uspantán. To get there, take the San Cristóbal Verapaz bus, 25 minutes, or take a bus heading to the capital, get off at the junction and walk 200 m into town. The local fiestas are 15, 20 January, 21-26 July with the *Palo Volador*. The devil-burning dance can be seen on 8 December. Six kilometres west towards Uspantán is **San Cristóbal Verapaz**, which has a large, white, colonial church. From the church, a 1-km long, straight, road (Calle del Calvario) slopes down and then curves upwards to a hilltop **Calvario Church**. At Easter, the whole road is carpeted in flowers that rival those on display in Antigua at this time of year. There is **Museo Katinamit** ⓘ *T7950-4039, cecep@intelnet. net.gt, Mon-Fri 0900-1200, 1500-1700,* run by the Centro Comunitario Educativo Poqomchi', dedicated to the preservation and learning of the Poqomchi' culture.

Cobán and around → *For listings, see pages 138-142. Altitude: 1320 m.*

The cathedral and centre of the Imperial City of Cobán (www.cobanav.net), is perched on a long, thin plateau with exceptionally steep roads climbing down from the plaza. To the south the roads are filled with the odd, well-preserved colonial building and a coffee *finca*. There is year-round soft rainfall, known as *chipi-chipi*, which is a godsend to the coffee and cardamom plants growing nearby. Most visitors use the city as a base for visiting sights in the surrounding area, trips to Semuc Champey, Languin and as a stepping off point for rafting trips on the Río Cahabón. English is spoken at the **city tourist office** ⓘ *Parque Central*, where they have lots of information and can help organize tours. **INGUAT office** ⓘ *7 Av 1-17, in Los Arcos shopping centre, T7951-0216, Mon-Fri 0800-1600, Sat 0900-1300,* is very helpful with leaflets and maps on the whole Verapaz region. For online information on northern Alta Verapaz and the southern Petén, check www.puertamundomaya.com.

Sights

The **cathedral** is on the east side of the Parque Central and dates from the middle of the 16th century. The chapel of **El Calvario**, in the northwest, has its original façade still intact. On the way up to the church are altars used by worshippers who freely blend Maya and

Roman Catholic beliefs. Its worth climbing the 142 steps to get a bird's-eye view of Cobán. The **Museo El Príncipe Maya** ① *6 Av, 4-26, Zona 3, Mon-Sat 0900-1300, 1400-1800, US$1.30*, is a private museum of pre-Columbian artefacts. The **Parque Nacional Las Victorias** ① *just west of El Calvario, daily 0700-1800, US$0.80*, has two little lagoons in its 84 ha. There are paths and you can picnic and camp, loos but no showers, but check with the tourist office about safety before going. The daily market is near the bus terminal. Starbucks coffee fans can check out where their mug of the old bean comes from – direct from **Finca Santa Margarita** ① *on the edge of town, 3 Calle, 4-12, Zona 2, T7951-3067, Mon-Fri 0800-1230, 1330-1700, Sat 0800-1200, 45-min tour with English/Spanish-speaking guides, US$2.50*. Don't miss a visit to the flower-filled world of **Vivero Verapaz** ① *2.5 km southwest of town, 40-min walk, or taxi ride, 0900-1200, 1400-1700 daily, US$1.30; US$1.30 for guided tour*, an orchid farm with more than 23,000 specimens, mostly flowering from December to February – the best time to go – with the majority flowering in January.

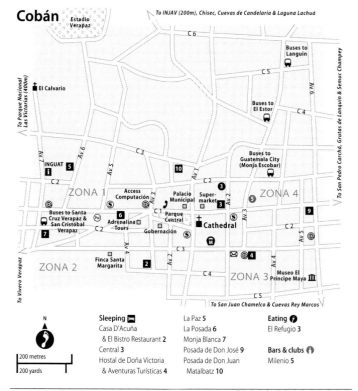

Cobán

To INJAV (200m), Chisec, Cuevas de Candelaria & Laguna Lachuá

Estadio Verapaz

To Parque Nacional Las Victorias (400m)

El Calvario

Buses to Lanquín

To San Pedro Carchá, Grutas de Lanquín & Semuc Champey

Buses to El Estor

Buses to Guatemala City (Monja Escobar)

INGUAT **5**

ZONA 1

Access Computación

Palacio Municipal

Super-market

ZONA 4

Buses to Santa Cruz Verapaz & San Cristóbal Verapaz

Adrenalina Tours

Parque Central

Gobernación

Cathedral

7

Finca Santa Margarita

ZONA 2

2

10

3

3

9

ZONA 3

Museo El Príncipe Maya

To Vivero Verapaz

To San Juan Chamelco & Cuevas Rey Marcos

N

200 metres
200 yards

Sleeping
Casa D'Acuña
& El Bistro Restaurant **2**
Central **3**
Hostal de Doña Victoria
& Aventuras Turísticas **4**

La Paz **5**
La Posada **6**
Monja Blanca **7**
Posada de Don José **9**
Posada de Don Juan
Matalbatz **10**

Eating
El Refugio **3**

Bars & clubs
Milenio **5**

Around Cobán

Southeast of Cobán (8 km) is **San Juan Chamelco** with an old colonial church. A one-hour walk from here is **Aldea Chajaneb** (see Sleeping). Along this road are the caves of **Grutas Rey Marcos** ① *US$1.30*, and **Balneario Cecilinda** ① *0800-1700*. **San Pedro Carchá** is 5 km east of Cobán on the main road and used to be famous for its pottery, textiles, wooden masks and silver, but only the pottery and silver are available now. The local food speciality here is *kaq Ik*, a turkey broth.

Lanquín and Semuc Champey → *For listings, see pages 138-142.*

Lanquín is surrounded by mountainous scenery reminiscent of an Alpine landscape. It nestles in the bottom of a valley, where a river runs. With this mountain ambience, caves and the clear water pools at Semuc Champey, it is worth kicking back for a few days and inhaling the high altitude air. Lanquín is 56 km east of Cobán, 10 km from the Pajal junction. Just before the town are the **Grutas de Lanquín** ① *0800-1600, US$3, 30-min walk from town*. The caves are lit for 200 m and strange stalactite shapes are given names, but it's worth taking a torch. The cave, whose ceiling hangs with thousands of stalactites, is dangerously slippery from guano mud, although handrails will help you out. The sight of the bats flying out at dusk is impressive. Outside the cave you can swim in the river and camp for free.

From Lanquín you can visit the natural bridge of **Semuc Champey** ① *0600-1800, US$6, parking available*, a liquid paradise stretching 60 m across the Cahabón Gorge. The limestone bridge is covered in stepped, glowing blue and green water pools, that span the length and breadth of it. Upstream you can see the water being channelled under the bridge. As it thunders through, it is spectacular. At its voluminous exit you can climb down from the bridge and see it cascading. You can swim in all the pools and little hot flows pour into some of them. Tours of Semuc Champey from Cobán cost around US$31.

Parque Nacional Laguna Lachuá

① *T5704 1509 to hire a guide for the day, US$4, main entrance, US$5.20, Mon-Sat 0900-1700.* Near **Playa Grande**, northwest of Cobán, is Parque Nacional Laguna Lachuá. The deep velvet-green lake, formed by a meteor impact, is 5 sq km and 220 m deep in places. It is surrounded by virtually unspoilt dense jungle, and the chances of seeing wildlife at dawn and dusk are high. There is a guided nature trail and camping and a basic guesthouse. In this area is the **Río Ikbolay**, a green river that runs underground through caves. When it emerges the other side it is blue. The river has changed its course over time leaving some of its run-through caves empty, making it possible to walk through them. The **Proyecto Ecológico Quetzal**, see page 140, runs jungle hikes in this area.

North of Cobán and southern Petén crossroads → *For listings, see pages 138-142.*

About 100 km northeast of Cobán is **Sebol**, reached via **Chisec** (www.visitchisec.com with information on the Grutas de Candelaria and Laguna Lachuá, see above) and unappealing **Raxrujá**. From here roads go north to Sayaxché and east to Modesto Méndez via Fray Bartolomé de las Casas. West of Raxrujá are the **Grutas de Candelaria** ① *US$5.35 including a guided tour*, an extensive cavern system with stalagmites. Tubing is available. Take the road to Raxrujá and look for the Candelaria Camposanto village at Km 310 between Chisec and Raxrujá or look for a sign saying 'Escuela de Autogestión Muqbilbe' and enter here to get to the caves and eco-hotel. Camping is possible. Both points of access offer activities for visitors. North of Raxrujá is the Maya site of **Cancuén** ① *www.puertamundomaya.com, ask in Cobán about tours*, reached by *lancha* in 30 minutes (US$40 for one to 12 people), from the village of La Unión (camping and meals are available at the site). Ten kilometres east of Sebol, and 15 minutes by bus, is **Fray Bartolomé de las Casas**, a town that is just a stop-off for travellers on the long run between Poptún and Cobán or Sayaxché. A road (that is nearly all tarmacked) links Fray Bartolomé de las Casas, Sebol and Sayaxché via Raxrujá. The scenery is beautiful with luscious palms, solitary sheer-sided hills and thatched-roofed homes.

The Verapaces listings

For Sleeping and Eating price codes and other relevant information, see pages 12-13.

⊜ Sleeping

Sierra de las Minas *p133*
$$ La Cabaña de Los Albores, Chilascó.
A 130-m-high waterfall, el salto de Chilascó, is near this ecotourism project with 2 cabins and 8 beds with shared hot water showers.

Biotopo del Quetzal *p133*
$$ Posada Montaña del Quetzal, at Km 156, www.hposadaquetzal.com. Bungalows or rooms with private bathrooms, hot water, café, bar, swimming pool and gardens.
$$ Ram Tzul, Km 185.5, T5908-4066, http://m-y-c.com.ar/ramtzul. Lovely bedrooms in wooden *cabañas*.
Dozens of excursions can be arranged.
$ Hospedaje Ranchitos del Quetzal, Km 160.8, near the Biotopo entrance, T7823-5860. Clean rooms with shared or private bathrooms, hot water, *comedor*.

Salamá, Rabinal and Cubulco *p133*
$ Posada San Pablo, 3 Av, 1-50, T7938-8025, Rabinal. Clean and friendly, will do laundry, but hard beds.
$ San Ignacio, 4 Calle "A", 7-09, Salamá, T7940-1797. Behind the Telgua building, with bath and TV, clean and friendly.

Santa Cruz Verapaz and around *p134*
$$ Hotel Park, Km 196, on the main road south of the junction to the Poqomchi' Maya village, Santa Cruz, Verapaz, T7952-0807, www.parkhotelresort.com. Rooms of varying prices with TV, restaurant, bar, gym and excellent gardens.
$ Eco Hotel Chi' Ixim, Km 182.5, just beyond Tactic, T7953-9198. Rooms with private bath, hot water and fireplaces, restaurant.
$ Hotel El Portón Real, 4 Av, 1-44, Zona 1, Santa Cruz Verapaz, T7950-4604. Dreary from

the outside, but inside this hotel is lovely with lots of wood furnishings. It's run by a very friendly *señora*. Rooms with bath, cheaper without, hot water and free drinking water. The hotel closes its doors at 2130.

Cobán *p134, map p135*
Accommodation is extremely hard to find on the Fri and Sat of **Rabin Ajau** (last week of Jul) and in Aug. For Rabin Ajau you need to be in town a few days beforehand to secure a room, or ring and reserve.
$$ Hotel Posada de Don Juan Matalbatz, 3 Calle, 1-46, Zona 1, T7952-1599, info@ discoveryguate.com. A colonial-style hotel with rooms set around a courtyard. Despite the nearby bus terminal it is very quiet and safe. All rooms have TV and there's a restaurant, pool table and parking. Tours offered.
$$ La Posada, 1 Calle, 4-12, Zone 2, T7952-1495, www.laposadacoban.com. 16 attractively decorated rooms all with private tiled bathrooms and fireplaces, colonial hotel with well-kept flourishing gardens, credit cards accepted, stylish restaurant with terrace and fireplace, stop by for a drink if nothing else. Café too, see Eating.
$ Casa D'Acuña, 4 Calle, 3-11, Zona 2, T7951-0482, casadeacuna@yahoo.com. 2 bunk beds to a room, ultra-clean bathrooms with hot water, laundry service, internet, excellent meals, tempting goodies and coffee in **El Bistro** restaurant in a pretty courtyard (see Eating). The owners run a tourist office, shop and tours. Recommended.
$ Central, 1 Calle, 1-79, T7952-1442. A stone's throw from the cathedral. 15 very clean large rooms, around a patio, with hot shower. Rooms with TV cost a little extra.
$ Hostal de Doña Victoria, 3 Calle, 2-38, Zona 3, T7951-4213. In a 400-year-old former Dominican convent with colonnaded gallery, attractive gardens and a good

restaurant (see Eating). Excursions arranged, recommended.

$ La Paz, 6 Av, 2-19, T7952-1358. Hot water, safe parking, pleasant, 35 rooms, cheaper without bath, laundry, café, garden, popular.

$ Monja Blanca, 2 Calle, 6-30 Zona 2, T7952-1712. All rooms are set around a pretty courtyard, very peaceful, old-fashioned dining room, breakfast good value. The place is run by a slightly eccentric *señora* and looks shut from the outside. Recommended.

$ Posada de Don José, 6 Av, 1-18, Zona 4, T7951-4760. 13 rooms with private bathroom, TV, cheaper without, clean general bathrooms, laundry, friendly, courtyard, good budget option.

Around Cobán *p136*
$$ Don Jerónimo's, Km 5.3 Carretera a Chamil, Aldea Chajaneb, T5301-3191, www.dearbrutus.com/donjeronimo. Bungalows to rent, with full board including 3 vegetarian meals a day and activities such as hiking, swimming and tubing included, massage available, a great place for relaxation. From Cobán in a taxi, 30 mins, about US$8. Or, take a bus from Cobán to Chamelco, then bus or pickup to Chamil and ask to be let off at Don Jerónimo's.

Lanquín and Semuc Champey *p136*
There is a backpackers' hostel at Semuc Champey (**$**). Otherwise try:

$$-$ El Retiro, 5 mins from Lanquín on the road to Cahabón, T4585-4684. Campsite, *cabañas*, dorms and restaurant, in a gorgeous riverside location. There's an open fire for cooking, hammocks to chill out in, and inner tubes for floating on the river. To get there don't get off in town, continue for 5 mins and ask to be dropped off. Highly recommended.

$ El Recreo, Lanquín, at the village entrance, T7983-0056, hotel_el_recreo@hotmail.com. Big, spacious wooden lodge in riverside grounds, with clean rooms, good meals, friendly; parking space. Recommended.

$ Hospedaje El Centro, Lanquín, close to the church. Friendly, good simple dinner, basic.

Camping
It is possible to camp for as long as you want at Semuc Champey once you've paid the entrance fee. There are toilets and cooking areas. Take insect repellent, a mosquito net, and all food and water. See also **El Retiro**, above.

Parque Nacional Laguna Lachuá *p136*
$ Finca Chipantun, on the borders of the national park on the bank of the Río Chixoy, T7951-3423, www.geocities.com/chipantun/main.html. With rooms, hammocks or camping space. 3 meals a day are provided at extra cost but at excellent value – the most expensive is dinner at US$3.50. Horse riding, boating, kayaking and guided tours possible.

$ National park accommodation, T5704-1509. Price per person. Bunk beds with mosquito netting or camping (tents available). Bring your own food and rubbish bags. There are fireplaces, showers and toilets.

North of Cobán and the southern Petén crossroads *p137*
$$-$ Complejo Cultural y Ecoturístico Cuevas de Candelaria, T7861-2203, www.cuevasdecandelaria.com. Thatched *cabañas* in a country setting with 1 large room with 10 beds and private rooms. Restaurant and café on site. Full board available.

$ Las Diamelas, Fray Bartolomé de las Casas, just off park, T5810-1785. Cleanest rooms in town. Restaurant food is OK and cheap.

$ Rancho Ríos Escondidos, near Grutas de Candelaria, on the main road. Camping possible at this farmhouse. Ask for Doña América.

☕ Eating

Cobán *p134, map p135*
$$$-$$ El Bistro, in Casa D'Acuña (see Sleeping), T7951-0482. Excellent menu and massive portions. Try the blueberry pancakes, great yogurt, don't walk through the restaurant without putting your nose into the cake cabinet! Recommended.
$$ El Refugio, 2 Av, 2-28, Zona 4, T7952-1338, 1030-2300. Excellent waiter service and substantial portions at good-value prices – steaks, fish, chicken and snacks, set lunch. Also cocktails, big screen TV and bar.
$$ Hostal de Doña Victoria (see Sleeping). Serves up breakfast, lunch and supper in a semi-open area with a pleasant, quiet ambience. Good Italian food, including vegetarian options, is the speciality of the house. Also mini cellar bar.

Cafés
Café Fantasia, 1 Calle, 3-13, western end of the main park. Handy spot open for breakfast. **Café La Posada**, part of La Posada (see Sleeping). Divine brownies and ice cream, sofas with a view of the Parque Central. Open afternoons.

Lanquín and Semuc Champey *p136*
There are *tiendas* in Lanquín selling good fruit and veg, and there are a couple of bakeries, all open early, for stocking up for a trip to Semuc Champey.
$ Comedor Shalom, Lanquín. Excellent value, if basic, including drink.

🎭 Entertainment

Cobán *p134, map p135*
Bars and clubs
Milenio, 3 Av 1-11, Zona 4, 5 rooms, dance floor, live music weekends, beer by the jug, pool table, big screen TV, week ends minimum consumption US$3, popular place with a mature crowd.

Cinema
At Plaza Magdalena, a few blocks west of town. Multi-screen cinema with latest releases usually showing.

🎉 Festivals and events

Cobán *p134, map p135*
Mar/Apr Holy Week.
Last week of Jul Rabin Ajau, the election of the Maya Beauty Queen. Around this time the **Paa banc** is also performed, when the chiefs of brotherhoods are elected for the year.
1-6 Aug Santo Domingo, the town's fiesta in honour of its patron.

🏔 Activities and tours

Cobán *p134, map p135*
Adrenalina Tours, west of the main square. Reliable tour operator, with a national presence.
Aventuras Turísticas, 3 Calle, 2-38, Zona 3, T7952-2213, www.aventurasturisticas.com. Also offers tourist information.
Proyecto Ecológico Quetzal, 2 Calle, 14-36, Zona 1, Cobán, T7952-1047, www.ecoquetzal.org. Contact David Unger. Trips are organized to the multicoloured Río Ikbolay, northwest of Cobán, see page 136, and the mountain community of Chicacnab.

⊖ Transport

Biotopo del Quetzal *p133*
Bus
From **Guatemala City**, take a Cobán bus with **Escobar-Monja Blanca** and ask to be let out at the Biotopo, hourly from 0400-1700, 3½ hrs, US$3.50. From **Cobán**, 1 hr, US$0.80, take any capital-bound bus or a minibus from Campo 2 near football stadium every 20 mins, US$0.80. From **El Rancho**–Biotopo, 1¼ hrs. Cobán–Purulhá, local buses ply this route between 0645-2000 returning until 1730, 1 hr 20 mins.

Salamá, Rabinal and Cubulco p133
Bus

Salamá-Rabinal, 1-1½ hrs. Rabinal is reached by travelling west from Salamá on a paved road. From **Guatemala City**, 5½ hrs, a beautiful, occasionally heart-stopping ride, or via El Progreso, and then Salamá by bus. Buses leave 0330-1600 to Guatemala City via Salamá from Cubulco. There is a bus between Rabinal and Cubulco, supplemented by pickup rides.

Santa Cruz Verapaz and around p134
Bus

From **Cobán** between 0600-1915 every 15 mins, US$0.700, 40 mins. All capital-bound buses from Cobán run through **Tactic**, or take a local bus between 0645-2000, returning between 0500-1730, 40 mins, US$0.80. Bus from Cobán to **Senahú**, 6 hrs, from opposite INJAV building, from 0600-1400, 4 daily, US$2.90. If you are coming from El Estor, get off at the Senahú turn-off, hitch or wait for the buses from Cobán. Trucks take this road, but there is little traffic, so you have to be at the junction very early to be in luck.

Cobán p134, map p135
Bus

The central bus terminal has attempted to group the multitude of bus stations into one place. While many now depart from this bus terminal, there are still a number of departure points scattered around town. Seek local advice for updates or changes.

To **Guatemala City** with Transportes Escobar-Monja Blanca, T7951-3571, every 30 mins from 0200-1600, 4-5 hrs, US$7, from its own offices near the terminal. **El Estor**, 4 daily from Av 5, Calle 4, first at 0830, and mostly morning departures, but check in the terminal beforehand, 7 hrs, US$5.60.

To **Fray Bartolomé de las Casas**, between 0600-1600 by bus, pickup and trucks, every 30 mins. Route **Raxrujá–**

Sayaxché–Flores there are minibuses **Micro buses del Norte** that leave from the terminal del norte near INJAV 0530 and 0630, 5 hrs, US$7.20. In Sayaxché you take a passenger canoe across the river (there is also a car ferry) where minibuses will whisk you to Flores on a tarmacked road in 45 mins. To **Uspantán**, 1000 and 1200, 5 hrs, US$2 from 1 Calle and 7 Av, Zona 2. Cobán can be reached from **Santa Cruz del Quiché** via Sacapulas and Uspantán, and from **Huehuetenango** via Aguacatán, Sacapulas and Uspantán.

Around Cobán p136
Bus

Every 20 mins from Cobán to **San Juan Chamelco**, US$0.25, 20 mins from Wasen Bridge, Diagonal 15, Zona 7 To **San Pedro Carchá**, every 15 mins, US$0.25, 20 mins from 2 Calle and 4 Av, Zona 4.

Lanquín and Semuc Champey p136
Bus

From **Cobán** there are minibuses that leave from the 3 Av, 5-6 Calle, 9 a day 0730-1745, US$3.80. From Lanquín to Semuc Champey hire a pickup, see below. From Lanquín to **Flores**, take a Cobán-bound bus to **Pajal**, 1 hr, then any passing bus or vehicle to **Sebol**, 2-2½ hrs (there are Las Casas–Cobán buses passing hourly in the morning only) and then pickup, hitch or bus to Sayaxché and then Flores.

Semuc Champey is a 10-km walk to the south from Lanquín, 3 hrs' walking along the road, which is quite tough for the 1st hr as the road climbs very steeply out of Lanquín. If planning to return to Lanquín the same day, start very early to avoid the midday heat. To get there in a pickup start early (0630), US$0.85, or ask around for a private lift (US$13 return). Transport is very irregular so it's best to start walking and keep your fingers crossed. By 1200-1300 there are usually people returning to town to hitch a lift with. If you are on your own and out of season, it would be wise to arrange a lift back.

Car
There is a gas station in Lanquín near the church.

Car hire Inque Renta Autos, T7952-1431, **Tabarini**, T7952-1504.

Parque Nacional Laguna Lachuá *p136*
Heading for **Playa Grande** from Cobán, also known as **Ixcan Grande**, ask the bus driver to let you off before Playa Grande at 'la entrada del parque', from where it's a 4.2-km (1-hr) walk to the park entrance. Minibuses leave Cobán every 30 mins via Chisec, 4 hrs, US$8 opposite INJAV.

North of Cobán and the southern Petén crossroads *p137*
Bus
Local transport in the form of minibuses and pickups connects most of these towns before nightfall.

Bus to **Poptún** from Fray Bartolomé de las Casas leaves at 0300 from the central park, 5¾ hrs, US$5.10. This road is extremely rough and the journey is a bone-bashing, coccyx-crushing one. Buses to **Cobán** at 0400 until 1100 on the hour. However, do not be surprised if one does not turn up and you have to wait for the next one. To **Flores** via Sebol, Raxrujá and Sayaxché

at 0700 (3½ hrs) a further 30 mins-1 hr to Flores. The road from **Raxrujá** via Chisec to Cobán is very steep and rocky. **Chisec** to Cobán, 1½ hrs. The Sayaxché–Cobán bus arrives at Fray Bartolomé de las Casas for breakfast and continues between 0800 and 0900. You can also go from here to Sebol to Modesto Méndez to join the highway to **Flores**, but it is a very slow, killer of a journey. Buses leave from Cobán for Chisec from Campo 2 at 0500, 0800, 0900.

❶ Directory

Cobán *p134, map p135*
Banks Most banks around the Parque Central will change money. MasterCard accepted at **G&T Continental**, corner of 1 Calle and 2 Av. **Internet** Access Computación, same building as Café Tirol. Fax and collect-call phone service only. Infocel, 3 Av, between 1-2 Calle, Zona 4. **Language schools** Active Spanish School, 3 Calle, 6-12, Zona 1, T7952-1432 (Nirma Macz). La Escuela de Español Muq'bil' B'e, 6 Av, 5-39, Zona 3, T7951-2459 (Oscar Macz), muqbilbe@yahoo.com. Offers Spanish and Q'eqchi'. **Laundry** Lavandería Providencia, opposite Café Tirol. **Medical services** Policlínica y Hospital Galen, a private institution on 3 Av, 1-47, Zona 3, T7951-2913. **Post** Corner of 2 Av and 3 Calle. **Telephone** You can make international calls from **Telgua** and **Access Computación** (see above).

El Petén

Deep in the lush lowland jungles of the Petén lie the lost worlds of Maya cities, pyramids and ceremonial centres, where layers of ancient dust speak ancient tales. At Tikal, where battles and burials are recorded in intricately carved stone, temples push through the tree canopy, wrapped in a mystical shroud. Although all human life has vanished from these once-powerful centres, the forest is humming with the latter-day lords of the jungle: the howler monkeys that roar day and night. There are also toucans, hummingbirds, spider monkeys, wild pig and coatimundi. Jaguar, god of the underworld in Maya religion, stalks the jungle but remains elusive, as does the puma and tapir. Further into the undergrowth away from Tikal, the adventurous traveller can visit El Mirador, the largest Maya stronghold, as well as El Zotz, El Perú, El Ceibal and Uaxactún by river, on foot and on horseback.

Ins and outs

Best time to visit The dry season and wet season offer different advantages and disadvantages. In the months of November through to early May, access to all sites is possible as tracks are bone-dry. There are also less mosquitoes and if you are a bird lover, the mating season falls in this period. In the rainy winter months, from May to November, tracks become muddy quagmires making many of them impassable, also bringing greater humidity and mosquitoes. Take plenty of repellent, and reapply frequently. It's also fiercely hot and humid at all times in these parts so lots of sun screen and drinking water are essential.

Background

Predominantly covered in jungle, the Petén is the largest department of Guatemala although it has the smallest number of inhabitants. The northern area was so impenetrable that its Maya settlers, the Itzás, were not conquered by the Spaniards until 1697. In 1990, 21,487 sq km of the north of the Petén was declared a *Reserva de la Biósfera Maya* (Maya Biosphere Reserve), by **CONAP**, the National Council for Protected Areas. It became the largest protected tropical forest area in Central America. Inside the boundaries of the biosphere are the Parque Nacional Tikal, Parque Nacional Mirador–Río Azul and Parque Nacional Laguna del Tigre.

Poptún

Poptún is best known for its association with **Finca Ixobel**, see Sleeping, page 157. Otherwise, it is just a staging-post between Río Dulce and Flores, or a stop-off to switch buses for the ride west to Cobán.

Flores and Santa Elena → *For listings, see pages 157-164.*

Flores is perched on a tiny island in Lake Petén Itzá. Red roofs and palm trees jostle for position as they spread up the small hill, which is topped by the white twin-towered cathedral. Some of the streets of the town are lined with houses and restaurants that have been given lashings of colourful paint, giving Flores a Caribbean flavour. A pleasant new lakeshore *malecón* has been built around the island, with benches, street lamps and jetties for swimming. *Lanchas*, drifting among the lilies and dragonflies, are pinned to the lake edges. Boat trips around the lake go from the Flores end of the causeway, about US$20 for 40 minutes, but it's worth bargaining.

Santa Elena is the dustier, less elegant and noisier twin town on the mainland where the cheapest hotels, banking services and bus terminal can be found.

Ins and outs
Getting there and around Flores is 2 km from the international airport on the outskirts of Santa Elena. The airport departures hall has an internet place. Tour operator and hotel representatives are based in the arrival halls. A causeway links Flores with Santa Elena. A taxi from the airport into Santa Elena or Flores costs US$1.30 and takes five minutes, but bargain hard. If you arrive by long-distance bus from Guatemala City, Mexico or Belize, the terminal is 10 blocks south of the causeway. There are hotels in Santa Elena and Flores across the causeway (10 to 15 minutes from Santa Elena). Chicken buses run between the two, US$0.35. Tuc-tucs charge US$0.90 for journeys between the two.

Tourist information INGUAT ① *in the airport, T7956-0533, daily 0700-1200, 1500-1800*. ProPetén ① *Calle Central, T7867-5155, www.propeten.org*, associated with **Conservation International**. CINCAP (Centro de Información sobre la Naturaleza, Cultura y Artesanía de Petén) ① *on the plaza, T7926-0718, www.alianzaverde.org*, has free maps of Tikal, and other local information. Housed in the same building is the **Alianza Verde** ① *closed Mon*, an organization promoting sustainable ecotourism. If you wish to make trips independently to remote Maya sites, check with **ProPetén** to see if they have vehicles making the journey.

Safety Roadside robbery used to be a problem on the road to Tikal and to Yaxhá. Get independent, up-to-date advice before visiting these places and leave all valuables at your hotel. Asistur, see Safety, page 16, can assist and have a base at Tikal.

Background
This jungle region was settled by the Maya Itzá Kanek in about AD 600, with their seat then known as La Isla de Tah Itzá (Tayasal in Spanish), now modern-day Flores. The Itzás were untouched by Spanish inroads into Guatemala until the Mexican conquistador Hernán Cortés and Spanish chronicler Bernal Díaz del Castillo dropped by in 1525 on their way from Mexico to Honduras. In 1697 Martín Urzua y Arismendi, the governor of the Yucatán, fought the first battle of the Itzás, crossing the lake in a galley killing 100 indigenous people in the ensuing battle, and capturing King Canek. He and his men destroyed the temples and palaces of Tayasal and so finished off the last independent Maya state.

Sights

The **cathedral**, Nuestra Señora de los Remedios y San Pablo del Itzá, is plain inside, and houses a Cristo Negro, part of a chain of Black Christs that stretches across Central America, with the focus of worship at Esquipulas. **Paraíso Escondido** is home to the **zoo** ① *US$2.70*. A dugout to the island costs US$16 round trip. Near the zoo is **ARCAS** (**Asociación de Rescate y Conservación de Vida Silvestre**) ① *T5208-0968, www.arcas guatemala.com, US$2*, where they care for rescued animals and release them back into the wild. Volunteers are welcome. There is a centre and interactive trails at the site. Boat tours of the whole lake cost from about US$10 per boat, calling at the zoo and **El Mirador** on the Maya ruin of **Tayasal** ① *US$2.70*. **Actún Kan caves** ① *0800-1700, US$2.70*, are a

Flores

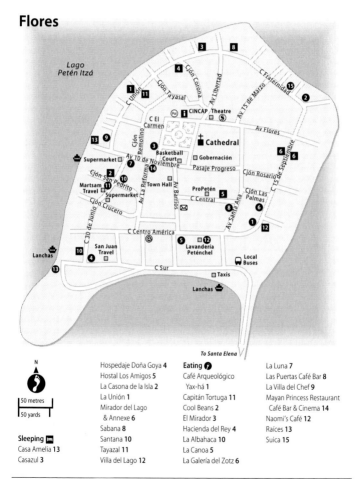

N

50 metres
50 yards

Sleeping 🛏
Casa Amelia **13**
Casazul **3**
Hospedaje Doña Goya **4**
Hostal Los Amigos **5**
La Casona de la Isla **2**
La Unión **1**
Mirador del Lago
  & Annexe **6**
Sabana **8**
Santana **10**
Tayazal **11**
Villa del Lago **12**

Eating 🍴
Café Arqueológico
  Yax-há **1**
Capitán Tortuga **11**
Cool Beans **2**
El Mirador **3**
Hacienda del Rey **3**
La Albahaca **10**
La Canoa **5**
La Galería del Zotz **6**

La Luna **7**
Las Puertas Café Bar **8**
La Villa del Chef **9**
Mayan Princess Restaurant
  Café Bar & Cinema **14**
Naomi's Café **12**
Raíces **13**
Suica **15**

fascinating labyrinth of tunnels where, legend has it, a large serpent lived. They are 3 km south of Santa Elena and a 30 to 45 minutes' walk. To get there take the 6 Avenida out of Santa Elena to its end, turn left at a small hill, then take the first road to the right where it is well marked. South of Santa Elena, at Km 468 is **Parque Natural Ixpanpajul** ① *T2336-0576, www.ixpanpajul.com*, where forest canopy Tarzan tours, zip-wire, night safari, birdwatching and horse riding and more are on offer. Local fiestas include 12-15 January, the Petén *feria*, and 11-12 December in honour of the Virgen de Guadalupe.

Around Lake Petén Itzá

San Andrés, 16 km by road from Santa Elena, enjoys sweeping views of Lake Petén Itzá, and its houses climb steeply down to the lake shore. There is a language school, see Directory. Adonis, a villager, takes good-value tours to El Zotz and El Mirador and has been recommended. Ask around for him; his house is close to the shoreline. You can also volunteer in the village with **Volunteer Petén** ① *Parque Nueva Juventud, T5711-0040, www.volunteerpeten.com*, a conservation and community project. The attractive village of **San José**, a traditional Maya Itzá village, where efforts are being made to preserve the Itzá language and revive old traditions, is 2 km further northeast on the lake from San Andrés. Its painted and thatched homes huddling steeply on the lake shore make it a

Santa Elena

Sleeping 🛏
Casa de Elena 1
Casona del Lago 6
Maya Internacional 2
Patio Tikal 3
Petén Espléndido 4
San Juan 5

Eating 🍴
El Petenchel 1
El Rodeo 2
Mijaro 3

much better day trip than San Andrés. Some 4 km beyond the village a signed track leads to the Classic period site of **Motul**, with 33 plazas, tall pyramids and some stelae depicting Maya kings. It takes 20 minutes to walk between the two villages. On 1 November San José hosts the **Holy Skull Procession**.

At the eastern side of Lake Petén Itzá is **El Remate**. The sunsets are superb and the lake is flecked with turquoise blue in the mornings. You can swim in the lake in certain places away from the local women washing their clothes and the horses taking a bath. There are many lovely places to stay, as it is also a handy stop-off point en route to Tikal. West of El Remate is the 700-ha **Biotopo Cerro Cahuí** ① *daily 0800-1600, US$2.70, administered by CECON*. It is a lowland jungle area where three species of monkey, deer, jaguar, peccary, ocellated wild turkey and some 450 species of bird can be seen. If you do not wish to walk alone, you can hire a guide. Ask at your *posada*.

Parque Nacional Tikal → *For listings, see pages 157-164.*

① *Open daily 0600-1800, US$19 per day, payable at the national park entrance, 18 km from the ruins (park administration, T7920-0025). An overall impression of the ruins may be gained in 5 hrs, but you need at least 2 days to see them properly. If you enter after 1600 your ticket is valid for the following day. If you stay the night in the park hotels, you can enter at 0500 once the police have scoured the grounds. This gives you at least a 2-hr head start on visitors coming in from Flores. At the visitor centre there is a post office, which stores luggage, a tourist guide service (see below), exchange facilities, toilets, a restaurant and a few shops that sell relevant guidebooks. Take a hat, mosquito repellent, water and snacks with you as it's extremely hot, drinks at the site aren't cheap and there's a lot of legwork involved.*

With its Maya skyscrapers pushing up through the jungle canopy, Tikal will have you transfixed. Steep-sided temples for the mighty dead, stelae commemorating the powerful rulers, inscriptions recording the noble deeds and the passing of time, and burials that were stuffed with jade and bone funerary offerings, make up the greatest Maya city in this tropical pocket of Guatemala.

Ins and outs
Getting there From Flores, it's possible to visit Tikal in a day. **San Juan Travel Agency** minibuses leave hourly between 0500 and 1000, one at 1400 and return at 1230 and hourly between 1400 and 1700 (though on the way back from Tikal, buses are likely to leave 10-15 minutes before scheduled), one hour, US$7.50 return. Several other companies also run trips such as **Línea Dorada** at 0500, 0830, 1530, returning 1400 and 1700. If you have not bought a return ticket you can often get a discounted seat on a returning bus if it's not full. Minibuses also meet Guatemala City–Flores flights. A taxi to Tikal costs US$60 one way. You can also visit Tikal with a one-day or two-day package tour from Guatemala City or Antigua.

Best time to visit Try to visit the ruins after 1400, or before 0900, as there are fewer visitors. From April to December it rains every day for a while; it is busiest November to January, during the Easter and summer holidays and most weekends. The best time for bird tours is December to April, with November to February being the mating season. Mosquitoes can be a real problem even during the day if straying away from open spaces.

Tourist information A guide is highly recommended as outlying structures can otherwise be missed. The official **Tourist Guide Association** offers tours of varying natures and in different languages. A private guide can be hired for US$60 or you can join up with a group for US$15 per person. Tours are available in Spanish, English, Italian, German and French. The guidebook *Tikal*, by W R Coe, in several languages, has an excellent map; or you can buy a reasonable leaflet/map at the entrance, US$2.50. Free transport around the site is available for elderly and disabled visitors, in an adapted pickup truck, with wheelchair access.

Tikal

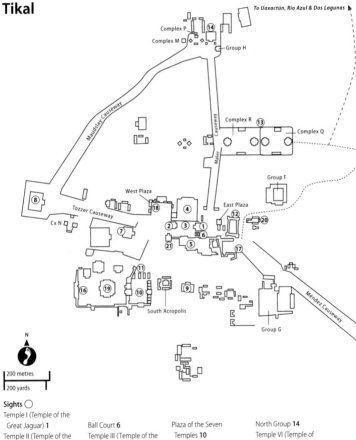

Sights ○

Temple I (Temple of the Great Jaguar) **1**	Ball Court **6**
Temple II (Temple of the Masks) **2**	Temple III (Temple of the Jaguar Priest) **7**
Great Plaza **3**	Temple IV (Temple of the Double-Headed Serpent) **8**
North Acropolis **4**	Temple V **9**
Central Acropolis **5**	

Plaza of the Seven Temples **10**	North Group **14**
Triple Ball Court **11**	Temple VI (Temple of Inscriptions) **15**
Market **12**	El Mundo Perdido (Lost World) **16**
Twin Pyramid Complexes Q & R **13**	

Background

At its height, the total 'urban' area of Tikal was more than 100 sq km, with the population somewhere between 50,000 and 100,000. The low-lying hill site of Tikal was first occupied around 600 BC during the pre-Classic era, but its buildings date from 300 BC. It became an important Maya centre from AD 300 onwards, which coincided with the decline of the mega power to the north, El Mirador. It was governed by a powerful dynasty of 30-plus rulers between about the first century AD until about AD 869, with the last known named ruler being Hasaw Chan K'awill II.

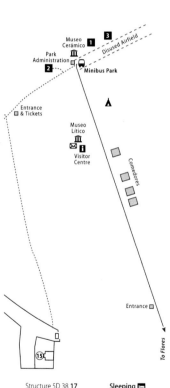

Structure 5D 38 **17**
Structure 5D II **18**
Great Pyramid **19**
Sweat House **20**
Structure 5D 73 **21**

Sleeping 🛏
Jaguar Inn **1**
Jungle Lodge **2**
Tikal Inn **3**

Tikal's main structures, which cover 2.5 sq km, were constructed from AD 550 to 900 during the Late-Classic period. These include the towering mega structures of temples – shrines to the glorious dead – whose roof combs were once decorated with coloured stucco figures of Tikal lords. Doorways on the temple rooms were intricately carved – using the termite-resistant wood of the sapodilla tree – with figures and symbols, known as lintels. Tikal's stelae tell of kings and accessions and war and death. Its oldest stela dates from AD 292. Many Central Mexican influences have been found on the stelae imagery, in burial sites at Tikal and in decorative architectural technique, which led archaeologists to conclude that the city was heavily influenced from the west by forces from the great enclave of Teotihuacán, now just outside Mexico City. This war-like state bred a cult of war and sacrifice and seemed intent on spreading its culture. After the collapse of Teotihuacán in AD 600, a renaissance at Tikal was achieved by the ruler Ah Cacao (Lord Cocoa, Ruler A, Moon Double Comb, Hasaw Chan K'awil I, Sky Rain) who succeeded to the throne in AD 682 and died sometime in the 720s. However, in the latter part of the eighth century the fortunes of Tikal declined. The last date recorded on a stela is AD 889. The site was finally abandoned in the 10th century. Most archaeologists now agree the collapse was due to warfare with neighbouring states, overpopulation, which resulted in environmental destruction, and drought.

Tikal's existence was first reported by Spanish monk Andrés de Avendaño, but its official discovery is attributed to Modesto Méndez, Commissioner of the Petén, and Ambrosio Tut, Governor of the Petén, in 1848. They were both accompanied by the artist Eusebio Lara.

Wildlife

Tikal is a fantastic place for seeing animal and bird life of the jungle. Wildlife includes spider monkeys, howler monkeys, three species of toucan (most prominent being the keel-billed toucan), deer, foxes and many other birds and insects. Pumas have been seen on quieter paths and coatimundis (*pizotes*), in large family groups, are often seen rummaging through the bins. The ocellated turkeys with their sky-blue heads with orange baubles attached are seen in abundance at the entrance, and at El Mundo Perdido.

The ruins

The **Great Plaza (3)** is a four-layered plaza with its earliest foundations laid around 150 BC and its latest around AD 700. It is dwarfed by its two principal temples – Temples I and II. On the north side of the plaza between these two temples are two rows of monuments. It includes Stela 29, erected in AD 292, which depicts Tikal's emblem glyph – the symbol of a Maya city – and the third century AD ruler Scroll Ahau Jaguar, who is bearing a two-headed ceremonial bar.

Temple I (Temple of the Great Jaguar) (1), on the east side of the Great Plaza, rises to 44 m in height with nine stepped terraces. It was ordered to be built by the ruler Ah Cacao, who ruled between AD 682 to around AD 720-724, who probably planned it for use as his shrine. His tomb, the magnificent Burial 116, was discovered beneath Temple I in 1962 with a wealth of burial goods on and around his skeleton. The display is reconstructed in the Museo Cerámico/Tikal.

Temple II (Temple of the Masks) (2) faces Temple I on the Great Plaza and rises to 38 m, although with its roof comb it would have been higher. It's thought Ah Cacao ordered its construction as well. The lintel on the doorway here depicted a woman wearing a cape, and experts have suggested that this could be his wife.

The **North Acropolis (4)** contains some 100 buildings piled on top of earlier structures in a 1-ha area and is the burial ground of all of Tikal's rulers until the break with royal practice made by Ah Cacao. In 1960, the prized Stelae 31, now in the Museo Cerámico/Tikal, see below, was found under the Acropolis. It was dedicated in AD 445. Its base was deliberately burnt by the Maya and buried under Acropolis buildings in the eighth century. This burning was thought to be like a 'killing', where the burning ritual would 'kill' the power of the ruler depicted on the monument, say, after death. It's thought to depict the ruler Siyah Chan K'awil (Stormy Sky), who died sometime around AD 457 having succeeded to the throne in AD 411. Yax Moch Xok (Great Scaffold Shark) is thought to be entombed in the first century AD grave, Burial 85. Surrounding the headless male body were burial objects and a mask bearing the royal head band. Under a building directly in the centre of this acropolis Burial 22 – that of ruler Great Jaguar Paw, who reigned in the fourth century, and died around AD 379 – was discovered. Also found here was Burial 10, thought to be the tomb of Nun Yax Ayin I (Curl Nose), who succeeded to the throne in AD 379 after Great Jaguar Paw. Inside were the remains of nine sacrificed servants as well as turtles and crocodile remains and a plethora of pottery pieces. The pottery laid out in this tomb had Teotihuacán artistic influences, demonstrating Tikal's links to the powers of Teotihuacán and Teotihuacán-influenced Kaminal Juyú. Burial 48 is thought to be the tomb of Curl Nose's son, Siyah Chan K'awil (Stormy Sky).

Central Acropolis (5) is made up of a complex of courts connected by passages and stairways, which have expanded over the centuries to cover 1.6 ha. Most of the building work carried out took place between AD 550-900 in the Late-Classic era. The **East Plaza** behind Temple I is the centre of the highway junctions of the Maler Causeway in the north, and the Méndez Causeway heading southeast.

On the western side of the **West Plaza** is structure 5D II under which Burial 77 was brought to light. The skeleton was adorned with a jade pendant, which was stolen from the site museum in the 1980s.

Temple III (Temple of the Jaguar Priest) (7) is so called because of the scene of a figure in a glamorous jaguar pelt on a lintel found on the temple. Some experts believe this figure is Ah Chitam (Nun Yax Ayin II, Ruler C), son of Yax Kin, and grandson of the great Ah Cacao, and so propose that this is his shrine, although there has been no confirmation of this. Temple III was constructed around AD 810 and is 55 m tall.

Temple IV (Temple of the Double-Headed Serpent) (8) is the highest building in Tikal at 70 m. It was built in the Late-Classic period around AD 741, as proven by hieroglyphic inscriptions and carbon dating. It's thought it was built to honour Yax Kin, the son of Ah Cacao, who became ruler in AD 734. A date on the lintel is AD 741, the same year that Temple I was dedicated.

Temple V (9), constructed between AD 700-750 during the reign of Yax Kin, is 58 m high. It is the mortuary temple of an unknown ruler.

El Mundo Perdido (The Lost World) (16). The **Great Pyramid** is at the centre of this lost world. At 30 m high, it is the largest pyramid at Tikal. It is flat topped and its stairways are flanked by masks. From the top a great view over the canopy to the tops of other temples can be enjoyed. Together with other buildings to the west, it forms part of an astronomical complex. The Lost World pyramid is a pre-Classic structure, but was improved upon in the Early Classic. East of El Mundo Perdido is the **Plaza of the Seven Temples (10)**, constructed during the Late Classic period (AD 600-800). There is a triple ball court lying at its northern edge.

Temple VI (Temple of the Inscriptions) (15) was discovered in 1951. The 12-m-high roof comb is covered on both sides in hieroglyphic text and is the longest hieroglyphic recording to date. It was carved in AD 766, but the temple was built under the rule of Yax Kin some years before. Altar 9 is at the base of the temple as is Stela 21, said to depict the sculptured foot of the ruler Yax Kin to mark his accession as ruler in AD 734. Unfortunately because of the location of this temple away from the rest of the main structures it has become a hideout for robbers and worse. Some guides no longer take people there. Take advice before going, if at all.

The North Group has several twin pyramid complexes, including Complexes Q and R, marking the passing of the *katun* – a Maya 20-year period.

The **Museo Cerámico (Museo Tikal)** ⓘ *near the Jungle Lodge, Mon-Fri 0900-1700, Sat and Sun, 0900-1600, US$1.30*, has a collection of Maya ceramics, but its prize exhibits are Stela 31 with its still clear carvings, and the reconstruction of the tomb of Tikal's great ruler, Ah Cacao. In the **Museo Lítico** ⓘ *inside the visitor centre, Mon-Fri 0900-1700, Sat and Sun, 0900-1600*, there are stelae and great photographs of the temples as they were originally found, and of their reconstruction, including the 1968 rebuild of the Temple II steps. **Note** Photography is no longer permitted in either of these museums.

Other Maya ruins → *For listings, see pages 157-164.*

There are literally hundreds of Maya sites in the Petén. Below are a handful of sites, whose ruins have been explored, and of whose histories something is known.

Uaxactún

In the village of Uaxactún (pronounced Waash-ak-tún) are ruins, famous for the oldest complete Maya astronomical complex found, and a stuccoed temple with serpent and jaguar head decoration. The village itself is little more than a row of houses either side of a disused airstrip. Uaxactún is one of the longest-occupied Maya sites. Its origins lie in the Middle pre-Classic (1000-300 BC) and its decline came by the early post-Classic (AD 925-1200) like many of its neighbouring powers. Its final stelae, dated AD 889, is one of the last to be found in the region. The site is named after a stela, which corresponds to Baktun 8 (8 x 400 Maya years), carved in AD 889 – *uaxac* means 8, *tun* means stone. South of the remains of a ball court, in **Group B**, a turtle carving can be seen, and Stela 5, which marks the takeover of the city, launched from Tikal. Next door to this stela under Temple B-VIII were found the remains of two adults, including a pregnant woman, a girl of about 15 and a baby. It is believed this may have been the governor and his family who were sacrificed in AD 378. From Group B, take the causeway to **Group A**. In Group A, Structure A-V had 90 rooms and there were many tombs to be seen. The highest structure in the complex is Palace A-XVIII, where red paint can still be seen on the walls. In **Group E** the oldest observatory (E-VII-sub) ever found faces structures in which the equinoxes and solstices were observed. When the pyramid (E-VII) covering this sub-structure was removed, fairly well preserved stucco masks of jaguar and serpent heads were found flanking the stairways of the sub-structure. The ruins lie either side of the village, the main groups (**Group A** and **Group B**) are to the northwest (take a left just before **Hotel El Chiclero** and follow the road round on a continuous left to reach this group). A smaller group (**Group E**) with the observatory is to the southwest (take any track, right off the airstrip, and ask. This group is 400 m away. The site is 24 km north of Tikal on an unpaved road. It is in fairly good condition taking less than one hour in any vehicle.

El Zotz

El Zotz, meaning bat in Q'eqchi', is so called because of the nightly flight from a nearby cave of thousands of bats. There is an alternative hiking route as well (see below). Incredibly, from Temple IV, the highest in the complex at 75 m, it is possible to see in the distance, some 30 km away, Temple IV at Tikal. The wooden lintel from Temple I (dated AD 500-550) is to be found in the Museo Nacional de Arqueología y Etnología in the capital. Each evening at about 1850 the sky is darkened for 10 minutes by the fantastic spectacle of tens of thousands of bats flying out of a cave near the camp. The 200-m-high cave pock-marked with holes is a half-hour walk from the camp. If you are at the cave you'll see the flight above you and get doused in falling excrement. If you remain at the campsite you will see them streaking the dark blue sky with black in straight columns. It's also accessible via Uaxactún. There is some basic infrastructure for the guards, and you can camp.

One of the best trips you can do in the Petén is a three-day hike to El Zotz and on through the jungle to Tikal. The journey, although long, is not arduous, and is accompanied by birds, blue morpho butterflies and spider monkeys chucking branches at you all the way.

El Perú and the Estación Biológica Guacamayo

A visit to El Perú is included in the **Scarlet Macaw Trail**, a two- to five-day trip into the **Parque Nacional Laguna del Tigre**, through the main breeding area of the scarlet macaw. There is little to see at the Maya site, but the journey to it is worthwhile. In 2004 the 1200 year old tomb and skeleton of a Maya queen were found. A more direct trip involves getting to the isolated Q'eqchi'-speaking community of **Paso Caballos** (1¾ hours). Here, the **Comité de Turismo** can organize transport by *lancha* along the Río San Pedro. From Paso Caballos it is one hour by *lancha* to the El Perú campsite and path. It's possible to stop off at the **Estación Biológica Guacamayo** ① *US$1.30, volunteers may be needed, contact Propeten, www.propeten.org*, where there is an ongoing programme to study the wild scarlet macaws (*ara macao*). The chances of seeing endangered scarlet macaws during March, April and May in this area is high because that's when they are reproducing. A couple of minutes upriver is the landing stage, where it's a 30-minute walk to the campsite of El Perú: howler monkeys, hummingbirds, oropendola birds and fireflies abound. From there, it is a two-hour walk to the El Perú ruins. Small coral snakes slither about, howler monkeys roar, spider monkeys chuck branches down on the path. White-lipped peccaries, nesting white turtles, eagles, fox and kingfishers have also been seen. The trip may be impossible between June and August because of rising rivers during the rainy season and because the unpaved road to Paso Caballos may not be passable. Doing it on your own is possible, although you may have to wait for connections and you will need a guide, about US$20 per day.

El Mirador, El Tintal and Nakbé

El Mirador is the largest Maya site in the country. It dates from the late pre-Classic period (300 BC-AD 250) and is thought to have sustained a population of tens of thousands. It takes five days to get to El Mirador. From Flores it is 2½ to three hours to the village of Carmelita by bus or truck, from where it is seven hours walking, or part horse riding to El Mirador. It can be done in four days – two days to get there and two days to return. The route is difficult and the mosquitoes and ticks and the relentless heat can make it a trying trip. Organized tours are arranged by travel agents in Flores – get reassurance that your agents have enough food and water. If you opt to go to El Mirador independently, ask in Carmelita for the **Comité de Turismo**, which will arrange mules and guides. Take water, food, tents and torches. It is about 25 km to El Tintal, a camp where you can sling a hammock, or another 10 km to El Arroyo, where there is a little river for a swim near a *chiclero* camp. It takes another day to El Mirador, or longer, if you detour via Nakbé. You will pass *chiclero* camps on the way, which are very hospitable, but very poor. In May, June and July there is no mud, but there is little chance of seeing wildlife or flora. In July to December, when the rains come, the chances of glimpsing wildlife is much greater and there are lots of flowers. It is a lot fresher, but there can be tonnes of mud, sometimes making the route impassable. The mosquitos are also in a frenzy during the rainy season. Think carefully about going on the trip (one reader called it "purgatory"). The site, which is part of the Parque Nacional Mirador-Río Azul, is divided into two parts with the **El Tigre Pyramid** and complex in the western part, and the **La Danta** complex, the largest in the Maya world, in the east, 2 km away. The larger of two huge pyramids – La Danta – is 70 m high; stucco masks of jaguars and birds flank the stairways of the temple complex. The other, El Tigre, is 55 m in height and is a wonderful place to be on top of at night, with a view of endless jungle and other sites, including Calakmul, in Mexico. In **Carmelita** ask around for space to sling your hammock or camp. There is a basic *comedor*. **El Tintal**, a day's hike from El Mirador, is said to be the second largest site in Petén, connected by a causeway to El Mirador, with great views from the top of the pyramids. **Nakbé**, 10 km southeast of El Mirador, is the earliest known lowland Maya site (1000-400 BC), with the earliest examples of carved monuments.

Río Azul and Kinal

From Uaxactún a dirt road leads north to the campamento of Dos Lagunas. It's a lovely place to camp, with few mosquitoes, but swimming will certainly attract crocodiles. The guards' camp at Ixcán Río, on the far bank of the Río Azul, can be reached in one long day's walk, crossing by canoe if the water is high. If low enough to cross by vehicle you can drive to the Río Azul site, a further 6 km on a wide, shady track. It is also possible to continue into Mexico if your paperwork is OK. A barely passable side track to the east from the camp leads to the ruins of Kinal. The big attraction at Río Azul are the famous black and red painted tombs, technically off limits to visitors without special permission, but visits have been known.

Yaxhá, Topoxte, Nakum and Melchor de Mencos

About 65 km from Flores, on the Belize road ending at Melchor de Mencos, is a turning left, a dry weather road, which brings you in 8.5 km to Laguna Yaxhá. On the northern shore is the site of Yaxhá (meaning Green Water), the third largest known Classic Maya site in the country, accessible by causeway. Open 0800-1700. This untouristy site is good for birdwatching and the views from the temples of the milky green lake are outstanding. The tallest structure, **Templo de las Manos Rojas**, is 30 m high In the lake is the unusual Late Post Classic site (AD120-1530) of Topoxte. (The island is accessible by boat from Yaxhá, 15 minutes.) About 20 km further north of Yaxhá lies Nakum, which it's thought was both a trading and ceremonial centre. You will need a guide and your own transport if you have not come on a tour. The group of sites has been designated as a national park, entry to each US$9 (T7861-0250, www.conap.com.gt).

Northwest Petén and the Mexican border

An unpaved road runs 151 km west from Flores to **El Naranjo** on the Río San Pedro, near the Mexican border. Close by is **La Joyanca**, a site where the chance of wildlife spotting is high. You can camp at the *cruce* with the guards.

Parque Nacional Laguna del Tigre and Biotopo

The park and biotopo is a vast area of jungle and wetlands north of El Naranjo. The best place to stay is the CECON camp, across the river below the ferry. This is where the guards live and they will let you stay in the bunk house and use their kitchen. Getting into the reserve is not easy and you will need to be fully equipped, but a few people go up the Río

Escondido. The lagoons abound in wildlife, including enormous crocodiles and spectacular bird life. Contact CECON.

Sayaxché

Sayaxché, south of Flores on the road to Cobán, has a frontier town feel to it as its focus is on a bend on the Río de la Pasión. It is a good base for visiting the southern Petén including a number of archaeological sites, namely El Ceibal. You can change US dollar bills and traveller's cheques at **Banoro**.

El Ceibal

This major ceremonial site is reached by a 45-minute *lancha* ride up the Río de la Pasión from Sayaxché. It is about 1.5 km from the left bank of Río de la Pasión hidden in vegetation and extending for 1.5 sq km. The height of activity at the site was from 800 BC to the first century AD. Archaeologists agree that it appears to have been abandoned in between about AD 500 and AD 690 and then repopulated at a later stage when there was an era of stelae production between AD 771 and 889. It later declined during the early decades of the 10th century and was abandoned. You can sling a hammock at El Ceibal and use the guard's fire for making coffee if you ask politely – a mosquito net is advisable, and take repellent for walking in the jungle surroundings. Tours can be arranged in Flores for a day trip to Sayaxché and El Ceibal (around US$65) but there is limited time to see the site. From Sayaxché the ruins of the **Altar de los Sacrificios** at the confluence of the Ríos de la Pasión and Usumacinta can also be reached. It was one of the earliest sites in the Péten, with a founding date earlier than that of Tikal. Most of its monuments are not in good condition. Also within reach of Sayaxché is **Itzán**, discovered in 1968.

Piedras Negras

Still further down the Río Usumacinta in the west of Petén is Piedras Negras, a huge Classic period site. In the 1930s Tatiana Proskouriakoff first recognized the periods of time inscribed on stelae here coincided with human life spans or reigns, and so began the task of deciphering the meaning of Maya glyphs. Advance arrangements are necessary with a rafting company to reach Piedras Negras. **Maya Expeditions** (see page 8) run expeditions, taking in Piedras Negras, Bonampak, Yaxchilán and Palenque. This trip is a real adventure. The riverbanks are covered in the best remaining tropical forest in Guatemala, inhabited by elusive wildlife and hiding more ruins. Once you've rafted down to Piedras Negras, you have to raft out. Though most of the river is fairly placid, there are the 30-m **Busilhá Falls**, where a crystal-clear tributary cascades over limestone terraces and two deep canyons, with impressive rapids to negotiate, before reaching the take-out two days later.

Petexbatún

From Sayaxché, the Río de la Pasión is a good route to visit other Maya ruins. From **Laguna Petexbatún** (16 km), a fisherman's paradise can be reached by outboard canoe from Sayaxché. Excursions can be made from here to unexcavated ruins that are generally grouped together under the title Petexbatún. These include **Arroyo de la Piedra**, Dos Pilas and Aguateca. **Dos Pilas** has many well-preserved stelae, and an important tomb of a king was found here in 1991 – that of its Ruler 2, who died in AD 726. Dos Pilas flourished in the Classic period when as many as 10,000 lived in the city. There are many carved monuments and hieroglyphic stairways at the site, which record the important events of city life. **Aguateca**, where the ruins are so far little excavated, gives a feeling of authenticity. The city was abandoned in the early ninth century for unknown reasons. Again, a tour is advisable. It's a boat trip and a short walk away. The site was found with numerous walls (it's known the city was attacked in AD 790) and a chasm actually splits the site in two. The natural limestone bridge connects a large plaza with platforms and buildings in the west with an area of a series of smaller plazas in the east. These places are off the beaten track and an adventure to get to.

El Petén listings

For Sleeping and Eating price codes and other relevant information, see pages 12-13.

😴 Sleeping

Poptún *p143*

$$-$ Finca Ixobel, T5410-4307, www.finca ixobel.com. A working farm owned by Carole Devine, widowed after the assassination of her husband in 1990. This highly acclaimed 'paradise' has become the victim of its own reputation and is frequently crowded especially at weekends. However, you can still camp peacefully and there are great treehouses, dorm beds, private rooms and bungalows. One of the highlights is the food. The *finca* offers a range of trips that could keep you there for days. Recommended.

Flores *p144, map p145*

$$ Hotel Casazul, Calle Fraternindad, T7867-5451, www.hotelesdepeten.com. 9 rooms, all blue and most with lakeside view. All with cable TV, a/c and fan.

$$ Hotel Santana, Calle 30 de Junio, T7867-5123, www.santanapeten.com. Lakeside restaurant, pool, clean rooms, all with their own terrace a/c, and TV.

$$ La Casona de la Isla, Callejón San Pedrito, on the lake, T7867-5163, www.hotelesdepeten.com. Elegant rooms, fans, TV, clean, friendly, good restaurant, nice breakfasts, bar, garden, pool.

$$ Sabana, Calle La Unión, T7867-5100. Huge, airy rooms, good service, clean, pleasant, with funky green wavy paintwork in lobby; good view, caters for European package tours, lakeside pool and restaurant.

$$ Villa del Lago, 15 de Septiembre, T7926-0508. Very clean rooms with a/c and fan, cheaper with shared bath, some rooms with lake view and balcony. Breakfast is served on a terrace with lake view, but the service is excruciatingly slow. The breakfast menu

is open to non-guests, but avoid it in high season unless you don't mind a long wait.

$ Hospedaje Doña Goya, Calle Unión, T7926-3538. 6 basic but clean rooms, 3 with private bath, cheaper without, 3 with balcony, terrace with superb views, internet, book exchange, kitchen, hammocks on thatched roof terrace; friendly, family-run.

$ Hostal Los Amigos, Calle Centro América and Av Barrios, T7867-5075, www.amigos hostel.com. Dorms with 20 beds, private rooms, luxury dorms and hammocks with a funky courtyard. Good, cheap restaurant; bar and internet available. Very helpful and friendly. Very popular with backpackers but can be crowded and noisy; highly recommended. It also rents out hammocks and mosquito nets for tours to Tikal.

$ La Unión, Calle La Unión, T7867-5531. Basic but clean rooms with tiny balcony and lake view, very friendly.

$ Mirador del Lago, Calle 15 de Septiembre, T7926-3276. Beautiful view of the lake and a jetty to swim from. All with private bathrooms and (irregular) hot water. One of the better budget hotels and it has lake access. The annexe opposite is quiet. All with fan.

$ Tayazal, Calle Unión, T7867-5333. Rooms of various sizes, a bit dingy but OK, with fan, showers downstairs, some with private bath as well as dorms, roof terrace, very accommodating, can arrange a Tikal trip. Travel agency in reception.

Santa Elena *p144, map p146*

$$$$ Hotel Casona del Lago, overlooking the lake, T7952-8700, www.hotelesde peten.com. 32 spacious rooms, some with balcony, in this lovely duck-egg blue and white hotel. Pool, restaurant, internet and travel agency.

$$$ Maya Internacional, lakefront, T7926-2083, www.villasdeguatemala.com.

Bungalows and rooms beautifully situated and with all services. Room 52 is particularly delightful. Restaurant and pool open to non-guests, 0630-2100.

$$$ Petén Espléndido, 1 Calle, T7926-0880, www.petenesplendido.com. Small but well-furnished rooms with a/c, TV and some with lake view. A great lakefront restaurant setting (0600-2200), with beautiful pool on the lake. Pool open to non-guests for a small fee. Range of business services available.

$$ Casa de Elena, Av 6, just before the causeway, T7926-2235. With a beautiful tiled staircase, rooms have cable TV, pool, restaurant 0630-2100.

$$ Hotel del Patio Tikal, corner of Calle 2 and Av 8, T7926-0104, www.hoteldelpatio.com.gt. Clean, modern rooms with a/c, TV, expensive restaurant, beautiful pool and gym. It's best booked as part of a package for cheaper rates.

$ San Juan, Calle 2, close to the Catholic church, T7926-0562, sanjuanttravel@hotmail.com.gt. Full of budget travellers in the older rooms, cheaper with shared bath, not always spotless. Some remodelled rooms with a/c and TV. Exchanges US dollars and Mexican pesos and buys Belizean dollars. It's not the nicest place to stay but it's safe, there's a public phone inside and parking. Note that the Tikal minibuses leave from 0500 so you will probably be woken early.

Around Lake Petén Itzá *p146*
To reach the lodgings along the north shore of the lake can be up to a 2-km walk from El Remate centre, depending on where you stay (turn left, west on the Flores–Tikal main road). There is street light up to the Biotopo entrance until 2200.

$$$$ Bahía Taitzá Hotel and Restaurant, Barrio El Porvenir, San José, T7928-8125, www.taitza.com. 8 lovely rooms decorated with local furnishings set behind a beautiful lawn that sweeps down to the lakeshore.

Rates include breakfast and transfer. Restaurant on site.

$$$$-$$$ La Lancha, T7928-8331, www.blancaneaux.com. Francis Ford Coppola's attractive, small hotel has 10 tastefully furnished rooms, 4 of which have lake views from balconies. There's a pool and terrace restaurant serving excellent local cuisine, and local arts and crafts have been used to decorate the rooms. Quiet and friendly in a lovely setting, with horse riding and kayaking trips available.

$$$ Camino Real, 1.8 km from the western entrance of Biotopo Cerro Cahuí, El Remate, T7926-0204, www.caminorealtikal.com.gt. All rooms have views, good restaurant, a/c, cable TV, lovely pool in an attractive setting.

$$$ Hotel Ni'tun, 2 km from San Andrés on the Santa Elena road, T5201-0759, www.nitun.com. Luxury *cabañas* on a wooded hillside above the lake, run by friendly couple Bernie and Lore, who cook fantastic vegetarian meals and organize expeditions to remote sites.

$$ Hotel Casa Amelia, Calle La Unión, T7867-5430, www.hotelcasamelia.com. Cheerful and friendly hotel with 15 comfortable, a/c rooms – 6 of which have lake views. Guests can enjoy a terrace and pool table.

$ El Mirador del Duende, on the main Flores–Tikal road in El Remate Village, T7926-0269, miradordelduende@gmail.com. Overlooks lake, camping, cabins, veggy food, jungle trips, canoes, boat trips, mountain bikes, horses and guides are available.

$ Hotel y Restaurante Mon Ami, on the El Remate side, T7928-8413, www.hotelmonami.com. Guided tours to Yaxhá and Nakum organized with the owner who is a conservationist. Lovely bungalows, dorms and hammocks for sleeping. English, French and Spanish spoken. Restaurant 0700-2130, with wines and seriously cheap chicken, pastas and other dishes served.

$ La Casa de Don David, 20 m from the main road, on the El Remate side, T7928-8469, www.lacasadedondavid.com. Clean and comfortable; all rooms with private bath and some with a/c. Great view from the terrace restaurant with cheap food, bike hire free. Transport to Tikal and other tours offered. There's a wealth of information here and helpful advice is offered.

$ La Casa de Don Juan, on the main Flores–Tikal road in El Remate Village, T5309-7172, casadonjuan@hotmail.com. Rooms out the back behind the restaurant. Owner Don Juan offers tours.

$ La Casa Doña Tonita, on the El Remate side, T5701-7114. One of the most chilled out places along the shore and popular, with a friendly, warm family running the place. Shared bathroom, rooms and a dorm. Enormous portions of good food. Highly recommended.

$ La Casa Roja, on the El Remate side, T5909-6999. A red house with a tranquil, oriental feel. Rooms are under thatched roofs, with separate bathrooms in attractive stone and wood design. The rooms don't have doors but there are locked trunks. Hammock space and camping possible. Kayaks for rent and trips arranged. Recommended.

$ La Unión, Calle Unión, T7867-5634, gulzam75@hotmail.com. Formerly a restaurant and now a hotel with 14 rooms, all with hot water and private bathroom. Internet café in lobby and also rents kayaks.

$ Sun Breeze Hotel, exactly on the corner, on the El Remate side, T7928-8044. Run by the very friendly Humberto Castro. Little wooden rooms with views over the lake. Fans and *mosquiteros* in each room. 2 rooms with private bathroom. He runs a daily service to Tikal and can run other trips.

Camping
Campsite with hammock facilities at El Sotz, just before El Remate.

Parque Nacional Tikal *p147*
You are advised to book when you arrive; in high season, book in advance. Take a torch: 24-hr electricity is not normally available.

$$$-$$ Jungle Lodge, T5361-4098, www.quik.guate.com/jltikal/index.html. Spacious, comfortable bungalows, with bath, 24-hr hot water and fan (electricity 0700-2100); pool; cheaper without bath. It will cash TCs, full board available (although we've had consistent reports of unsatisfactory food, slow service and small portions). **Jungle Lodge**'s Tikal tours have been recommended.

$$$-$$ Tikal Inn, T7926-1917. Bungalows and rooms, hot water 1800-1900, electricity 0900-1600, 1800-2200, beautiful pool for guest use only. Natural history tours at 0930 for US$10, minimum 2 people, helpful.

$$ Jaguar Inn, T7926-0002, www.jaguartikal.com. Full board, less without food. There is also a dorm with 6 beds. Hammocks with mosquito nets and lockers. Electricity 1800-2200, hot water in the morning or on request Mar-Oct and Nov-Feb, 0600-2100. It will provide a picnic lunch and stores luggage.

Camping
$ Camping Tikal, run by the **Restaurante del Parque**, reservations T2370-8140, or at the **Petén Espléndido**, T7926-0880. If you have your own tent or hammock it is US$5. If you need to rent the gear it is US$8. There are also *cabañas* with mattresses and mosquito nets for US$7 per person. It also does deals that include breakfast, lunch and dinner ranging from US$15-30 for a double. Communal showers available. Take your own water as the supply is very variable.

Uaxactún *p152*
$ Aldana's Lodge, T5801-2588, edeniaa@yahoo.com. Little white *casitas*, tent and hammock space behind **El Chiclero**. Just before **El Chiclero** take a left on the road to the ruins and then first right until you

see a whitewashed *casita* on the right
(2 mins). Clean and run by a friendly family.
$ El Chiclero, T7926-1095. Neat and clean,
hammocks and rooms in a garden, also
good food by arrangement.

Sayaxché *p155*
$ Guayacán, close to ferry, T7928-6111.
Owner Julio Godoy is a good source
of information.
$ Hotel Posada Segura, turn right from
the dock area and then 1st left, T7928-6162.
Some rooms with bath, TV, clean; one of the
best options in town.

Petexbatún *p155*
$$$ Chiminos Island Lodge, T2335-3506,
www.chiminosisland.com. Remote, small
ecolodge close to a Maya site on a peninsula
on the river. Great for exploring local sites,
fishing and wildlife spotting. Includes all food.
$$$ Posada Caribe, T7928-6117, including
3 meals, comfortable *cabañas* with bath-
room and shower, excursion to **Aguateca**
by launch and a guide for excursions.

Camping
Camping is possible at Escobado,
on the lakeside.

🍴 Eating

Flores *p144, map p145*
$$$-$$ Raíces, T5521-1843,
raicesrestaurante@gmail.com. Excellent
waterfront restaurant beside the *lanchas*
near the far west end of Calle Sur. Specialities
include *parillas* and kebabs. Great seafood.
$$-$ Café Arqueológico Yax-há, Calle15
de Septiembre, T5830-2060, www.cafeyaxha.
com. Cheap daily soups, Maya specialities,
such as chicken in tamarind sauce, great
smoothies, and home-made nachos. German
owner Dieter offers tours to little-known
Maya sites (speaks English too) and works
with local communities to protect them.

$$-$ Capitán Tortuga, Calle 30 de junio.
Pizzas, pasta and bar snacks, with dayglo
painted walls and lakeside terrace.
$$-$ Hacienda del Rey, Calle Sur. Expensive
Argentine steaks are on the menu, but the
breakfasts are seriously cheap.
$$-$ La Albahaca, Calle 30 de Junio. 1st-
class home-made pasta and chocolate cake.
$$-$ La Galería del Zotz, 15 de Septiembre.
A wide range of food, delicious pizzas, good
service and presentation, popular with locals.
$$-$ La Luna, Av 10 de Noviembre. Closed
Sun. Refreshing natural lemonade, range
of fish, meat and vegetarian dishes. The
restaurant has a beautiful courtyard with
blue paintwork set under lush pink
bougainvillea. Recommended.
$$-$ Las Puertas Café Bar, Av Santa Ana
and Calle Central, T7867-5242. Closes at 2300
for food and 2400 completely. Closed Sun.
Cheap breakfasts, huge menu, good large
pasta portions. It's popular at night with
locals and travellers and is in an airy building,
chilled atmosphere, games available.
$$ La Villa Del Chef, T4366-3822,
lavilladelchef guatemala@yahoo.com.
Friendly German-owned restaurant at the
South end of Calle Unión that specializes in
pescado blanco. Has a happy hour and also
rents canoes for lake tours. Recommended.
**$$ Mayan Princess Restaurant Café Bar
and Cinema**, Reforma and 10 de Noviembre.
Closed Sun. Has the most adventurous menu
on the island including daily specials, many
with an Asian flavour, relaxed atmosphere,
with bright coloured textile cloths on the
tables. Internet and free films.
$ Café Uka, Calle Centro América. Open
from 0600. Filling breakfasts and meals.
$ Cool Beans, Calle Fraternidad, T5571-9240,
coolbeans@itelgua.com. Cheap food with
home-made bread and pastries.
$ El Mirador, overlooking the lake but view
obscured by restaurant wall. Seriously cheap
food and snacks but service slow.

$ La Canoa, Calle Centro América. Good breakfasts (try the pancakes), dinners start at US$1.50, with good *comida típica*, very friendly owners.

$ Suica, Calle Fraternidad. Small place serving an unusual mix of sushi, tempura and curries (open 1200-1900, closed Sun).

Santa Elena *p144, map p146*
$$ El Rodeo, 1 Calle. Excellent, reasonable prices, classical music and sometimes impromptu singing performances.

$ El Petenchel, Calle 2. Vegetarian food served here as well as conventional meats and meals. Excellent breakfasts. Good-value *menú del día*. Music played, prompt service.

$ Restaurante Mijaro, Calle 2 and Av 8. Great filling breakfasts and a bargain *menú del día* at US$1.70, all in a thatched-roofed roadside location.

Uaxactún *p152*
$ Comedor Imperial, at village entrance. Bargain *comida típica* for US$1.30.

Sayaxché *p155*
$$$ El Botanero Café Restaurante and Bar, straight up from the dock and 2nd left. A funky wooden bar with logs and seats carved from tree trunks.

$ Restaurant La Montaña, near dock. Cheap food, local information given.

$ Yakín, near dock. Cheap, good food; try the *licuados*.

▲ Activities and tours

Flores and Santa Elena *p144, maps p145 and 146*
Conservation Tours Tikal, Calle 15 de Septiembre, opposite Oficina Contable Tayasal, run by Lucía Prinz, T7926-0670, nermeild@yahoo.com.gt. (or ask at Las Puertas). This organization, funded by UNESCO, employs people from Petén communities to take visitors on tours to local sites. English and Spanish spoken.

Also walking tours in the jungle, bird-watching, horse and kayak tours also. 5% of profits go to conservation.

Equinoxio, Calle Unión, T4250-6384, sergioequinoxio@yahoo.es. Bus and airline tickets as well as Tikal tours.

Explore, 2a Calle 3-55, Sta Elena, T7926-2375, www.exploreguate.com. Very helpful, reliable and professional operator offering tours to Tikal, Aguateca, Dos Pilas, Ceibal and Yaxhá.

Martsam Travel, Calle 30 de Junio, T7867-5377, www.martsam.com. Guided tours to Tikal, El Zotz, El Mirador, El Perú, Yaxhá, Nakum, Aguateca, Ceibal and Uaxactún. Guides with wildlife and ornithological knowledge in addition to archaeological knowledge. Highly recommended.

San Juan Travel Agency, T7926-0042, www.corporacionsanjuandelnorte.com, offers transport (US$7.50 return) to Tikal and excursions to Ceibal, Uaxactún, and Yaxhá (US$80). Service to Belize, US$20, 0500 and 0700, 5 hrs, pickup from hotels Also to Chetumal, Mexico, at 0500 and 0730, US$20, 7 hrs. To Palenque at 0500, US$35, 7 hrs.

Tikal Connection, International Airport, T7926-1537, www.tikalcnx.com, runs tours to El Perú, El Mirador, Nakbé, El Zotz, Yaxhá, Dos Aguadas, Uaxactún. It also sells bus tickets.

Viajes de Tivoli, Calle Centroamerica, T5436-6673, www.tivoli.com.gt. Trips to local sites as well as general agency services.

Uaxactún *p152*
For guided walks around the ruins ask for one of the trained guides, US$10. For expeditions further afield, contact Elfido Aldana at **Posada Aldana**. Neria Baldizón at **El Chiclero** has high-clearance pickups and plenty of experience in organizing both vehicle and mule trips to any site. She charges US$200 per person to go to Río Azul.

Sayaxché *p155*
Viajes Don Pedro, on the river front near the dock, T7928-6109, runs launches to El Ceibal

---

(US$35 for up to 3), Petexbatún and Aguateca (US$60 for up to 5), Dos Pilas (US$50 for small group). Trip possible by jeep in the dry season, Altar de los Sacrificios (US$100 minimum 2 people) and round trips to Yaxchilán for 3 days (US$400). Mon-Sat 0700-1800, Sun 0700-1200.

🚌 Transport

Poptún p143
Bus

Take any **Fuente del Norte** bus or any bus heading to the capital from **Flores**, 2 hrs. To Flores catch any Flores-bound bus from the capital. To **Río Dulce**, 2 hrs. Buses will drop you at the driveway to **Finca Ixobel** if that's your destination, just ask. From there it's a 15-min walk. Or, get off at the main bus stop and arrange a taxi there or through **Finca Ixobel**. To **Guatemala City** there are plenty daily, 7-8 hrs, US$10-13. The only bus that continues to **Fray Bartolomé de las Casas** (Las Casas on the bus sign) leaves at 1030, 5¾ hrs, US$8.

Flores and Santa Elena p144,
maps p145 and p146
Air

Be early for flights, as overbooking is common. The cost of a return flight is between US$180-220, shop around. **Grupo Taca**, T2470-8222, www.taca.com, leaves **Guatemala City** daily at 0645, 0955, 1725, 1 hr, returns 0820, 1605 and 1850. **Tag**, T2360-3038, www.tag.com.gt, flies at 0630 returning 1630. To **Cancún**, Grupo Taca. To **Belize City**, Tropic Air, www.tropicair.com.

Boat

Lanchas moor along Calle Sur, Flores; behind the **Hotel Santana**; from the dock behind **Hotel Casona de Isla**; and beside the arch on the causeway.

Bus

Local Local buses (chicken buses), US$0.26, Flores to Santa Elena, leave from the end of the causeway in Flores.

Long distance All long-distance buses leave from the relocated bus terminal, 6 blocks south of the Calle Principal in Santa Elena. It has a snack bar, toilets, seating and ATM. Opposite are restaurants, *comedores*, and a bakery. Banrural is down the side. To **Guatemala City**, Línea Dorada, daily office hours 0500-2200, www.tikalmayan world.com, leaves 1000, 2100, 1st class, US$30; 2200, US$16, 8 hrs. **Autobuses del Norte (ADN)**, T7924-8131, www.adnauto busesdelnorte.com, luxury service, 1000, 2100, 2300, US$23. **Fuente del Norte**, T7926-0666, office open 24 hrs, buses every 45 mins-1 hr, 0330-2230, US$12, 9 hrs. At 1000, 1400, 2I00, 2200, US$20, 7-8 hrs. 2nd-class buses, **Rosita**, T7926-5178 and **Rápidos del Sur**, T7924-8072, also go to the capital, US$13. If you are going only to **Poptún**, 2 hrs, or **Río Dulce**, 3½-4 hrs, make sure you do not pay the full fare to Guatemala City. To **Sayaxché** with Pinita, T9926-0726, at 1100, returns next day at 0600, US$2.50. With **Fuente del Norte** at 0600, US$1.70, returning 0600. *Colectivos* also leave every 15 mins 0530-1700, US$2.40. Buses run around the lake to **San Andrés**, with one at 1200 with Pinita continuing to **Cruce dos Aguadas,** US$2.90 and **Carmelita**, US$3.30 for access to El Mirador. Returning from Carmelita at 0500 the next day. Minibuses also run to San Andrés. To **Chiquimula**, take Transportes María Elena, T5550-4190, at 0400, 0800, 1300, US$3. The María Elena bus continues onto **Esquipulas**, 9 hrs, US$12. **Fuente del Norte** to **Cobán**, 0530, 0630, 1230, 1330, 5 hrs, US$8. Or take a minibus to Sayaxché and change. Shuttle transfers may also be possible. To **Jutiapa**, 0500, 0530, 7 hrs, returning 0900, US$10-12.

International To **Melchor de Mencos** at the Belize border, 0500, 0600, 1630, 2300, 1½ hrs, US$3.30. Returning 0200, 0500, 0600, 1630, 2300. Also with **Línea Dorada** and on to **Chetumal, Mexico**

To **Copán Ruinas, Honduras**, take **Transportes María Elena**, T5550-4190, to Chiquimula at 0400, 0800, 1300, US$13 then from Chiquimula to El Florido and finally on to Copán Ruinas. Alternatively, take any bus to the capital and change at Río Hondo. To **San Salvador**, 0600, 8 hrs, US$26.70.

Car
There are plenty of agencies at the airport, mostly Suzuki jeeps, which cost about US$65-80 per day. **Hertz**, at the airport, T7926-0332. **Garrido** at Sac-Nicte Hotel, Calle 1, Santa Elena, T7926-1732.

Petrol Available in Santa Elena at the 24-hr Texaco garage on the way to the airport.

Around Lake Petén Itzá *p146*
Boat
Public *lanchas* from San Benito have virtually come to a stop. Visitors can still charter a *lancha* from Flores for about US$10.

Bus
There's a bus ticket and internet office opposite the turning to El Remate. Any bus/shuttle heading for Tikal can stop at El Remate, US$2.50, last bus around 1600; taxi around US$10. Returning to **Flores**, pick up any shuttle heading south (this is a lot easier after 1300 when tourists are returning). There is a bus service heading to **Flores** from El Remate at 0600, 0700, 0830, 0930, 1300 and 1400. Shuttles leave every 30 mins for San Andrés, US$0.70, 30 mins and go on to San José.

Uaxactún *p152*
Bus To Uaxactún from Santa Elena at 1200 arriving between 1600-1700, US$2.60, returning 0500 with **Transportes Pinita**.

Foreigners have to pay US$2 to pass through Parque Nacional Tikal on their way to Uaxactún, payable at the main entrance to Tikal.

El Mirador, El Tintal and Nakbé *p153*
Bus 1 bus daily with **Transportes Pinita** to **Carmelita**. See Flores for information.

Northwest Petén and the Mexican border *p154*
Boat and bus To **El Naranjo** at 0500 and 1000, returning at 0500, 1100 and 1300, US$4. Or hire a *lancha* from Paso Caballos.

Sayaxché *p155*
Bus There are buses to **Flores**, 0600, 0700, 1-2 hrs, and microbuses every 30 mins. To **Raxrujá** and on to **Cobán** via **Chisec** at 0400, US$.80, 6½ hrs direct to Cobán. There are pickups after that hourly and some further buses direct and not via Chisec. For **Lanquín** take the bus to Raxrujá, then a pickup to Sebol, and then a pickup to Lanquín, or the Lanquín *cruce* at Pajal, and wait for onward transport. If you are heading to **Guatemala City** from here it could be quicker to head north to Flores rather than take the long road down to Cobán. However, this road has now been entirely tarmacked.

Petexbatún *p155*
Boat It is 30-40 mins in *lancha* from Sayaxché to the stop for **Dos Pilas** to hire horses. It's 50 mins-1 hr to **Chiminos** lodge and 1 hr 20 mins to the **Aguateca** site. To Dos Pilas and Aguateca from Chiminos, US$27 return to each site.

ⓘ Directory

Flores and Santa Elena *p144, maps p145 and 146*
Banks **Banrural**, Flores, next to the church. TCs only. **Banco del Café**, Santa Elena, best rates for Amex TCs. Do not use its ATM: it eats cards by the dozen. **Banco de los**

Trabajadores, Santa Elena, MasterCard accepted. **Banco Agromercantil**, Santa Elena, open until 1800. **Banco Industrial**, MasterCard only. The major hotels and travel agents change cash and TCs. There's a bank opposite the bus terminal. **Immigration** at the airport, T7926-0984. **Internet** There are plenty of places. Hotel internet terminals tend to have fairer prices than the internet shops. **Laundry** Lavandería Petenchel, wash and dry. Open 0800-1900. **Medical services** Hospital Nacional, in San Benito, T7926-1333, open 24 hrs. **Centro Médico Maya**, 4 Av 335, Santa Elena, T7926-0810, speaks some English. Recommended.

Post In Flores and in Santa Elena.
Telephone Telgua in Santa Elena and some travel agencies. **Volunteering** See ARCAS, page 18. Also www.volunteerpeten. com, and Women's **Association for the Revival of Traditional Medicine**, T5514-8889.

Around Lake Petén Itzá *p146*
Language schools Eco-Escuela Español, San Andrés, T5940-1235, www.ecoescuela espanol.org. 20 hrs of classes, homestay and extra curricular activities for a week, US$150. The **Escuela Bio-Itzá**, San José, www.ecobioitza.org offers classes, homestay and camping for the same price.

Contents

Footnotes

Basic Spanish for travellers

Learning Spanish is a useful part of the preparation for a trip to Latin America and no volumes of dictionaries, phrase books or word lists will provide the same enjoyment as being able to communicate directly with the people of the country you are visiting. It is a good idea to make an effort to grasp the basics before you go. As you travel you will pick up more of the language and the more you know, the more you will benefit from your stay.

General pronunciation

Whether you have been taught the 'Castilian' pronunciation (*z* and *c* followed by *i* or *e* are pronounced as the *th* in think) or the 'American' pronunciation (they are pronounced as *s*), you will encounter little difficulty in understanding either. Regional accents and usages vary, but the basic language is essentially the same everywhere.

Vowels

a	as in English *cat*
e	as in English *best*
i	as the *ee* in English *feet*
o	as in English *shop*
u	as the *oo* in English *food*
ai	as the *i* in English *ride*
ei	as *ey* in English *they*
oi	as *oy* in English *toy*

Consonants

Most consonants can be pronounced more or less as they are in English. The exceptions are:

g	before *e* or *i* is the same as *j*
h	is always silent (except in *ch* as in *chair*)
j	as the *ch* in Scottish *loch*
ll	as the *y* in *yellow*
ñ	as the *ni* in English *onion*
rr	trilled much more than in English
x	depending on its location, pronounced *x*, *s*, *sh* or *j*

Spanish words and phrases

Greetings, courtesies

hello	*hola*	please	*por favor*
good morning	*buenos días*	thank you (very much)	*(muchas) gracias*
good afternoon/		I don't speak Spanish	*no hablo español*
evening/night	*buenas*	do you speak English?	*¿habla inglés?*
	tardes/noches	I don't understand	*no comprendo*
goodbye	*adiós/chao*	please speak slowly	*hable despacio por*
pleased to meet you	*mucho gusto*		*favor*
see you later	*hasta luego*	I am very sorry	*lo siento mucho*
how are you?	*¿cómo está?*	what do you want?	*¿qué quiere?*
	¿cómo estás?		*¿qué quieres?*
I'm fine, thanks	*estoy muy bien, gracias*	I want	*quiero*
I'm called...	*me llamo...*	I don't want it	*no lo quiero*
what is your name?	*¿cómo se llama?*	leave me alone	*déjeme en paz/*
	¿cómo te llamas?		*no me moleste*
yes/no	*sí/no*	good/bad	*bueno/malo*

Questions and requests

Have you got a room for two people?
¿Tiene una habitación para dos personas?
How do I get to_? *¿Cómo llego a_?*
How much does it cost?
¿Cuánto cuesta? ¿cuánto es?
I'd like to make a long-distance phone call
Quisiera hacer una llamada de larga distancia
Is service included? *¿Está incluido el servicio?*
Is tax included? *¿Están incluidos los impuestos?*

When does the bus leave (arrive)?
¿A qué hora sale (llega) el autobús?
When? *¿cuándo?*
Where is_? *¿dónde está_?*
Where can I buy tickets?
¿Dónde puedo comprar boletos?
Where is the nearest petrol station?
¿Dónde está la gasolinera más cercana?
Why? *¿por qué?*

Basics

bank	*el banco*	market	*el mercado*
bathroom/toilet	*el baño*	note/coin	*el billete/la moneda*
bill	*la factura/la cuenta*	police (policeman)	*la policía (el policía)*
cash	*el efectivo*	post office	*el correo*
cheap	*barato/a*	public telephone	*el teléfono público*
credit card	*la tarjeta de crédito*	supermarket	*el supermercado*
exchange house	*la casa de cambio*	ticket office	*la taquilla*
exchange rate	*el tipo de cambio*	traveller's cheques	*los cheques de*
expensive	*caro/a*		*viajero/los travelers*

Getting around

aeroplane	*el avión*	insured person	*el/la asegurado/a*
airport	*el aeropuerto*	to insure yourself against	*asegurarse contra*
arrival/departure	*la llegada/salida*	luggage	*el equipaje*
avenue	*la avenida*	motorway, freeway	*el autopista/la*
block	*la cuadra*		*carretera*
border	*la frontera*	north, south, west, east	*norte, sur,*
bus station	*la terminal de*		*oeste (occidente),*
	autobuses/camiones		*este (oriente)*
bus	*el bus/el autobús/*	oil	*el aceite*
	el camión	to park	*estacionarse*
collective/		passport	*el pasaporte*
fixed-route taxi	*el colectivo*	petrol/gasoline	*la gasolina*
corner	*la esquina*	puncture	*el pinchazo/*
customs	*la aduana*		*la ponchadura*
first/second class	*primera/segunda clase*	street	*la calle*
left/right	*izquierda/derecha*	that way	*por allí/por allá*
ticket	*el boleto*	this way	*por aquí/por acá*
empty/full	*vacío/lleno*	tourist card/visa	*la tarjeta de turista*
highway, main road	*la carretera*	tyre	*la llanta*
immigration	*la inmigración*	unleaded	*sin plomo*
insurance	*el seguro*	to walk	*caminar/andar*

Accommodation

air conditioning	*el aire acondicionado*	power cut	*el apagón/corte*
all-inclusive	*todo incluido*	restaurant	*el restaurante*
bathroom, private	*el baño privado*	room/bedroom	*el cuarto/l*
bed, double/single	*la cama matrimonial/ sencilla*		*a habitación*
		sheets	*las sábanas*
blankets	*las cobijas/mantas*	shower	*la ducha/regadera*
to clean	*limpiar*	soap	*el jabón*
dining room	*el comedor*	toilet	*el sanitario/excusado*
guesthouse	*la casa de huéspedes*	toilet paper	*el papel higiénico*
hotel	*el hotel*	towels, clean/dirty	*las toallas limpias/ sucias*
noisy	*ruidoso*		
pillows	*las almohadas*	water, hot/cold	*el agua caliente/fría*

Health

aspirin	*la aspirina*	diarrhoea	*la diarrea*
blood	*la sangre*	doctor	*el médico*
chemist	*la farmacia*	fever/sweat	*la fiebre/el sudor*
condoms	*los preservativos, los condones*	pain	*el dolor*
		head	*la cabeza*
contact lenses	*los lentes de contacto*	period/	*la regla/*
contraceptives	*los anticonceptivos*	sanitary towels	*las toallas femeninas*
contraceptive pill	*la píldora anti- conceptiva*	stomach	*el estómago*
		altitude sickness	*el soroche*

Family

family	*la familia*	boyfriend/girlfriend	*el novio/la novia*
brother/sister	*el hermano/la hermana*	friend	*el amigo/la amiga*
daughter/son	*la hija/el hijo*	married	*casado/a*
father/mother	*el padre/la madre*	single/unmarried	*soltero/a*
husband/wife	*el esposo (marido)/ la esposa*		

Months, days and time

January	*enero*	November	*noviembre*
February	*febrero*	December	*diciembre*
March	*marzo*		
April	*abril*	Monday	*lunes*
May	*mayo*	Tuesday	*martes*
June	*junio*	Wednesday	*miércoles*
July	*julio*	Thursday	*jueves*
August	*agosto*	Friday	*viernes*
September	*septiembre*	Saturday	*sábado*
October	*octubre*	Sunday	*domingo*

at one o'clock	*a la una*	it's six twenty	*son las seis y veinte*
at half past two	*a las dos y media*	it's five to nine	*son las nueve menos*
at a quarter to three	*a cuarto para las tres/*		*cinco*
	a las tres menos quince	in ten minutes	*en diez minutos*
it's one o'clock	*es la una*	five hours	*cinco horas*
it's seven o'clock	*son las siete*	does it take long?	*¿tarda mucho?*

Numbers

one	*uno/una*	sixteen	*dieciséis*
two	*dos*	seventeen	*diecisiete*
three	*tres*	eighteen	*dieciocho*
four	*cuatro*	nineteen	*diecinueve*
five	*cinco*	twenty	*veinte*
six	*seis*	twenty-one	*veintiuno*
seven	*siete*	thirty	*treinta*
eight	*ocho*	forty	*cuarenta*
nine	*nueve*	fifty	*cincuenta*
ten	*diez*	sixty	*sesenta*
eleven	*once*	seventy	*setenta*
twelve	*doce*	eighty	*ochenta*
thirteen	*trece*	ninety	*noventa*
fourteen	*catorce*	hundred	*cien/ciento*
fifteen	*quince*	thousand	*mil*

Food

avocado	*el aguacate*	fish	*el pescado*
baked	*al horno*	fork	*el tenedor*
bakery	*la panadería*	fried	*frito*
banana	*el plátano*	garlic	*el ajo*
beans	*los frijoles/*	goat	*el chivo*
	las habichuelas	grapefruit	*la toronja/el pomelo*
beef	*la carne de res*	grill	*la parrilla*
beef steak or pork fillet	*el bistec*	grilled/griddled	*a la plancha*
boiled rice	*el arroz blanco*	guava	*la guayaba*
bread	*el pan*	ham	*el jamón*
breakfast	*el desayuno*	hamburger	*la hamburguesa*
butter	*la mantequilla*	hot, spicy	*picante*
cake	*el pastel*	ice cream	*el helado*
chewing gum	*el chicle*	jam	*la mermelada*
chicken	*el pollo*	knife	*el cuchillo*
chilli or green pepper	*el ají/pimiento*	lime	*el limón*
clear soup, stock	*el caldo*	lobster	*la langosta*
cooked	*cocido*	lunch	*el almuerzo/la comida*
dining room	*el comedor*	meal	*la comida*
egg	*el huevo*	meat	*la carne*

minced meat	el picadillo	sausage	la longaniza/el chorizo
onion	la cebolla	scrambled eggs	los huevos revueltos
orange	la naranja	seafood	los mariscos
pepper	el pimiento	soup	la sopa
pasty, turnover	la empanada/	spoon	la cuchara
	el pastelito	squash	la calabaza
pork	el cerdo	squid	los calamares
potato	la papa	supper	la cena
prawns	los camarones	sweet	dulce
raw	crudo	to eat	comer
restaurant	el restaurante	toasted	tostado
salad	la ensalada	turkey	el pavo
salt	la sal	vegetables	los legumbres/vegetales
sandwich	el bocadillo	without meat	sin carne
sauce	la salsa	yam	el camote

Drink

beer	la cerveza	ice/without ice	el hielo/sin hielo
boiled	hervido/a	juice	el jugo
bottled	en botella	lemonade	la limonada
camomile tea	la manzanilla	milk	la leche
canned	en lata	mint	la menta
coffee	el café	rum	el ron
coffee, white	el café con leche	soft drink	el refresco
cold	frío	sugar	el azúcar
cup	la taza	tea	el té
drink	la bebida	to drink	beber/tomar
drunk	borracho/a	water	el agua
firewater	el aguardiente	water, carbonated	el agua mineral con gas
fruit milkshake	el batido/licuado	water, still mineral	el agua mineral sin gas
glass	el vaso	wine, red	el vino tinto
hot	caliente	wine, white	el vino blanco

Key verbs

to go	**ir**
I go	voy
you go (familiar)	vas
he, she, it goes, you (formal) go	va
we go	vamos
they, you (plural) go	van

to have (possess)	**tener**
I have	tengo
you (familiar) have	tienes
he, she, it, you (formal) have	tiene
we have	tenemos
they, you (plural) have	tienen

there is/are	hay
there isn't/aren't	no hay

to be	**ser**	estar
I am	soy	estoy
you are	eres	estás
he, she, it is, you (formal) are	es	está
we are	somos	estamos
they, you (plural) are	son	están

This section has been assembled on the basis of glossaries compiled by André de Mendonça and David Gilmour of South American Experience, London, and the Latin American Travel Advisor, No 9, March 1996

Index